Mometrix

TEST PREPARATION

AEPA®

Foundations of Reading (190) Secrets Study Guide

ACCESS YOUR ONLINE RESOURCES

DON'T MISS OUT ON THE ONLINE RESOURCES INCLUDED WITH YOUR PURCHASE!

Your purchase of this product unlocks access to our Online Resources page. Elevate your study experience with our **interactive practice test interface**, along with all of the additional resources that we couldn't include in this book.

Flip to the Online Resources section at the end of this book to find the link and a QR code to get started!

Mometrix
TEST PREPARATION

DEAR FUTURE EXAM SUCCESS STORY

First of all, **THANK YOU** for purchasing Mometrix study materials!

Second, congratulations! You are one of the few determined test-takers who are committed to doing whatever it takes to excel on your exam. **You have come to the right place.** We developed these study materials with one goal in mind: to deliver you the information you need in a format that's concise and easy to use.

In addition to optimizing your guide for the content of the test, we've outlined our recommended steps for breaking down the preparation process into small, attainable goals so you can make sure you stay on track.

We've also analyzed the entire test-taking process, identifying the most common pitfalls and showing how you can overcome them and be ready for any curveball the test throws you.

Standardized testing is one of the biggest obstacles on your road to success, which only increases the importance of doing well in the high-pressure, high-stakes environment of test day. Your results on this test could have a significant impact on your future, and this guide provides the information and practical advice to help you achieve your full potential on test day.

Your success is our success

We would love to hear from you! If you would like to share the story of your exam success or if you have any questions or comments in regard to our products, please contact us at **800-673-8175** or **support@mometrix.com**.

Thanks again for your business and we wish you continued success!

Sincerely,
The Mometrix Test Preparation Team

Need more help? Check out our flashcards at:
http://MometrixFlashcards.com/AEPA

Written and edited by the Mometrix Exam Secrets Test Prep Team
Printed in the United States of America

Table of Contents

Introduction

Thank you for purchasing this resource! You have made the choice to prepare yourself for a test that could have a huge impact on your future, and this guide is designed to help you be fully ready for test day. Obviously, it's important to have a solid understanding of the test material, but you also need to be prepared for the unique environment and stressors of the test, so that you can perform to the best of your abilities.

For this purpose, the first section that appears in this guide is the **Secret Keys**. We've devoted countless hours to meticulously researching what works and what doesn't, and we've boiled down our findings to the five most impactful steps you can take to improve your performance on the test. We start at the beginning with study planning and move through the preparation process, all the way to the testing strategies that will help you get the most out of what you know when you're finally sitting in front of the test.

We recommend that you start preparing for your test as far in advance as possible. However, if you've bought this guide as a last-minute study resource and only have a few days before your test, we recommend that you skip over the first two Secret Keys since they address a long-term study plan.

If you struggle with **test anxiety**, we strongly encourage you to check out our recommendations for how you can overcome it. Test anxiety is a formidable foe, but it can be beaten, and we want to make sure you have the tools you need to defeat it.

Review Video Directory

As you work your way through this guide, you will see numerous review video links interspersed with the written content. If you would like to access all of these review videos in one place, click on the video directory link found on the online resources page: **mometrix.com/resources719/aepafoundread**

Secret Key #1 – Plan Big, Study Small

There's a lot riding on your performance. If you want to ace this test, you're going to need to keep your skills sharp and the material fresh in your mind. You need a plan that lets you review everything you need to know while still fitting in your schedule. We'll break this strategy down into three categories.

Information Organization

Start with the information you already have: the official test outline. From this, you can make a complete list of all the concepts you need to cover before the test. Organize these concepts into groups that can be studied together, and create a list of any related vocabulary you need to learn so you can brush up on any difficult terms. You'll want to keep this vocabulary list handy once you actually start studying since you may need to add to it along the way.

Time Management

Once you have your set of study concepts, decide how to spread them out over the time you have left before the test. Break your study plan into small, clear goals so you have a manageable task for each day and know exactly what you're doing. Then just focus on one small step at a time. When you manage your time this way, you don't need to spend hours at a time studying. Studying a small block of content for a short period each day helps you retain information better and avoid stressing over how much you have left to do. You can relax knowing that you have a plan to cover everything in time. In order for this strategy to be effective though, you have to start studying early and stick to your schedule. Avoid the exhaustion and futility that comes from last-minute cramming!

Study Environment

The environment you study in has a big impact on your learning. Studying in a coffee shop, while probably more enjoyable, is not likely to be as fruitful as studying in a quiet room. It's important to keep distractions to a minimum. You're only planning to study for a short block of time, so make the most of it. Don't pause to check your phone or get up to find a snack. It's also important to **avoid multitasking**. Research has consistently shown that multitasking will make your studying dramatically less effective. Your study area should also be comfortable and well-lit so you don't have the distraction of straining your eyes or sitting on an uncomfortable chair.

The time of day you study is also important. You want to be rested and alert. Don't wait until just before bedtime. Study when you'll be most likely to comprehend and remember. Even better, if you know what time of day your test will be, set that time aside for study. That way your brain will be used to working on that subject at that specific time and you'll have a better chance of recalling information.

Finally, it can be helpful to team up with others who are studying for the same test. Your actual studying should be done in as isolated an environment as possible, but the work of organizing the information and setting up the study plan can be divided up. In between study sessions, you can discuss with your teammates the concepts that you're all studying and quiz each other on the details. Just be sure that your teammates are as serious about the test as you are. If you find that your study time is being replaced with social time, you might need to find a new team.

Secret Key #2 – Make Your Studying Count

You're devoting a lot of time and effort to preparing for this test, so you want to be absolutely certain it will pay off. This means doing more than just reading the content and hoping you can remember it on test day. It's important to make every minute of study count. There are two main areas you can focus on to make your studying count.

Retention

It doesn't matter how much time you study if you can't remember the material. You need to make sure you are retaining the concepts. To check your retention of the information you're learning, try recalling it at later times with minimal prompting. Try carrying around flashcards and glance at one or two from time to time or ask a friend who's also studying for the test to quiz you.

To enhance your retention, look for ways to put the information into practice so that you can apply it rather than simply recalling it. If you're using the information in practical ways, it will be much easier to remember. Similarly, it helps to solidify a concept in your mind if you're not only reading it to yourself but also explaining it to someone else. Ask a friend to let you teach them about a concept you're a little shaky on (or speak aloud to an imaginary audience if necessary). As you try to summarize, define, give examples, and answer your friend's questions, you'll understand the concepts better and they will stay with you longer. Finally, step back for a big picture view and ask yourself how each piece of information fits with the whole subject. When you link the different concepts together and see them working together as a whole, it's easier to remember the individual components.

Finally, practice showing your work on any multi-step problems, even if you're just studying. Writing out each step you take to solve a problem will help solidify the process in your mind, and you'll be more likely to remember it during the test.

Modality

Modality simply refers to the means or method by which you study. Choosing a study modality that fits your own individual learning style is crucial. No two people learn best in exactly the same way, so it's important to know your strengths and use them to your advantage.

For example, if you learn best by visualization, focus on visualizing a concept in your mind and draw an image or a diagram. Try color-coding your notes, illustrating them, or creating symbols that will trigger your mind to recall a learned concept. If you learn best by hearing or discussing information, find a study partner who learns the same way or read aloud to yourself. Think about how to put the information in your own words. Imagine that you are giving a lecture on the topic and record yourself so you can listen to it later.

For any learning style, flashcards can be helpful. Organize the information so you can take advantage of spare moments to review. Underline key words or phrases. Use different colors for different categories. Mnemonic devices (such as creating a short list in which every item starts with the same letter) can also help with retention. Find what works best for you and use it to store the information in your mind most effectively and easily.

Secret Key #3 – Practice the Right Way

Your success on test day depends not only on how many hours you put into preparing, but also on whether you prepared the right way. It's good to check along the way to see if your studying is paying off. One of the most effective ways to do this is by taking practice tests to evaluate your progress. Practice tests are useful because they show exactly where you need to improve. Every time you take a practice test, pay special attention to these three groups of questions:

- The questions you got wrong
- The questions you had to guess on, even if you guessed right
- The questions you found difficult or slow to work through

This will show you exactly what your weak areas are, and where you need to devote more study time. Ask yourself why each of these questions gave you trouble. Was it because you didn't understand the material? Was it because you didn't remember the vocabulary? Do you need more repetitions on this type of question to build speed and confidence? Dig into those questions and figure out how you can strengthen your weak areas as you go back to review the material.

Additionally, many practice tests have a section explaining the answer choices. It can be tempting to read the explanation and think that you now have a good understanding of the concept. However, an explanation likely only covers part of the question's broader context. Even if the explanation makes perfect sense, **go back and investigate** every concept related to the question until you're positive you have a thorough understanding.

As you go along, keep in mind that the practice test is just that: practice. Memorizing these questions and answers will not be very helpful on the actual test because it is unlikely to have any of the same exact questions. If you only know the right answers to the sample questions, you won't be prepared for the real thing. **Study the concepts** until you understand them fully, and then you'll be able to answer any question that shows up on the test.

It's important to wait on the practice tests until you're ready. If you take a test on your first day of study, you may be overwhelmed by the amount of material covered and how much you need to learn. Work up to it gradually.

On test day, you'll need to be prepared for answering questions, managing your time, and using the test-taking strategies you've learned. It's a lot to balance, like a mental marathon that will have a big impact on your future. Like training for a marathon, you'll need to start slowly and work your way up. When test day arrives, you'll be ready.

Start with the strategies you've read in the first two Secret Keys—plan your course and study in the way that works best for you. If you have time, consider using multiple study resources to get different approaches to the same concepts. It can be helpful to see difficult concepts from more than one angle. Then find a good source for practice tests. Many times, the test website will suggest potential study resources or provide sample tests.

Practice Test Strategy

If you're able to find at least three practice tests, we recommend this strategy:

Untimed and Open-Book Practice

Take the first test with no time constraints and with your notes and study guide handy. Take your time and focus on applying the strategies you've learned.

Timed and Open-Book Practice

Take the second practice test open-book as well, but set a timer and practice pacing yourself to finish in time.

Timed and Closed-Book Practice

Take any other practice tests as if it were test day. Set a timer and put away your study materials. Sit at a table or desk in a quiet room, imagine yourself at the testing center, and answer questions as quickly and accurately as possible.

Keep repeating timed and closed-book tests on a regular basis until you run out of practice tests or it's time for the actual test. Your mind will be ready for the schedule and stress of test day, and you'll be able to focus on recalling the material you've learned.

Secret Key #4 – Pace Yourself

Once you're fully prepared for the material on the test, your biggest challenge on test day will be managing your time. Just knowing that the clock is ticking can make you panic even if you have plenty of time left. Work on pacing yourself so you can build confidence against the time constraints of the exam. Pacing is a difficult skill to master, especially in a high-pressure environment, so **practice is vital**.

Set time expectations for your pace based on how much time is available. For example, if a section has 60 questions and the time limit is 30 minutes, you know you have to average 30 seconds or less per question in order to answer them all. Although 30 seconds is the hard limit, set 25 seconds per question as your goal, so you reserve extra time to spend on harder questions. When you budget extra time for the harder questions, you no longer have any reason to stress when those questions take longer to answer.

Don't let this time expectation distract you from working through the test at a calm, steady pace, but keep it in mind so you don't spend too much time on any one question. Recognize that taking extra time on one question you don't understand may keep you from answering two that you do understand later in the test. If your time limit for a question is up and you're still not sure of the answer, mark it and move on, and come back to it later if the time and the test format allow. If the testing format doesn't allow you to return to earlier questions, just make an educated guess; then put it out of your mind and move on.

On the easier questions, be careful not to rush. It may seem wise to hurry through them so you have more time for the challenging ones, but it's not worth missing one if you know the concept and just didn't take the time to read the question fully. Work efficiently but make sure you understand the question and have looked at all of the answer choices, since more than one may seem right at first.

Even if you're paying attention to the time, you may find yourself a little behind at some point. You should speed up to get back on track, but do so wisely. Don't panic; just take a few seconds less on each question until you're caught up. Don't guess without thinking, but do look through the answer choices and eliminate any you know are wrong. If you can get down to two choices, it is often worthwhile to guess from those. Once you've chosen an answer, move on and don't dwell on any that you skipped or had to hurry through. If a question was taking too long, chances are it was one of the harder ones, so you weren't as likely to get it right anyway.

On the other hand, if you find yourself getting ahead of schedule, it may be beneficial to slow down a little. The more quickly you work, the more likely you are to make a careless mistake that will affect your score. You've budgeted time for each question, so don't be afraid to spend that time. Practice an efficient but careful pace to get the most out of the time you have.

Secret Key #5 – Have a Plan for Guessing

When you're taking the test, you may find yourself stuck on a question. Some of the answer choices seem better than others, but you don't see the one answer choice that is obviously correct. What do you do?

The scenario described above is very common, yet most test takers have not effectively prepared for it. Developing and practicing a plan for guessing may be one of the single most effective uses of your time as you get ready for the exam.

In developing your plan for guessing, there are three questions to address:

- When should you start the guessing process?
- How should you narrow down the choices?
- Which answer should you choose?

When to Start the Guessing Process

Unless your plan for guessing is to select C every time (which, despite its merits, is not what we recommend), you need to leave yourself enough time to apply your answer elimination strategies. Since you have a limited amount of time for each question, that means that if you're going to give yourself the best shot at guessing correctly, you have to decide quickly whether or not you will guess.

Of course, the best-case scenario is that you don't have to guess at all, so first, see if you can answer the question based on your knowledge of the subject and basic reasoning skills. Focus on the key words in the question and try to jog your memory of related topics. Give yourself a chance to bring the knowledge to mind, but once you realize that you don't have (or you can't access) the knowledge you need to answer the question, it's time to start the guessing process.

It's almost always better to start the guessing process too early than too late. It only takes a few seconds to remember something and answer the question from knowledge. Carefully eliminating wrong answer choices takes longer. Plus, going through the process of eliminating answer choices can actually help jog your memory.

Summary: Start the guessing process as soon as you decide that you can't answer the question based on your knowledge.

How to Narrow Down the Choices

The next chapter in this book (**Test-Taking Strategies**) includes a wide range of strategies for how to approach questions and how to look for answer choices to eliminate. You will definitely want to read those carefully, practice them, and figure out which ones work best for you. Here though, we're going to address a mindset rather than a particular strategy.

Your odds of guessing an answer correctly depend on how many options you are choosing from.

Number of options left	5	4	3	2	1
Odds of guessing correctly	20%	25%	33%	50%	100%

You can see from this chart just how valuable it is to be able to eliminate incorrect answers and make an educated guess, but there are two things that many test takers do that cause them to miss out on the benefits of guessing:

- Accidentally eliminating the correct answer
- Selecting an answer based on an impression

We'll look at the first one here, and the second one in the next section.

To avoid accidentally eliminating the correct answer, we recommend a thought exercise called **the $5 challenge**. In this challenge, you only eliminate an answer choice from contention if you are willing to bet $5 on it being wrong. Why $5? Five dollars is a small but not insignificant amount of money. It's an amount you could afford to lose but wouldn't want to throw away. And while losing $5 once might not hurt too much, doing it twenty times will set you back $100. In the same way, each small decision you make—eliminating a choice here, guessing on a question there—won't by itself impact your score very much, but when you put them all together, they can make a big difference. By holding each answer choice elimination decision to a higher standard, you can reduce the risk of accidentally eliminating the correct answer.

The $5 challenge can also be applied in a positive sense: If you are willing to bet $5 that an answer choice *is* correct, go ahead and mark it as correct.

Summary: Only eliminate an answer choice if you are willing to bet $5 that it is wrong.

Which Answer to Choose

You're taking the test. You've run into a hard question and decided you'll have to guess. You've eliminated all the answer choices you're willing to bet $5 on. Now you have to pick an answer. Why do we even need to talk about this? Why can't you just pick whichever one you feel like when the time comes?

The answer to these questions is that if you don't come into the test with a plan, you'll rely on your impression to select an answer choice, and if you do that, you risk falling into a trap. The test writers know that everyone who takes their test will be guessing on some of the questions, so they intentionally write wrong answer choices to seem plausible. You still have to pick an answer though, and if the wrong answer choices are designed to look right, how can you ever be sure that you're not falling for their trap? The best solution we've found to this dilemma is to take the decision out of your hands entirely. Here is the process we recommend:

Once you've eliminated any choices that you are confident (willing to bet $5) are wrong, select the first remaining choice as your answer.

Whether you choose to select the first remaining choice, the second, or the last, the important thing is that you use some preselected standard. Using this approach guarantees that you will not be enticed into selecting an answer choice that looks right, because you are not basing your decision on how the answer choices look.

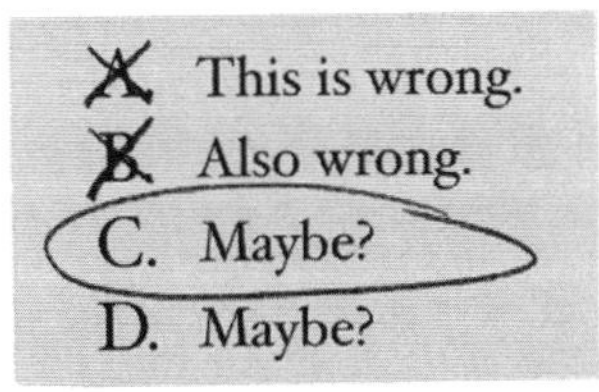

This is not meant to make you question your knowledge. Instead, it is to help you recognize the difference between your knowledge and your impressions. There's a huge difference between thinking an answer is right because of what you know, and thinking an answer is right because it looks or sounds like it should be right.

Summary: To ensure that your selection is appropriately random, make a predetermined selection from among all answer choices you have not eliminated.

Test-Taking Strategies

This section contains a list of test-taking strategies that you may find helpful as you work through the test. By taking what you know and applying logical thought, you can maximize your chances of answering any question correctly!

It is very important to realize that every question is different and every person is different: no single strategy will work on every question, and no single strategy will work for every person. That's why we've included all of them here, so you can try them out and determine which ones work best for different types of questions and which ones work best for you.

Question Strategies

☑ Read Carefully

Read the question and the answer choices carefully. Don't miss the question because you misread the terms. You have plenty of time to read each question thoroughly and make sure you understand what is being asked. Yet a happy medium must be attained, so don't waste too much time. You must read carefully and efficiently.

☑ Contextual Clues

Look for contextual clues. If the question includes a word you are not familiar with, look at the immediate context for some indication of what the word might mean. Contextual clues can often give you all the information you need to decipher the meaning of an unfamiliar word. Even if you can't determine the meaning, you may be able to narrow down the possibilities enough to make a solid guess at the answer to the question.

☑ Prefixes

If you're having trouble with a word in the question or answer choices, try dissecting it. Take advantage of every clue that the word might include. Prefixes can be a huge help. Usually, they allow you to determine a basic meaning. *Pre-* means before, *post-* means after, *pro-* is positive, *de-* is negative. From prefixes, you can get an idea of the general meaning of the word and try to put it into context.

☑ Hedge Words

Watch out for critical hedge words, such as *likely, may, can, often, almost, mostly, usually, generally, rarely,* and *sometimes.* Question writers insert these hedge phrases to cover every possibility. Often an answer choice will be wrong simply because it leaves no room for exception. Be on guard for answer choices that have definitive words such as *exactly* and *always.*

☑ Switchback Words

Stay alert for *switchbacks.* These are the words and phrases frequently used to alert you to shifts in thought. The most common switchback words are *but, although,* and *however.* Others include *nevertheless, on the other hand, even though, while, in spite of, despite,* and *regardless of.* Switchback words are important to catch because they can change the direction of the question or an answer choice.

✓ Face Value

When in doubt, use common sense. Accept the situation in the problem at face value. Don't read too much into it. These problems will not require you to make wild assumptions. If you have to go beyond creativity and warp time or space in order to have an answer choice fit the question, then you should move on and consider the other answer choices. These are normal problems rooted in reality. The applicable relationship or explanation may not be readily apparent, but it is there for you to figure out. Use your common sense to interpret anything that isn't clear.

Answer Choice Strategies

✓ Answer Selection

The most thorough way to pick an answer choice is to identify and eliminate wrong answers until only one is left, then confirm it is the correct answer. Sometimes an answer choice may immediately seem right, but be careful. The test writers will usually put more than one reasonable answer choice on each question, so take a second to read all of them and make sure that the other choices are not equally obvious. As long as you have time left, it is better to read every answer choice than to pick the first one that looks right without checking the others.

✓ Answer Choice Families

An answer choice family consists of two (in rare cases, three) answer choices that are very similar in construction and cannot all be true at the same time. If you see two answer choices that are direct opposites or parallels, one of them is usually the correct answer. For instance, if one answer choice says that quantity *x* increases and another either says that quantity *x* decreases (opposite) or says that quantity *y* increases (parallel), then those answer choices would fall into the same family. An answer choice that doesn't match the construction of the answer choice family is more likely to be incorrect. Most questions will not have answer choice families, but when they do appear, you should be prepared to recognize them.

✓ Eliminate Answers

Eliminate answer choices as soon as you realize they are wrong, but make sure you consider all possibilities. If you are eliminating answer choices and realize that the last one you are left with is also wrong, don't panic. Start over and consider each choice again. There may be something you missed the first time that you will realize on the second pass.

✓ Avoid Fact Traps

Don't be distracted by an answer choice that is factually true but doesn't answer the question. You are looking for the choice that answers the question. Stay focused on what the question is asking for so you don't accidentally pick an answer that is true but incorrect. Always go back to the question and make sure the answer choice you've selected actually answers the question and is not merely a true statement.

✓ Extreme Statements

In general, you should avoid answers that put forth extreme actions as standard practice or proclaim controversial ideas as established fact. An answer choice that states the "process should be used in certain situations, if..." is much more likely to be correct than one that states the "process should be discontinued completely." The first is a calm rational statement and doesn't even make a definitive, uncompromising stance, using a hedge word *if* to provide wiggle room, whereas the second choice is far more extreme.

⊘ Benchmark

As you read through the answer choices and you come across one that seems to answer the question well, mentally select that answer choice. This is not your final answer, but it's the one that will help you evaluate the other answer choices. The one that you selected is your benchmark or standard for judging each of the other answer choices. Every other answer choice must be compared to your benchmark. That choice is correct until proven otherwise by another answer choice beating it. If you find a better answer, then that one becomes your new benchmark. Once you've decided that no other choice answers the question as well as your benchmark, you have your final answer.

⊘ Predict the Answer

Before you even start looking at the answer choices, it is often best to try to predict the answer. When you come up with the answer on your own, it is easier to avoid distractions and traps because you will know exactly what to look for. The right answer choice is unlikely to be word-for-word what you came up with, but it should be a close match. Even if you are confident that you have the right answer, you should still take the time to read each option before moving on.

General Strategies

⊘ Tough Questions

If you are stumped on a problem or it appears too hard or too difficult, don't waste time. Move on! Remember though, if you can quickly check for obviously incorrect answer choices, your chances of guessing correctly are greatly improved. Before you completely give up, at least try to knock out a couple of possible answers. Eliminate what you can and then guess at the remaining answer choices before moving on.

⊘ Check Your Work

Since you will probably not know every term listed and the answer to every question, it is important that you get credit for the ones that you do know. Don't miss any questions through careless mistakes. If at all possible, try to take a second to look back over your answer selection and make sure you've selected the correct answer choice and haven't made a costly careless mistake (such as marking an answer choice that you didn't mean to mark). This quick double check should more than pay for itself in caught mistakes for the time it costs.

⊘ Pace Yourself

It's easy to be overwhelmed when you're looking at a page full of questions; your mind is confused and full of random thoughts, and the clock is ticking down faster than you would like. Calm down and maintain the pace that you have set for yourself. Especially as you get down to the last few minutes of the test, don't let the small numbers on the clock make you panic. As long as you are on track by monitoring your pace, you are guaranteed to have time for each question.

⊘ Don't Rush

It is very easy to make errors when you are in a hurry. Maintaining a fast pace in answering questions is pointless if it makes you miss questions that you would have gotten right otherwise. Test writers like to include distracting information and wrong answers that seem right. Taking a little extra time to avoid careless mistakes can make all the difference in your test score. Find a pace that allows you to be confident in the answers that you select.

⊘ KEEP MOVING

Panicking will not help you pass the test, so do your best to stay calm and keep moving. Taking deep breaths and going through the answer elimination steps you practiced can help to break through a stress barrier and keep your pace.

Final Notes

The combination of a solid foundation of content knowledge and the confidence that comes from practicing your plan for applying that knowledge is the key to maximizing your performance on test day. As your foundation of content knowledge is built up and strengthened, you'll find that the strategies included in this chapter become more and more effective in helping you quickly sift through the distractions and traps of the test to isolate the correct answer.

Now that you're preparing to move forward into the test content chapters of this book, be sure to keep your goal in mind. As you read, think about how you will be able to apply this information on the test. If you've already seen sample questions for the test and you have an idea of the question format and style, try to come up with questions of your own that you can answer based on what you're reading. This will give you valuable practice applying your knowledge in the same ways you can expect to on test day.

Good luck and good studying!

Foundations of Reading Development

Phonetics, Phonics, and Print Concepts

Building Rapid Word Identification and Automaticity

Rapid word identification and **automaticity** refer to the quick, effortless, and accurate recognition of individual words when reading. Speed and accuracy are strong predictors of comprehension, so the ability to identify words automatically plays an important role in reading development.

When readers come to unfamiliar words in texts, they pause to use reading strategies. This includes applying phonics skills and using semantic and syntactic clues. Using these strategies takes time, which may cause the reader to slow down. Applying strategies to decode words also requires significant processing in working memory, which is limited. This diverts attention away from comprehending the text, and comprehension may be negatively affected. When readers develop the ability to accurately and automatically identify words, they free up space in working memory to use for comprehension. This shift often occurs around second and third grade.

It is also important to remember that rapid word identification and automaticity are necessary for fluency but not sufficient on their own. Fluency also involves reading with appropriate phrasing and intonation.

Strategies to Build Automatic Recognition of High-Frequency Sight Words

Readers need several opportunities to see words before they can automatically recognize them. Therefore, providing opportunities for repeated exposure to high-frequency sight words is an important goal of reading instruction and should be included along with explicit phonics instruction.

Sight words are commonly introduced to students a few at a time. The most frequently used words, such as *a*, *you*, and *the*, are typically introduced first. Some reading programs coordinate sight word lists with weekly texts, ensuring that students will have frequent exposure to each set of words as they are introduced.

There are several types of activities that can be done to build sight word recognition. Having students go on "word hunts" to locate and circle sight words in texts is one activity. Sight words can be built using magnetic letters or spelled in the air with fingers or wands. Activities that require students to read, build, and write each word are also commonly used. Additionally, flash card drills can be incorporated into the school day.

Typical Progression of Phonological Awareness Skills

One of the earliest phonological awareness skills children develop is the ability to recognize rhyming words. After recognizing rhyming words heard in stories, songs, and poems, children begin to produce their own sets of rhyming words. Alliteration, or identifying and producing words with the same initial sounds, is another early phonological awareness skill.

Later, children develop awareness of syllables. This involves both the ability to blend syllables to form whole words and the ability to break whole words into syllables. They also develop the ability to blend and segment onsets and rimes. **Onsets** are composed of the initial consonants or consonant blends in syllables, whereas **rimes** consist of the vowels and remaining consonants that follow. For example, in the word *star*, /st/ is the onset, and /ar/ is the rime. Phonemic awareness is the most advanced phonological awareness skill, and it is usually developed after the others.

RELATIONSHIP BETWEEN PHONOLOGICAL AWARENESS AND PHONEMIC AWARENESS

Although they are often used interchangeably, phonological awareness and phonemic awareness are distinct terms. **Phonological awareness** is a broader term that refers to the ability to identify and manipulate sounds in spoken language. This can refer to identifying and manipulating sounds at the word, syllable, or phoneme level. Example activities include rhyming, alliteration, breaking words into syllables, dividing syllables into onsets and rimes, and blending and segmenting phonemes.

Phonemic awareness is one specific component of phonological awareness. It focuses on the ability to identify and manipulate sounds at the phoneme level only. Phonemes are the smallest units of speech, and phonemic awareness is therefore the most advanced component of phonological awareness. It usually develops after other phonological awareness skills.

Review Video: Phonological and Phonemic Awareness, and Phonics
Visit mometrix.com/academy and enter code: 197017

PHONEMIC AWARENESS SKILLS

One early phonemic awareness skill is **phoneme isolation**, which is the ability to identify specific phonemes in spoken words. This includes identifying beginning (initial), middle (medial), and ending (final) sounds. Another skill is **phoneme identification**, which involves identifying the common sound in a list of words that have either the same beginning, middle, or ending sound. In phoneme categorization, students are given a set of words in which all but one have the same beginning, middle, or ending phoneme, and they must identify the word that doesn't belong.

In **blending**, a more complex skill, students are given the phonemes that make up a word in isolation. They must then identify the whole word formed by putting the phonemes together. In **segmentation**, students are given a whole word and must identify the individual phonemes that make up that word. **Phoneme deletion** involves removing one phoneme from a word and identifying what new word was formed. **Phoneme substitution** involves changing one phoneme in a word and identifying what new word was formed.

ACTIVITIES USED TO TEACH PHONEME BLENDING AND SEGMENTATION

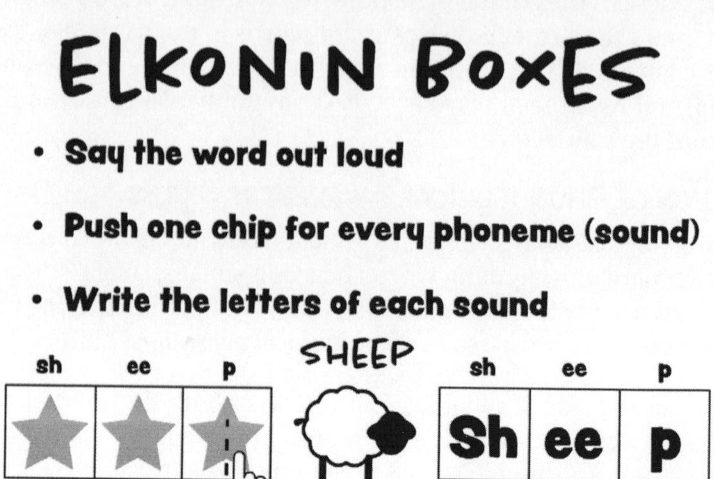

Children often benefit from a multisensory approach to phonemic blending and segmentation. **Elkonin boxes** are one tool that can be used. Elkonin boxes consist of a series of connected boxes on paper. Students listen to a word and slide a penny or other token into a box each time they hear a new sound. For example, while listening to the word *cat*, students would slide three pennies into the boxes.

Students can also be given strings of beads, and they can move one bead for every sound, or phoneme, they hear. They can slide the beads back together as they blend the sounds to form the whole words again. Rubber bands can be used in a similar manner. Students can say whole words with the rubber bands un-stretched and then slowly stretch the bands as they segment the sounds. They can then push the rubber bands back together again as they blend the sounds to form the whole words.

Phonics

Phonics refers to the relationship between letters and the sounds they make. After children learn to identify letter names, they learn that each letter makes a predictable sound. They later learn that groups of letters, such as consonant blends and digraphs, make predictable sounds as well. This understanding of letter-sound relationships is known as phonics.

Understanding the predictable relationship between letters and the sounds they make is important for the development of both decoding and encoding skills. When early readers come across unfamiliar words, they use knowledge of letter-sound relationships to decode the words as one common reading strategy. For early readers, this is especially helpful for unknown words that follow predictable spelling patterns, such as CVC words. When children are engaging in early writing activities, they use knowledge of letter-sound relationships to write words, which is known as **encoding**.

Phonemic Awareness Vs. Phonics

Phonemic awareness and phonics are commonly confused terms, but they are not the same. **Phonemic awareness** refers to identifying and manipulating phonemes in spoken language. **Phonics** refers to the relationship between letters and the sounds they make. A key question to ask when deciding if an activity is related to phonemic awareness or phonics is whether or not any letters are involved. If letters and their sounds are involved, the activity is related to phonics rather than phonemic awareness.

For example, asking students what sounds they hear in the word *cat* is a phonemic awareness activity because they are identifying sounds in a spoken word. However, asking students to decode the word *cat* when it is written in a text is a phonics activity because students must use their understanding of letter-sound relationships to successfully decode the word. Students are also using phonics skills if they write the word *cat* by identifying the sounds that they hear and writing the letters that make those sounds.

Fluency

Fluency is defined as reading accurately with the appropriate speed and intonation. Beginning readers typically have to stop and decode unknown words frequently, which affects both speed and intonation. Over time, as readers develop rapid word recognition, their reading speed increases. Appropriate intonation is also developed through frequent shared and guided reading experiences.

Relationship Between Fluency and Comprehension

Research has shown that reading fluency is one major predictor of reading comprehension. Non-fluent readers burden their working memories with decoding. Sentences are read in a fragmented way, making it difficult for the brain to organize and make sense of what was read. After expending the energy to decode difficult words, they may forget what they have previously read. Fluent readers are free to use working memory for comprehending the text. They read using smooth, continuous phrasing, making it easier for the brain to make sense of what has been read.

Using Syntactic and Semantic Cues to Figure out Unknown Words

Readers can use multiple cueing systems to figure out unknown words and make meaning from texts. When readers use **syntactic cues**, they use knowledge about correct oral language structures and the ways sentences are put together to decode and make meaning. For example, readers may use knowledge about subject-verb agreement and word order to decode new words and make meaning from sentences. When readers use **semantic cues**, they use prior knowledge from personal experiences along with meaning contained in the text and pictures to make sense of what they are reading. When they are stuck on unknown words, they consider what they already know about the topic or look to context clues or pictures for hints. While many readers still will use cueing systems to help them read unknown words, the best practice is to teach students to decode words using systematic and explicit phonics instruction rather than cueing systems.

Decoding Vs. Encoding

Decoding refers to the process of translating print to speech, which is done by translating graphemes into phonemes. **Graphemes** are letters or groups of letters that represent a single sound, and phonemes are the smallest units of sound in language. When a reader uses strategies to read the printed word *chair*, he or she is decoding the word.

Encoding refers to the process of translating sounds to print using knowledge of letter-sound relationships. This is done by translating phonemes to graphemes. When a writer uses knowledge of the sounds letters make to write the word *hop*, he or she is encoding the word.

Review Video: Phonics (Encoding and Decoding)
Visit mometrix.com/academy and enter code: 821361

Observing how a developing writer spells can be used to assess phonics knowledge. It can provide information about the writer's understanding of when to apply certain spelling patterns. By observing the writer's work over time, a teacher can determine which phonics strategies the writer has mastered and which are still developing. This information can be used to plan individualized phonics instruction. For example, if a writer frequently spells CVCe words without the e at the end, the teacher may focus on this spelling pattern during guided reading lessons with the student.

Review Video: Print Awareness and Alphabet Knowledge
Visit mometrix.com/academy and enter code: 541069

Instructional Strategies Used to Teach Decoding of Common Spelling Patterns

Blending is a common strategy to teach decoding of CVC words. Students say the sound represented by each letter in the word and then state the whole word they made. To increase fluency, students can be encouraged to increase the speed of blending over time. Once CVC words have been mastered and students have been introduced to consonant blends and digraphs, they can use the same blending process with CVCC words.

For CVVC and CVCe words that cannot be decoded using blending, students can be introduced to the sounds made by each spelling pattern. They can then build and explore word families that contain the same spelling pattern, changing the initial sounds to build new, related words. For example, after identifying the sound that /ake/ makes, students can build *rake*, *cake*, and *lake* using letter tiles or magnetic letters.

Instructional Strategies Used to Teach Decoding of Multisyllabic Words

Although decoding instruction typically tapers off around second grade, it is at this point that students begin reading texts with more complex, multisyllabic words. Therefore, it is important to teach specific strategies that readers can use to decode these types of words.

One strategy is to teach students to identify the different syllables present in a word. This can be done by clapping each syllable or saying the word while looking in a mirror and observing how many times the mouth opens. Students can then be taught to recognize common syllable spelling patterns and the sounds that they make. These common syllable spelling patterns include the following:

- closed syllables, which end in a consonant and usually have a short vowel sound (e.g., rabbit)
- open syllables, which end in a vowel and usually have a long vowel sound (e.g., bagel)
- r-controlled vowels (e.g., carpet)
- vowel digraph pairs (e.g., detain)
- vowel-consonant-silent-e syllables, which usually have a long vowel sound (e.g., athlete)
- consonant-le words, which are usually found at the end of a word (e.g., maple)

Readers can also be taught to look for known parts of words, such as known prefixes and suffixes.

Consonant Blends and Consonant Digraphs

A **consonant blend** is a group of two or three consonants that blend together to make a sound, but each individual letter sound is still heard. Examples include *bl*, *fr*, and *sw*. Blends are typically introduced after readers have learned to decode basic CVC words, and they are introduced in groups according to the second consonant they contain. Blends containing two consonants are usually introduced before blends containing three consonants. When introducing each blend, the teacher shows students how the sounds of each consonant are blended together to form the new sound. Common words containing the blend can be listed, and students can go on word hunts to find additional examples of words containing the blend. Students can also sort cards containing pictures of objects whose names are spelled with consonant blends.

A **consonant digraph** is a group of two consonants that form a new consonant sound when combined. Examples include *th*, *sh*, and *ch*. Digraphs are also typically introduced a few at a time, with beginning digraphs introduced before ending digraphs. Creating lists of example words, going on word hunts, and completing matching and sorting activities can also be used to teach digraphs.

R-Controlled Vowels

R-controlled vowels are vowels that appear before the letter r in a word. Words containing this spelling pattern are sometimes referred to as bossy-r words, because the letter r changes the sound of the vowel. The r-controlled vowel pairs are *ar*, *ir*, *or*, and *er*.

To teach decoding of words containing r-controlled vowels, teachers can model blending of simple words containing these spelling patterns by sliding their fingers along the words as they blend them. For each word, they can point out that the vowel and r together make one sound, and they can generate a list of other words containing the same letter pair and sound. Students can also be given word or picture cards to sort according to which r-controlled vowel sound they contain. Another strategy is to provide a picture of an object that contains an r-controlled vowel in its name. The word can be written below the picture, with the r-controlled vowel omitted. Students can be asked to provide the missing letters to complete the word.

BENEFITS OF EXPLICIT PHONICS INSTRUCTION

Research has shown that early readers benefit from an explicit and systematic approach to phonics instruction. Developing readers who receive explicit and systematic phonics instruction at an early age often show increased ability to decode and spell, along with increased reading comprehension skills when older.

Explicit instruction means that phonics lessons are purposely planned to address specific skills rather than waiting until problems arise with decoding words while reading. For example, a teacher may plan to focus on a set of consonant blends during one week of reading instruction. Systematic instruction means that the lessons follow a carefully planned scope and sequence, with phonics lessons progressing from basic to advanced. Early phonics lessons for kindergarteners may focus on letter-sound relationships, whereas first grade students may focus on decoding different spelling patterns.

ROLE OF PHONOLOGICAL AWARENESS AND PHONICS SKILLS IN READING DEVELOPMENT

ENGLISH LANGUAGE LEARNERS

For English language learners (ELLs), research has shown that **phonological awareness** in a reader's first language is a **strong predictor** of his or her ability to learn to read in a second language. This is especially true when the native language is closely related to English. Despite the fact that phonological awareness in the native language can be beneficial when learning English, it may lead to **overgeneralization** of rules of the native language. Continued language experiences in the native language along with language scaffolding can be beneficial to ELLs as they learn English.

Some ELLs may also speak native languages in which there is not a **one-to-one correspondence** between letters and phonemes. They may also speak languages that use the same alphabet as English but where the letters represent different sounds. It is important for teachers to understand their ELLs' prior knowledge and consider this when planning appropriate phonics instruction.

Additionally, some English phonemes may not be used in other languages. Introducing English vocabulary words that contain these phonemes helps give these sounds a meaningful context. Using poems and songs with repetition and rhyme can also be helpful.

Review Video: ESL/ESOL/Second Language Learning
Visit mometrix.com/academy and enter code: 795047

STRUGGLING AND PROFICIENT STUDENTS

Research has shown that phonological awareness and phonics skills are important predictors of reading success. For struggling readers, daily phonological awareness and phonics practice are important. Explicit and systematic instruction should be tailored to the individual needs of each student and based upon observation and assessment data. Once a teacher has determined which skills the student needs to improve, instruction should be regularly included to target these skills until mastered. Ongoing reading assessments and flexible groupings can help make sure that struggling readers' individual needs are consistently met.

Phonological awareness and phonics assessments are important for proficient readers as well. Some proficient readers have developed strong rapid word identification skills without mastering the underlying phonological awareness and phonics skills. When they get into older grade levels and more frequently encounter unfamiliar vocabulary, they will have difficulty decoding the text. Assessment data can be used to identify specific skills to practice in small-group instruction with these proficient readers.

Role of Natural Exposure to Phonics in Early Reading Development

Like explicit phonics instruction, natural exposure to phonics also plays a role in early reading development. This exposure occurs when children are involved in natural reading experiences, and they come across words they are unable to decode. Phonics instruction is provided in the moment to address the unknown words.

This type of phonics instruction is known as **implicit** instruction. It differs from explicit instruction, which progresses from part (letter sounds) to whole (whole words). Implicit instruction progresses from whole (unknown words encountered in text) to part (breaking down the words in order to decode them).

Implicit phonics instruction has some benefits. Because it occurs during natural reading experiences, the phonics skills are taught **in context** rather than in isolation. Readers are motivated to learn the skills needed to decode the unknown words and continue reading. Teachers can allow time to address unknown words while reading aloud or listening to students reading independently. However, research has shown that it is still important to schedule time for explicit and systematic phonics instruction as well.

Strategies to Teach Letter Identification

Most reading programs introduce letters gradually. Some suggest introducing letters that have high value to learners first, such as the first letters of their names. Others focus on letters that play prominent roles in the books they are reading for the week, whereas others sequence letters by physical characteristics. In general, it is best to avoid teaching commonly confused letter pairs simultaneously, such as b and d.

To develop **letter recognition**, students can be given texts and instructed to circle certain letters. They can play alphabet bingo and cover specific letters when they are called. They can sing the alphabet song while pointing to each letter. Additionally, they can go on letter hunts, where they search the classroom or building to find examples of specific letters in environmental print. To practice recognizing capital and lowercase forms of letters, students can play memory and find matches consisting of both letter forms.

Strategies to Teach Letter Formation

To teach letter formation, students can be given letter stencils to trace with pencils. They can also be provided cutout letters made from different materials, such as felt and sandpaper, to trace with their fingers. Later, they can attempt to write letters independently on writing paper following the school's selected handwriting program guidelines.

To practice letter formation using a **multisensory approach**, students can write letters with shaving cream or fingerpaint. They can also write letters in containers filled with salt or sand. Wax craft sticks, modeling dough, and pipe cleaners can be used to construct letter models. Large-sized letters can also be drawn using sidewalk chalk, and students can hop along the letter shapes to trace them. They can also trace letter shapes in the air with their fingers or toy wands. Additionally, students can be given outlines of letters, which they can fill in with buttons, dried beans, or other common objects.

Strategies to Teach Letter-Sound Relationships

Once students understand that letters are combined to form words that convey meaning in print, they begin learning that each letter makes a predictable sound. This is known as the **alphabetic principle**. Although different reading programs introduce the letters and sounds in different orders, most introduce the letter-sound relationships gradually.

In some reading programs, each letter has a song, poem, or chant that incorporates repetition of the letter name and sound. In others, a letter character or visual is produced, which includes a hint about the sound it makes. The visual often includes a picture of a common object that starts with the letter. Students can also be encouraged to find objects beginning with the letter sound they are learning. Tactile activities, such as building letters out of wax craft sticks or writing them in shaving cream while repeating the names and sounds, are also commonly used. Bingo and other similar games that require matching letters to their sounds can also be used.

Concepts of Print That Collectively Form a Foundation for Early Reading Instruction

Concepts of print are the conventions used to convey meaning in printed text. Children begin developing an understanding of these concepts from an early age through shared reading experiences with others and interactions with printed materials.

Understanding concepts of print includes recognizing the front cover, back cover, and title of a book. It also includes recognizing that the print, rather than the pictures, carries the message. Additionally, it includes directionality concepts, such as knowing that you read from left to right and from the top of the page to the bottom, with a return sweep at the end of each line of text. One-to-one correspondence between written and spoken words is another concept of print. Letter concepts are also important, such as knowing that words are made up of individual letters, identifying letter names, and identifying both capital and lowercase letters. Identifying the names and purposes of common punctuation marks used to end sentences is also a key concept of print.

Strategies to Teach Print Awareness

Starting at an early age, caregivers and teachers can begin introducing children to concepts of print. While reading storybooks and big books aloud, they can model how to hold the books, where the front and back covers and titles are located, and where to begin reading. They can also model directionality by following the text with their fingers as they read, showing the left-to-right movement and return sweep. They can point out different text features, such as capital letters and punctuation marks, and discuss their purposes.

When students are interacting with texts independently, teachers can ask them questions regarding concepts of print. For example, they can instruct students to follow the text with their fingers and pause after encountering punctuation marks at the ends of sentences. Teachers can also point out text features in environmental print, such as hallway signs.

Morphology and Word Analysis Skills

Homographs

Homographs are words that are spelled the same but may be pronounced differently and have different meanings. An example of a homograph pair is *bat* (baseball bat) and *bat* (the flying mammal).

After explaining the meaning of homographs, teachers can assist students with generating lists of homograph pairs. Teachers can provide sentences using homographs, and students can identify them and their meanings. Students can also look for homographs in texts and play matching games to find cards with two different definitions for the same word.

Homographs have different meanings, so it is important for readers to be able to identify which meanings are being used when they encounter homographs in texts. Readers can be encouraged to use context clues to assist with determining the meanings. Readers can also be encouraged to self-monitor their understanding of each homograph's meaning by asking themselves if what they have read makes sense. Because homograph pairs can also be pronounced differently, readers can be encouraged to try reading the sentences with each possible pronunciation and ask themselves which one sounds right.

Compound Words

A **compound word** is formed by combining two or more words to form one word with a new, unique meaning. Examples of compound words include *houseboat*, *moonlight*, and *basketball*.

Identifying compound words rapidly can assist readers with decoding multisyllabic words. Identifying the smaller, known words contained in the compound words will help students decode the words quickly and maintain fluency.

To teach students to identify compound words, they can practice breaking them into parts. Compound words can be provided using letter tiles, magnetic letters, or in writing, and students can be asked to split them into the two smaller word parts. Puzzle cards can be created with which two smaller words join together to create a compound word. Readers can also be asked to find and mark compound words in texts. When students struggle to decode compound words while reading independently, teachers can ask what smaller, known words they see in the unknown words.

Types of Context Clues

- There are several different types of context clues that are often provided in sentences. One common type is a **definition clue**. In this type of clue, a definition for the unfamiliar word is provided somewhere within the same sentence; for example, *the precocious toddler surprised her parents by learning to read at a much earlier age than her peers.*
- Another type of context clue is an **antonym clue**. In this type of clue, an antonym or contrasting definition of the unfamiliar word is provided somewhere within the same sentence; for example, *unlike his amiable coworker, Mark was quite unfriendly when interacting with customers.*
- **Synonym clues** are a third type of context clue. In this type, a synonym for the unfamiliar word is provided somewhere within the same sentence; for example, *the altruistic donor was so selfless that she donated all of her lottery winnings to her favorite charity.*

- **Inference clues** are another type of context clue. With this type of clue, the unknown word's meaning is not explicitly given, and the reader must infer it from the context of the sentence; for example, *Sam was thirsty after hiking the three-mile trail, so he ordered a cold beverage at the café.*

AFFIXES

Affixes are letters or groups of letters that are added to root words. **Prefixes** and **suffixes** are two common types of **affixes**. Root words may have one or multiple affixes attached to them.

Learning to identify affixes and understand their meanings is important for both fluency and comprehension. Because the same affixes are used repeatedly in English, immediately recognizing them and knowing how they are pronounced can assist readers with decoding multisyllabic words. Decoding the words quickly will help the readers maintain fluency. Because affixes also have predictable meanings, understanding these meanings can help readers comprehend new words in texts and build vocabulary. For example, if readers encounter the word *declutter*, they may know that *de* means the opposite of something, and *clutter* means a messy collection of things. Using this knowledge, they can put the parts together and determine the meaning of *declutter*.

Review Video: Affixes
Visit mometrix.com/academy and enter code: 782422

PREFIXES

A **prefix** is a letter or group of letters added to the beginning of a root word. The prefix modifies the existing word's meaning, and a new word is formed. For example, the prefix *dis-* can be added to the word *respect* to form the new word *disrespect.*

Students need to understand the difference between a prefix and base word. It should be emphasized that the base is a whole word, whereas the prefix is a letter or group of letters that cannot stand alone. Examples of words containing prefixes can be provided, and students can practice identifying both the prefixes and root words. Non-examples can also be provided, such as the word *decal. De-* is not a prefix in this example because *cal* is not a word on its own.

The meanings of different prefixes can then be introduced. Root words can be presented, and their meanings discussed. Prefixes can then be added, and students can discuss how the meanings of the words change. They can list other words containing the same prefixes, along with their meanings.

Students can also be encouraged to find examples of words containing prefixes in texts independently and use clues to determine their meanings.

SUFFIXES

A **suffix** is a letter or group of letters added to the end of a root word. When added, it sometimes changes the meaning of the root word and forms a new word. It may also change the part of speech of the root word. An example of a suffix is *-ful.* When added to the end of the root word *thank*, it forms the word *thankful*, which means full of thanks.

To introduce the topic, students can be given lists of words containing suffixes and asked to identify what the words have in common. The suffixes can then be identified, and teachers can explain how the suffixes change the root words. Three-column charts can be created, with columns dedicated to suffixes, their meanings, and example words. Students can be given cards containing root words and suffixes, and they can experiment with pairing them. They can explain whether the combinations form real or nonsense words and define any real words they create. Students can be encouraged to find examples of words containing suffixes and identify their meanings based on context clues in the texts.

Derivational vs. Inflectional Affixes

- **Derivational affixes** are letters or groups of letters added to root words to change the meanings of the words or the parts of speech.For example, if the affix *un-* is added to the root *kind*, the new word *unkind* is formed. Both the original and newly formed words are adjectives, but the meanings of the two words are different. However, if the affix *-ment* is added to the root word *fulfill*, the new word *fulfillment* is formed. The original word is a verb, and the newly formed word is a noun. Both of these examples demonstrate derivational affixes.
- **Inflectional affixes** do not change the part of speech of a word, but they do serve a grammatical function. Inflectional affixes include the suffixes *-s*, *-ed*, *-ing*, *-en*, *-'s*, *-er*, and *-est*. For example, adding an inflectional affix can change the word *walk* to *walked*. The part of speech does not change as both words are verbs. The affix only changes the tense of the verb. Inflectional affixes can indicate whether a noun is singular or plural, the verb tense, superlatives, or possessives.

Relationship Between Knowledge of Roots and Affixes

Knowledge of roots and affixes and the use of **context clues** are closely related. Proficient readers use a combination of these strategies to determine the meanings of unknown words, check their initial guesses, and revise their guesses if necessary.

- When encountering an unknown multisyllabic word, a reader may first look for kno**wn parts** of the word. This may lead the reader to break the word down into the root and affixes. Using knowledge of what each of these components means, the reader may then guess the word's meaning.
- However, both roots and affixes can have multiple meanings. The reader's initial guess may not make sense in this particular context. Therefore, it is important for the reader to also consider **context clues** to check the conjectured meaning. If it does not fit the context, the reader may consider other meanings of the root and affixes that better fit the context clues.
- The reader may also begin by guessing the word's meaning using context clues and then use knowledge of the root and affixes to check the initial conjecture. Teachers should encourage readers to use both of these strategies to **check** and **self-correct** their deductions.

Supporting Vocabulary Development

Encouraging Vocabulary Acquisition Through Reading and Writing Activities

If a new text contains unfamiliar vocabulary words that are central to the meaning and/or may be difficult to decode, a teacher may **preview** the words with the group. After introducing the topic of the text, the teacher may flip to the words, show students their spellings, and ask students to share what the words may mean based on prior knowledge and picture clues. Exposure to these words before reading will build readers' confidence and help them recognize and decode the words faster, maintaining fluency. Knowing the meanings in advance will also assist with comprehension.

When reading aloud to students, teachers may pause at new vocabulary words and model how to use context clues, prior knowledge, and picture support to decode and comprehend the new words. Students can be encouraged to use these strategies when reading independently.

Readers need repeated exposure to vocabulary words to develop automatic recognition and comprehension. Teachers may display classroom charts containing vocabulary words and their meanings, possibly using picture clues for young readers.

Students can also be encouraged to incorporate vocabulary words in their own writing. Word walls or charts containing the words can assist students with spelling and remembering the meanings of the words.

Helping Readers Explore the Meanings of Unknown Vocabulary Words

First, it is important for students to identify unknown vocabulary words when reading. Readers who are not monitoring their own comprehension may decode the words and continue reading, even if they do not understand their meanings. Teachers can model how to stop when they reach words they don't understand, even if they can decode them, and encourage students to do the same.

Next, readers need to determine which unknown words are central to the meanings of the text and worth exploring further. This is important because there may be many unknown words and, if readers stop extensively at each one, fluency and comprehension may be interrupted. Therefore, students can be encouraged to consider whether or not they can comprehend the sentences and overall meanings of the texts without devoting more energy to these particular unknown words.

If readers determine that the unknown words are central to the meaning of the text, they can be encouraged to use strategies such as using context clues, looking for known roots or affixes, or consulting dictionaries. Overall, readers should be encouraged to monitor their own reading and comprehension and determine when to apply known strategies.

Review Video: Acknowledging the Unknown When Reading
Visit mometrix.com/academy and enter code: 712339

Supporting Vocabulary Acquisition and Use Through Listening and Speaking

Young children begin their vocabulary development through listening well before they begin to read and write. Through listening to family members, caregivers, and others, children develop their meaning (oral) vocabularies. These are words that children understand when heard and eventually use in their own speech. These vocabularies can be developed by talking to the children frequently and for a variety of purposes, reading to them, exposing them to songs, rhymes, and poems, and many other language activities.

Children continue to build vocabulary through listening and speaking activities when they begin school. Teachers can read aloud to students often, varying the genres and purposes for listening. Engaging students in discussions about what was read aloud can give students a purpose for listening and opportunities to use text-related vocabulary in their own oral responses. Teachers can also incorporate key vocabulary words in class discussions.

Students should also have frequent opportunities to speak in the classroom. In addition to informal class discussions, students can present projects to classmates and explain their thinking during problem-solving. They should be encouraged to use content-specific vocabulary when appropriate.

Teaching Word Analysis Skills and Vocabulary to English Language Learners

Focusing on cognates is one way to help build word analysis skills and vocabulary for English language learners (ELLs). Cognates are words in different languages that share the same roots. For example, the English word *directions* and the Spanish word *direcciones* are cognates. ELLs can be encouraged to look for known parts of unfamiliar words. They can then use knowledge about the meanings in their native languages to determine the meanings of the English words. This strategy builds upon ELLs' prior knowledge. Explicitly teaching common roots and affixes can help ELLs quickly increase their vocabularies as well.

Scaffolding should also be provided when introducing ELLs to new words. This can be done using visuals that help demonstrate the meanings of the words. Real objects, pictures, and gestures can all be used. Graphic organizers can also be used to show how new words are related and how they connect to specific topics.

Teaching Word Analysis Skills to Struggling Readers

Struggling readers require consistent and explicit instruction, which often includes a combination of both whole-class instruction and targeted individual or small-group instruction daily. They also need frequent opportunities to manipulate words. Both building and breaking apart related words using letter tiles can help struggling readers develop understandings of patterns in the ways words are made.

Struggling readers can also benefit from explicit instruction on chunking words into component parts. Depending on the ages and prior knowledge of the students, this might include identifying syllable patterns, onsets and rimes, roots and affixes, or smaller sight words that are part of the larger words.

Struggling readers also need frequent opportunities to practice their word analysis skills using real texts. After explicit instruction on recognizing prefixes in words, for example, students can read texts that contain several prefixes. They can identify these words and their meanings. This will help them transfer their word analysis skills to realistic contexts. Scaffolding can be provided through anchor charts, graphic organizers, and teacher support during these independent reading experiences to provide reminders of known strategies.

Teaching Word Analysis Skills to Highly Proficient Readers

Proficient readers still have a need for differentiated reading instruction, even if they are meeting or exceeding grade-level expectations. They can benefit from developing the same word analysis skills as other readers, such as looking for known parts in unfamiliar vocabulary words, breaking words into components, and finding relationships between the meanings and spellings of different words. These strategies should be presented using materials and interactions that are both engaging and appropriately challenging for proficient readers. Use of texts that have some unfamiliar words will ensure that readers have opportunities to apply these strategies and continue to increase their vocabularies. Using assessments to determine reading levels or teaching readers to self-select appropriate texts can help ensure that the selected materials offer some challenges and learning opportunities for proficient readers.

Because proficient readers often devote less energy to decoding words than struggling readers, they are able to allocate more energy to reading comprehension, analysis, and reflection. Proficient readers can be asked to evaluate authors' word choices and discuss the effect that certain words have on the meaning or tone of the texts.

UNDERSTANDING GRAPHOPHONICS, SYNTAX, AND SEMANTICS

Reading strategies can be used and applied to different situations as needed. The types of text a student reads may differ greatly in terms of vocabulary, quality of context clues, picture support, and connections to the reader's prior knowledge. Therefore, the strategies that work to determine an unknown word in any one sentence or text may not work as well in another. These strategies are often unreliable. Instead, teachers should encourage readers to use phonics knowledge to decode unknown words. Proficient and skilled readers do not rely on cues when identifying an unknown word.

While these reading strategies are not recommended for instructional purposes, it is important to know the difference between strategies a reader may be using. Decoding words using graphophonic clues is a strategy where readers consider the letter-sound relationships in the word. Another strategy is to consider syntax, or how the word sounds in the sentence and fits into the overall sentence structure. A third strategy is to consider semantics, or the meaning of the text, to guess the unknown word. Basically, the reader is trying to determine if the unknown word looks right (graphophonics), sounds right (syntax), and makes sense (semantics).

When it comes to reading unknown words, it is best practice for students to use phonetic knowledge to decode words. Students who lack a basic understanding of phonics may rely on cues while reading unknown words. Thus, explicit and systematic phonics instruction is necessary in order to develop proficient readers.

HELPING STUDENTS USE CONTEXT CLUES

Teachers should explicitly introduce students to different types of context clues, including definition, antonym, synonym, and inference clues. Examples of sentences containing each type can be provided, and students can be asked to mark the clues, label each type, and explain the meanings of the unknown words. They can also be asked to find examples of each of these types of context clues in other texts. An anchor chart listing the different types of context clues and examples of each can also be posted in the classroom.

Students can also be given sets of words that are related in some way, such as pairs of synonyms or antonyms. They can be asked to write sentences that incorporate the word pairs, creating context clues for other readers. The students can then share their sentences with peers, asking them to identify the context clues and meanings of the unknown words.

Review Video: Reading Comprehension: Using Context Clues
Visit mometrix.com/academy and enter code: 613660

IMPORTANCE OF KNOWING LATIN AND GREEK ROOTS

Many English words are formed from Latin and Greek **roots**. Therefore, recognizing these roots and knowing their meanings can help readers with both decoding and comprehending.

When readers automatically recognize Latin and Greek roots, they will be able to quickly decode the main parts of words that contain them. If they automatically recognize the affixes as well, they will be able to break words into parts and decode them effortlessly. This will allow the readers to maintain speed and fluency while reading.

The roots also hold most of the meaning in words and form the bases of entire word families. Knowing the meanings of these roots will help readers quickly determine the meanings of many newly encountered words, especially if they also know the meanings of any attached affixes. For example, if readers know that the Latin root *port* means to carry, they will have clues about the meanings of the words *transport*, *transportation*, *import*, and *export* as well.

Helping Readers Identify Latin and Greek Roots in Unfamiliar Words

When teaching readers about Latin and Greek roots in English words, one strategy is to help them see the relationships between words in the same word families. This can be done by creating charts or other visual representations of word families and their meanings. For example, a root and its meaning can be written in the middle of a web, and words containing the root and their meanings can be written in circles branching off from the root.

Another strategy is to create three sets of cards, including prefixes, suffixes, and roots. Students can experiment with combining the sets of cards to try to form real words. When real words are created, students can explain their meanings. Students can also be given words containing prefixes, roots, and suffixes. They can be asked to break the words into their components and identify the meanings of each part.

Additionally, students can be encouraged to locate words containing Latin and Greek roots in the texts they read independently. They can use their knowledge of the roots to define the words.

Approaches to Vocabulary Learning

- A **definitional approach** to vocabulary learning is the most traditional. Students are either provided definitions of words or look them up in a dictionary, and they are drilled until they commit the meanings to memory.
- A **structural approach** to vocabulary learning emphasizes the morphological features of words—the roots, prefixes, and suffixes. Once students learn the recurring morphemes in English, they can deduce the meaning of a word in isolation without relying on its context.
- A **contextual approach** to vocabulary learning provides the students with multiple examples of a word used in realistic contexts, allowing them to infer the meaning without resorting to a dictionary or an explicit definition.
- A **categorical approach** to vocabulary learning groups words into categories based on a semantic similarity. For example, a student might be given a list of words associated with driving a car, such as "steering wheel," "to brake," "to accelerate," and "gear shift."
- A **mnemonic approach** to vocabulary learning builds associations between target words and mental images so that hearing a target word evokes the image, facilitating recall of the word's meaning.

Review Video: Types of Vocabulary Learning (Broad and Specific)
Visit mometrix.com/academy and enter code: 258753

Role of Non-Contextual Strategies in Vocabulary Development

Non-contextual strategies are used when new vocabulary is learned without seeing or hearing the words in context. For example, teachers may give students lists of new vocabulary words they have not yet encountered in texts. The teachers may ask students to define the words, use them in sentences, and memorize them. Quizzes may then be given in which students must match the words to their definitions or provide examples of the terms.

There are times teachers may use non-contextual vocabulary strategies, such as when students are learning content-specific words that are not often found naturally in texts. When studying parts of speech, for example, teachers may have students memorize the definitions of *noun*, *verb*, and *adjective*. These words are important for students' understanding of sentence structure, yet students are not likely to encounter these words written in texts with contextual clues. However, it is recommended that teachers do use contextual strategies whenever possible.

Students can be taught to use tools such as dictionaries to define unknown words when contextual clues are not available. They can be prompted to draw pictures to explain word meanings or use graphic organizers to show the relationships among words.

Role of Contextual Strategies in Vocabulary Development

Contextual strategies are used to determine the meanings of unknown vocabulary words when they are encountered in context. The ability to use these strategies to quickly determine word meanings is important for both reading fluency and comprehension. Because words can have multiple meanings, readers also need to use contextual strategies to determine which meaning makes sense in a given sentence.

Teachers can explicitly teach students about the different types of contextual clues often found in sentences. They can encourage students to highlight the words and phrases that provide clues about meanings of the vocabulary words.

Contextual clues often include synonyms or antonyms for the unknown vocabulary words. Therefore, when introducing new words, teachers can assist students with creating lists of synonyms and antonyms. Teachers can also ask students to solve analogies or determine which word does not belong when given a group of related words. These activities will help students recognize synonyms and antonyms and understand relationships among words when they are encountered in context.

Criteria for Selecting Vocabulary Words for Instruction

Vocabulary words can be divided into three tiers. Teachers should consider these tiers when determining which words to focus on during instruction.

- **Tier one words** are common words used in everyday speech. They are typically learned by the early grades through normal conversation. Explicit instruction on the meanings of these words is seldom needed.
- **Tier two words** are found in both fiction and nonfiction texts and are common enough that readers will likely encounter them in multiple texts. Tier two words carry a lot of meaning and can negatively affect comprehension if they are not understood by readers. When deciding which tier two words to focus on, teachers should consider how the words affect the overall meanings of the texts and their morphologies. They should consider if students will be able to form connections between these words and other words, helping them understand unfamiliar words encountered in the future.
- **Tier three words** are mostly found in nonfiction texts and are domain-specific. These words are important for understanding the texts and their domains. Because students are unlikely to have encountered these words before, explicit instruction is needed. This often includes pre-teaching the words and analyzing them in context.

Components of Reading Comprehension

Reading Comprehension

A basic definition of **reading comprehension** is understanding what has been read. However, reading comprehension is quite complex. It involves both taking meaning from the text and creating meaning by integrating the text with prior knowledge. It is an active process that requires the use of multiple skills and strategies, such as decoding, fluency, understanding word meanings, predicting, inferring, and more. It involves different levels of understanding, including comprehending both the literal meanings of the words and the unstated themes and implications of the text. Comprehension is one of the main goals of reading instruction.

Comprehension is essential to developing proficient readers. If readers are able to decode the words but cannot comprehend the messages, they won't make any meaning from the texts and will become easily frustrated. Because comprehension is an **active process**, it is also important for developing engaged readers who enjoy reading for a variety of purposes.

Literal Comprehension

Literal comprehension refers to understanding the written meaning of a text. It involves a basic understanding of the text's vocabulary, events, main ideas, and other features. Literal comprehension is important because it is the foundation upon which deeper levels of comprehension are formed.

Promoting Literal Comprehension

Answering **literal comprehension questions** using text evidence is one strategy to support development of this skill. This can be done through class discussions or written activities. Readers can be asked to identify the setting of the story, main characters, sequence of events, or other topics where the answers can be found directly in the text. Readers should be asked to provide text evidence for their answers, which might involve marking the sentences where the answers are found. Graphic organizers, such as story maps and problem/solution charts, can also help students develop literal comprehension skills.

To **scaffold** the development of literal comprehension, the teacher can begin by asking questions about a portion of the text immediately after it is read, using the same wording as the text. Over time, the wording can be varied and the teacher can wait for longer intervals before asking the questions.

Inferential Comprehension

Inferential comprehension is a deeper level of understanding than literal comprehension. It requires inferring what the author meant. The answers to inferential comprehension questions are not found directly in the text. Readers must instead make inferences, draw conclusions, determine points of view, and make other informed decisions based upon the evidence provided in the text.

Promoting Inferential Comprehension

To develop **inferential comprehension skills**, readers can be asked to make **predictions** or **inferences** and **draw conclusions**. This can be done using class discussions, written activities, or graphic organizers. For predictions, inferences, and conclusions, readers should be asked to provide text evidence to support their choices. This may involve marking parts of the text or recording relevant sentences. They should then be encouraged to evaluate their predictions, inferences, and conclusions as they continue reading. If new evidence conflicts with their initial predictions, inferences, or conclusions, readers should be encouraged to revise them as needed. Proficient readers self-monitor their comprehension and continually revise their understanding as additional evidence is gathered.

Evaluative Comprehension

Evaluative comprehension is a deeper level of understanding than literal comprehension and goes further than inferential comprehension. It requires readers to make judgments and share opinions about what they have read based upon evidence found in the text and prior knowledge. For example, evaluative comprehension questions might ask readers to consider if they would have handled an event in the text differently or explain whether they agree or disagree with the author's point of view.

Promoting Evaluative Comprehension

Because evaluative comprehension requires deeper thinking than literal comprehension, it is helpful for teachers to frequently model their thinking when responding to these types of questions. They can model how to identify relevant information within the text and draw upon prior experiences to form judgments about topics.

It is also helpful to provide readers with evaluative question stems they can reference when reading independently. These question stems can also be displayed on charts in the classroom.

Summarization

Summarization refers to providing a concise description of the main idea and key details of a text. Summarization assists with comprehension by helping readers separate important information and vocabulary from unimportant information. It also helps readers remember what they have read.

Summarization is often a difficult skill for students to learn. Their initial summaries may provide too few or too many details from the text. Modeling and explicit instruction can help students learn to provide **effective summaries**. Students can be taught to reread a text and cross off unimportant or repetitive information. They can then be encouraged to locate and mark the main idea and key details that are essential to understanding the meaning of the text. Additionally, they can be encouraged to substitute general words for lists of related words in a category. For example, rather than listing all of the animals belonging to a character's family, students could use the word *pets* instead.

Readers can also complete **graphic organizers** to develop their summaries. One common type of graphic organizer asks students to complete the following sentence stems to form summaries: Someone, Wanted, But, So, Then.

Review Video: Summarizing Text
Visit mometrix.com/academy and enter code: 172903

Role of Prior Knowledge in Reading Comprehension

Research has shown that students learn best when they can relate new information to existing knowledge already stored in long-term memory. This helps them organize and make sense of the new information and apply it in future situations. When reading, prior knowledge can help students determine the meaning of unfamiliar vocabulary words, form predictions about what might happen next, make inferences, and make sense of story events. All of these skills are important for comprehension.

To activate students' prior knowledge, the teacher can ask what students already know about a topic when it is introduced. Students' contributions can be listed on a chart or graphic organizer.

Know, want, and learned (KWL) charts can be completed, listing what students already know, want to know, and learned about the topic. The teacher can also ask students to make comparisons by asking how the new topic is similar to and different from something they have already learned.

Denotative vs. Connotative Meanings

Words often have multiple meanings. **Denotative** meanings are the literal meanings of words. **Connotative** meanings are the secondary meanings of words and refer to the positive and negative associations that arise from them. For example, the denotative meaning of the word *heart* is a muscular organ in the circulatory system that pumps blood. A connotative meaning of the word *heart* is love.

There are several reference tools that can be used to locate the meanings of words. Dictionaries can be used to find the denotative and connotative meanings of words, along with other information like word origin and pronunciation. Thesauri can be used to find lists of synonyms for words, and antonyms are sometimes included as well. Glossaries list the definitions of important vocabulary words and are often found at the end of texts. All of these reference tools can be found in both print and digital forms.

Review Video: Denotation and Connotation
Visit mometrix.com/academy and enter code: 310092

Helping Learners Retell Fictional Stories

There are specific steps teachers can take to focus readers' attention on key parts of stories to assist with retelling. Teachers can preview the stories with students and point out the key events they should listen for before they begin reading. During reading, they can pause and ask students to summarize the key events they have heard in the stories so far. After reading, teachers can lead students in shared retellings or ask students to retell the stories independently.

Students can fill out graphic organizers or create flip books that describe what happened in the beginning, middle, and end. They can also draw or act out the main story events. Additionally, students can be given sentence strips containing the main story events in a mixed-up order and asked to sequence them. Story ropes can also be used, where students tell story events in order as they move their hands along sets of beads or knots on ropes.

Retelling is important for story comprehension because it requires readers to identify and sequence the main story events. Readers must also consider other story elements, such as characters, setting, and plot, during retellings.

Purposes for Reading

One purpose of reading is for entertainment, which is known as **aesthetic reading**. Sometimes readers select texts because they look interesting to read, and they read them just for fun. Selecting a fairy tale from the library for silent reading time and choosing a bedtime story are examples of times students read for entertainment.

Additionally, sometimes people read for information. This is known as **efferent reading**. It occurs when readers select nonfiction texts to learn something new. This might include learning new facts about a topic or learning the steps needed to accomplish a task. Selecting a book about whales while studying ocean life is an example of reading for information. Reading a recipe to prepare dinner is also an example of reading for information.

Reading to learn opinions is another purpose for reading. This type of reading occurs when people are trying to make decisions about things and look to others for advice. Reading online reviews before purchasing a product is an example of reading for opinions.

Assisting with Comprehension by Recognizing the Author's Purpose

Recognizing the author's purpose can assist with comprehension in multiple ways. First, it can offer the readers clues about the text structures and features they are likely to encounter. If readers recognize that the author is writing to inform, they will know to look for features of informational texts, such as headings and content-specific vocabulary words. If readers recognize that the author is writing to entertain, they will know to pay attention to character traits, plot development, and other features of entertaining texts.

Additionally, knowing the **author's purpose** can help the reader evaluate the text more effectively. If readers recognize that the author is trying to persuade them, they will know to think critically about any claims that the author makes rather than accepting them at face value.

Knowing the author's purpose can also assist readers with determining if texts will meet their needs. For example, students may need to gather factual background information for a science experiment they are completing. They may preview a text and recognize that it is written for entertainment. They may then decide that the text is not suited to meet their needs in this circumstance.

> **Review Video: Understanding the Author's Intent**
> Visit mometrix.com/academy and enter code: 511819

Teaching Readers to Recognize an Author's Purpose

The author's purpose may be stated either explicitly or implicitly in a text. Readers can be taught to recognize text structures and features that help identify the author's purpose. Texts that are written to entertain often contain interesting characters and engaging plots. They may contain entertaining phrases and humor, and illustrations may be present.

Texts written to persuade usually contain evidence to support the author's points of view. This may include statistics, facts, and/or personal opinions. Readers can be asked if the authors appear to be for or against something to determine if texts are written to persuade.

Texts written to inform often include facts, which may be stated using text, charts, graphs, or other features. These texts may contain captioned photographs to provide additional information about the topics. Content-specific vocabulary words are often present. Readers can be asked if the authors appear to be trying to teach them about something to determine if texts are written for this purpose.

It is also important for readers to recognize that authors may have multiple purposes for writing. Readers may recognize text structures and features characteristic of two or more purposes within one text.

Making Predictions

When making predictions, readers gather evidence from the text and pictures to make inferences. They sequence story events and make connections between the text and prior experiences to predict what might happen next. Continually making and revising predictions also helps keep readers engaged. All of these activities support reading comprehension.

To help learners make predictions before shared reading experiences, teachers can conduct picture walks of texts. While showing the pictures, teachers can provide brief overviews of the stories, asking students to contribute their predictions about what each section might be about. During reading, teachers can pause to ask students to summarize what has happened so far and predict what might happen next. Teachers can model using prior experiences, picture and context clues, and memories of similar texts when making predictions.

Readers should be taught to evaluate their predictions to determine if they were correct. They should also be taught to look for additional information that might cause them to revise their original predictions. Readers can fill out charts listing their predictions, the evidence used to support these predictions, and what actually happened in the texts.

Review Video: Predictive Reading
Visit mometrix.com/academy and enter code: 437248

Inferring

Authors sometimes provide clues in their writing rather than stating things explicitly. When this occurs, readers must make **inferences** or draw conclusions based on facts, prior knowledge, or text evidence rather than explicit statements. For example, an author might state that a character marched off and slammed the door. Although the author did not state it directly, readers may infer that the character is angry based on his actions.

- Making **inferences** is important for comprehension because much of the meaning in a text can be stated indirectly. If readers comprehend only direct statements, they may miss out on major themes or events in the story.
- Because **prior knowledge** can be used to make inferences, it is helpful for teachers to activate students' prior knowledge before reading through previewing and discussing what is known about the topic. Providing students with frequent opportunities to read varied texts can also build prior knowledge that will assist with inferring.
- Teachers can also show **pictures** to students and ask what inferences they can make based upon picture clues. Additionally, teachers can model **thinking aloud** while reading, discussing what inferences they are making and what prior knowledge, facts, or text clues they are using as evidence.

Review Video: Inference
Visit mometrix.com/academy and enter code: 379203

Drawing Conclusions

Drawing conclusions is important for reading comprehension because it helps readers understand important events or concepts in a text that are not directly stated. Drawing conclusions about an author's purpose for writing can also help readers better evaluate the text because they will be aware of potential bias.

To help readers learn to draw conclusions, teachers can provide students with several supporting details about common topics and ask what conclusions they can draw. For example, they could describe a house with balloons, streamers, presents, and a cake in the kitchen, leading to a conclusion that it is somebody's birthday. A graphic organizer can be used to organize this information, with the conclusion in the middle and the supporting details branching off from this conclusion. This process can then be repeated using details found in texts. This will show readers how they can use prior knowledge and text evidence to form conclusions when they read independently.

Metacognition

Metacognition is when readers think about their own thinking. Proficient readers continuously self-monitor their own reading. They ensure that they are making meaning from the text. If things do not make sense, they use strategies to self-correct the issues. Metacognitive strategies are important for reading comprehension because they ensure that readers are actively engaged while reading and that they understand what they have read. Modeling these strategies by thinking aloud is an important way to help students learn and apply these strategies in their independent reading.

Metacognitive strategies before reading include previewing the text, making predictions, and setting a purpose for reading. Metacognitive strategies during reading include visualizing, making connections, rereading to clarify confusion, and asking self-monitoring questions. Readers also utilize text features to locate and make sense of key information. Metacognitive strategies after reading include summarizing, drawing conclusions, and determining if any unanswered questions remain that need additional clarification.

Comparing and Contrasting

Readers can **compare and contrast** many things when reading, such as characters, settings, story events, multiple texts, and more. This supports comprehension because readers must recall details and find text evidence to compare and contrast. Comparing and contrasting also requires higher-level thinking skills, can help readers organize information, and can clarify confusion between two things.

Venn diagrams are a common way to help readers **compare and contrast** information. Text evidence and prior knowledge can be used to identify features that are the same and different between two things, and they can then be listed in the appropriate sections of the diagram.

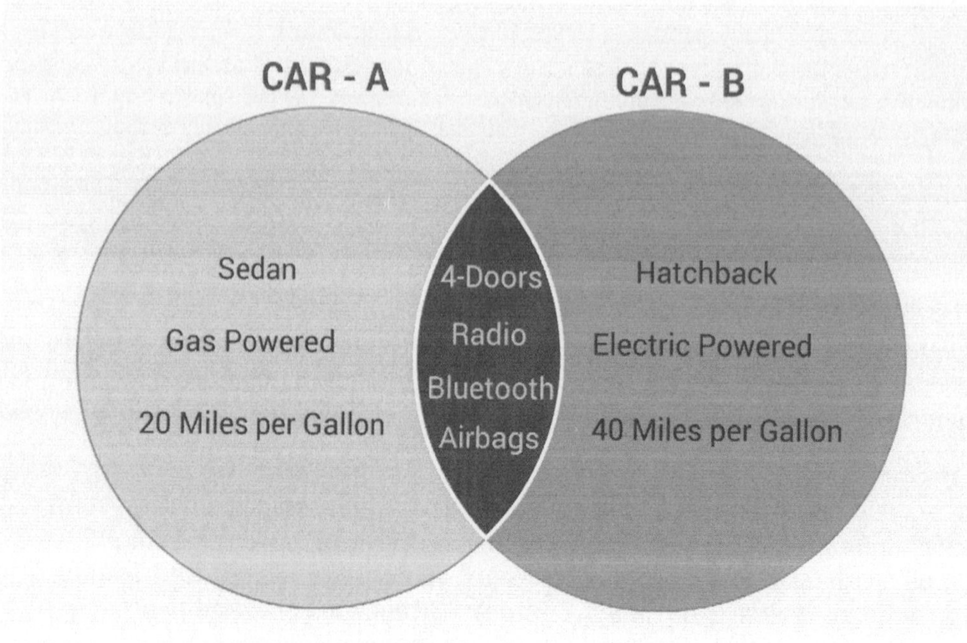

Students can also be taught to identify key words that signal whether two things in a text are the same or different. Word such as *similarly* and *like* signal that two things are the same, whereas words and phrases such as *although* and *on the other hand* signal that two things are different. A chart that lists these key words and phrases can be displayed in the classroom as a reminder for students to use when reading.

Review Video: Compare and Contrast
Visit mometrix.com/academy and enter code: 798319

Recognizing Main Ideas and Details

The ability to recognize the main ideas and supporting details of texts assists with comprehension. Main ideas and supporting details help readers identify what the texts are covering and determine what message an author is trying to send.

Understanding paragraph structure can help readers locate the main idea and supporting details. Readers can be taught that the main idea is typically located in either the first or last sentence of the paragraph.

Readers can be encouraged to locate the main idea and mark it and then locate all supporting details and mark them in a different way. Main ideas and details can also be written on webs or other graphic organizers to help readers comprehend what they have read. Scaffolding can be provided when readers are first learning to complete these graphic organizers and then gradually withdrawn.

Prereading activities, such as discussing the title and previewing the pictures, can also help readers form initial thoughts about the main idea of a text. They can revise their initial thoughts as they read.

Distinguishing Between Facts and Opinions

Facts are statements that can be proven to be true. For example, stating that George Washington was the first president of the United States is a fact. **Opinions** are statements that cannot be proven true or false. They represent people's judgements or views of something. Stating that cats are easier to take care of than dogs is an opinion.

It is important for readers to distinguish between facts and opinions. Recognizing when statements are opinions can help readers identify any biases the authors may have and recognize that the authors may be trying to persuade them. Distinguishing between facts and opinions is important when reading any text, but it necessitates special consideration when using digital sources. Anyone can post information online, and readers must be able to evaluate the sources effectively to determine if they are based on fact or opinion.

To teach students to identify facts and opinions, teachers can introduce the terms and provide examples of each. Students can be asked to mark examples of facts and opinions in texts using different colors. They can also be encouraged to look for key words that signal opinions, such as *think*, *believe*, *feel*, *best*, and *favorite*.

Review Video: Distinguishing Fact and Opinion
Visit mometrix.com/academy and enter code: 870899

ANALYZING AND INTERPRETING AN AUTHOR'S CRAFT AND STRUCTURE

An **author's craft** refers to an author's style of writing. It includes all of the choices an author makes when writing a text, such as word choice, text structure, point of view, use of literary elements, message, tone, and more. When focusing on an author's craft, readers analyze all of these choices and consider the effects they have on readers.

Analyzing and interpreting an author's craft and structure helps readers reach a deeper level of comprehension than surface comprehension. It aids them in understanding how different elements of the text work together to convey a certain meaning and tone. It helps them recognize that authors make several deliberate choices throughout the writing process about how to convey their messages most effectively, which will assist readers with making choices in their own writing. Additionally, it encourages active engagement with the text because readers are continuously analyzing and interpreting while they read. Comparing and contrasting an author's craft using different texts and other authors can also help readers make connections.

CLOSE READING

Close reading refers to reading and analyzing a text in a thoughtful manner to develop a deep understanding of its meaning, theme, use of language, and other elements. When close reading, readers first read through the text to determine the general meaning. They then reread the text to analyze the use of language and theme. They also make connections between the text and themselves, other texts, or real-world events and form evaluations. The goal of close reading is to develop independent readers who are able to gather deep meaning from texts with little or no scaffolding. Therefore, close reading activities do not involve previewing, picture walks, or other prereading activities.

Not all texts are ideal for close reading activities. Teachers should choose texts with deep meaning and multiple elements to discuss and analyze. They should consider the **complexity** of vocabulary, syntax, and meaning when choosing appropriate texts for close reading. Teachers should also consider the complexity of text features and structures.

Teachers can model how to reread texts and analyze different elements each time. They can guide students in this process by asking questions that require increasingly higher-level thinking skills after each reading of the text.

IMPORTANCE OF BEING ABLE TO SYNTHESIZE

Synthesis is the ability to gather information from multiple sources and combine it to make meaning. It is important because it requires readers to think critically about which parts of texts hold key information. Synthesis also requires readers to summarize and put ideas into their own words rather than repeat the texts verbatim. All of these skills assist with comprehension. Synthesis is also important when readers need to gather information about topics from multiple sources. The sources may differ in format and viewpoint, and readers must be able to find and combine the important points from each.

To teach students to **synthesize**, teachers can model tracking their thinking throughout the reading of a text and explain how it changes as new information is gathered. They can use phrases such as, "I used to think ____, but now I think ____. My thinking changed because____." Text evidence can be cited to explain the changes.

Readers can also be given **graphic organizers** to fill out as they read, recording key points in their own words. After compiling the key points, students can explain the main ideas they learned from the texts and how their thinking changed as they read.

Figurative Language

Types of Figurative Language

- **Similes** are one common type of figurative language used to compare two things using the terms *like* or *as*; for example, the child grew as fast as a weed.
- **Metaphors** are another common type of figurative language used to compare two things. Unlike similes, metaphors do not use the terms *like* or *as*. They simply state that one thing is another; for example, the star was a glistening diamond.
- **Personification** is a type of figurative language that gives human characteristics to nonhuman things, such as animals, objects in nature, or ideas; for example, the creek danced across the prairie.
- **Hyperbole** is a type of figurative language that uses exaggeration for effect. The exaggeration is so excessive that it is not intended to be taken literally; for example, if I don't eat now, I will starve to death.
- **Symbolism** is another type of figurative language. In symbolism, a writer uses a physical object as a representation of something other than its literal meaning. The symbol often represents something abstract, such as a feeling or idea; for example, diverging physical paths in a text can represent two people making different life choices.

Review Video: Figurative Language
Visit mometrix.com/academy and enter code: 584902

Helping Students Recognize and Interpret Figurative Language

Some types of figurative language can be identified by recognizing **key words**. For example, students can be taught to recognize the words *like* and *as* in examples of similes. Students can be taught to recognize sound words, such as *buzz*, in examples of onomatopoeia. Charts displaying these key words can be displayed in the classroom.

Figurative language can also be explicitly taught, with teachers explaining each type and providing examples. Mentor texts can be used to provide examples of each type of figurative language, and students can be encouraged to locate additional examples on their own. When examples are identified, students can analyze the messages the authors are trying to convey through the use of figurative language.

Authors use figurative language to make their writing more descriptive and interesting. Because phrases containing figurative language cannot be literally translated, readers must have adequate background knowledge and/or use context clues to determine their meanings. The ability to recognize and interpret figurative language ensures that readers understand the authors' intended messages and are able to comprehend the depth of the story beyond the literal, surface meanings of the phrases.

Allusions

When authors use **allusions**, they refer to well-known people or events familiar to readers without describing them explicitly. For example, a character being warned to avoid opening Pandora's box is an example of an allusion. It refers to a commonly known story in Greek mythology, and readers are expected to know the meaning of the statement without any further explanation. Biblical, mythological, historical, and literary allusions are four common types. Allusions are commonly found in similes and metaphors.

To help readers recognize allusions, students can be asked to find examples of allusions in texts and discuss their types and meanings. Additionally, they can explore and evaluate the effects that allusions have on the meanings and tones of stories. Students can also be taught strategies for researching the meaning of unknown allusions they encounter while reading independently.

Review Video: Allusions
Visit mometrix.com/academy and enter code: 294065

Idioms

Idioms are a type of figurative language. They are expressions that have unique meanings that differ from the literal meanings of their component words. They are typically passed down within cultures. For example, "It's raining cats and dogs" is an idiom that means it is raining hard.

Idioms can be introduced to students a few at a time, with students contrasting the literal and figurative meanings. They can practice using context clues to determine the meanings of unknown idioms, and they can look for examples of idioms in texts. They can also explore the ways that idioms make writing interesting. For example, they can write a paragraph using the idiom, "It's raining cats and dogs." They can then rewrite the paragraph, substituting the words, "It's raining hard." They can compare the effects of each option on readers.

Special consideration should be given when using idioms with ELLs in the early stages of English language acquisition. Because vocabulary knowledge cannot be used to assist with comprehension of idioms, students may miss the meanings and become frustrated.

Proverbs

Proverbs are short, well-known sayings that offer wisdom or advice. They are commonly passed down within cultures using oral language. An example of a proverb is: "Actions speak louder than words." Proverbs often use figurative language, and their literal meanings do not make sense. Therefore, students need to be taught to recognize proverbs and understand their figurative meanings to comprehend the overall messages of the texts containing them.

When introducing proverbs, teachers can help students understand the cultural and historical significance behind them. For example, the proverb "Don't look a gift horse in the mouth" refers to the historical practice of assessing a horse's teeth to determine its age. The proverb refers to being grateful for what you are given rather than assessing the worth of a gift. Teachers can help students research these proverbs to provide historical contexts for their meanings.

Students can write proverbs on graphic organizers and list both their literal and figurative meanings. They can analyze what the proverbs have in common, such as offering wisdom or advice about life. Additionally, when they are encountered in texts, readers can analyze how the meanings of the proverbs contribute to the meanings of the stories.

Role of Grammar in Reading Comprehension

Understanding English Grammar/Usage and Comprehension

There is evidence that having a strong understanding of English grammar and usage assists with reading comprehension. When readers are able to untangle complex sentences in texts and understand how the components work together to form meaning, they are better able to comprehend what was read. When answering comprehension questions, they are better able to locate key information within complex sentences. Readers are also better able to incorporate complex sentence structure in their own writing.

Understanding English grammar and usage includes knowledge of parts of speech, the roles that they play, and how they are arranged in English sentences. It also includes knowledge of how simple sentences can be combined to form complex sentences. Readers with strong syntactic knowledge are able to self-monitor their reading and recognize when something does not sound right due to decoding errors. The ability to self-monitor and make corrections when needed is important for comprehension.

Review Video: Grammar Skills and Reading Comprehension
Visit mometrix.com/academy and enter code: 411287

Teaching English Grammar and Usage to Aid Comprehension

One strategy to teach English grammar and usage to aid comprehension is to **break sentences apart** and analyze their components. Depending on the age and prior knowledge of the student, this may include **sentence diagramming**, dividing sentences into subjects and predicates, and splitting compound sentences into simple sentences. Students may also be asked to label sentence types—choosing from simple, compound, and complex sentences.

An alternative strategy is to combine words to form different types of sentences. Young readers may begin by combining only subjects and predicates to form the most basic types of sentences. As new parts of speech are learned, students can add additional words to form more complex sentences. Students can also be given word cards containing scrambled sentences. They can be asked to arrange the cards to form sentences, analyzing each attempt by asking if the sentences they have built sound right and make sense.

When given comprehension questions about texts, students can also highlight the parts of the sentences that contain the relevant information needed to respond.

Spoken vs. Written English

Although there are some occasions for formal, scripted speech, most spoken English is informal and conversational in nature. Speech often includes a mixture of fragments and complete sentences and may include interrupting and switching between speakers. Grammar in spoken English tends to be less strict, and there is more flexibility in word order. There may be differences in pronunciation, pacing, and intonation among speakers, and listeners must adjust to these differences to comprehend what was said. Speakers can gauge the understanding of listeners and rephrase or re-explain when necessary. Unlike written text, there is no formal record of what was said to review later unless notes were taken or the speech was recorded. If speaking is part of an instructional lesson, listeners may benefit from being given overviews of the topics and guiding questions in advance to help focus their attention on key information.

On the other hand, written English allows for careful and deliberate organization. It is typically more formal and features more complex structures than spoken English. Word order is more rigid. Writers cannot gauge readers' understanding or re-explain if necessary, so the meaning needs to be clear. Readers are able to review the text later to further clarify information.

Role of Frequent and Varied Reading Experiences

Frequent and varied reading experiences allow readers to see diverse examples of how authors write. They can compare and contrast different writing styles and analyze how the audience, topic, and purpose of writing may affect formality and structure. For example, expository science texts will likely differ from graphic novels in formality. The science texts may also include more content-specific vocabulary words and use sentence patterns designed to present facts rather than resemble conversations. Additionally, readers can see vocabulary words and different parts of speech in context and observe how they work together to build meaning. They can also see the effects of different writers' word choices on the moods of the texts. Overall, frequent and varied reading experiences help readers become more comfortable with language.

Being exposed to varied texts also provides students with models of sentence structure and writing styles to emulate in their own writing. Students often consider examples of familiar texts that fit certain genres or themes, called mentor texts, when they write their own. Being exposed to a variety of reading experiences gives students more examples to draw upon when they are writing.

Inductive vs. Deductive Methods of Teaching Grammar

- In **inductive** teaching, students read and analyze texts that contain similarities. They look for patterns and identify grammar rules by themselves. For example, a teacher might give students several compound sentences that contain semicolons to join the two component sentences. Students might be asked to determine what the sentences have in common, leading them to identify and discuss the use of semicolons to join two simple sentences. Benefits include active participation by students to determine the grammar rules and use of critical thinking skills.
- **Deductive** teaching is another method. In deductive teaching, students are explicitly told grammatical concepts and rules before being asked to apply them to their own reading and writing. For example, a teacher might present a lesson on using semicolons to create compound sentences and then ask students to look for examples of this rule during independent reading experiences. One benefit of this approach is that it can be quicker than inductive teaching. Some students may also be more accustomed to this teacher-centered type of approach.

Both methods of teaching grammar can be useful, and teachers often use a combination of both in their teaching.

Many teachers also use writing workshops to introduce grammar through mini-lessons and conferences with students. Using students' writing as informal assessment tools, teachers can determine which grammatical concepts and rules individual students need to practice.

Role of Grammar in Helping ELLs with Comprehension

Understanding grammar can assist English language learners (ELLs) with reading comprehension. It helps them comprehend different types of sentences. Understanding punctuation marks and word order of different types of sentences helps ELLs determine if something is a statement, a command, or a question.

Additionally, discerning the functions of different **parts of speech** helps ELLs identify the parts of sentences that carry the most meaning. This aids in focusing their attention on the most important words in each sentence. Recognizing words and affixes that signal verb tense also helps ELLs determine when the action takes place. For example, an ELL might recognize that the verbs in a text end in *-ed* and realize that the story takes place in past tense.

Using **syntactic clues** is one important strategy readers use to make meaning from texts. To use syntactic clues, readers must have an understanding of what sounds right in English. When ELLs develop an understanding of English grammar and word order, they are better able to self-monitor their reading and determine if something sounds right. They are also better able to use context clues if they have an understanding of correct word order in English sentences.

Teaching ELLs English Grammar and Usage

English language learners (ELLs) should be taught grammar and usage skills in realistic contexts rather than in isolation. It is also helpful to design grammar lessons around familiar topics and vocabulary so learners can focus on the grammar and usage concepts rather than trying to decipher the meaning.

Teachers should frequently **model** correct grammar and sentence structure through listening, reading, and speaking activities. One strategy is to read texts that model a specific grammar rule and ask ELLs to listen for examples of its use or apply it in their own writing. They can also be encouraged to look for patterns in grammar and usage, such as *-ed* and *-ing* endings.

Teachers need to carefully consider when and how to address grammatical and usage errors made by ELLs. Frequent and immediate corrections can cause **frustration**. However, if specific errors are not addressed over time, they may become **fossilized** and difficult to correct. One strategy is to note repeated errors and address them later in mini-lessons rather than at the time they are made. Teachers can also pick a small number of errors to focus on at any one time.

English Language Parts of Speech

The following are the eight parts of speech in the English language:

1. **Nouns** describe people, places, and things, for example, he ate a chocolate **cupcake**.
2. **Verbs** describe action or being; for example, the dog **chased** the squirrel around the yard.
3. **Pronouns** are words used in place of nouns, for example, **she** works in the office building downtown.
4. **Adjectives** describe nouns or pronouns. They usually describe which one, what kind, or how many of something, for example, the **yellow** house is located on the corner.
5. **Adverbs** describe verbs, adjectives, or other adverbs. They usually describe when, where, why, or how something happens, and they often end in *-ly*; for example, the fish swam **quickly** away from the shark.
6. **Prepositions** are words that relate nouns or pronouns to other words in the sentence; for example, the chef put the dough **in** the oven.
7. **Conjunctions** join words, phrases, or clauses; for example, the teacher **and** the principal attended the meeting.
8. **Interjections** show emotion in sentences; for example**, ouch**—I bumped my elbow.

When readers come across words whose meanings they do not know, knowing the parts of speech can help them determine the function of the words in the sentences. This will make it easier to guess the meanings using context clues.

> **Review Video: Parts of Speech**
> Visit mometrix.com/academy and enter code: 899611
>
> **Review Video: Nouns**
> Visit mometrix.com/academy and enter code: 344028

Teaching Students to Recognize Different Parts of Speech

Parts of speech are typically introduced one or a few at a time. **Nouns** and **verbs** are often introduced first because they can be used as the building blocks of basic sentences. If an inductive method is used, students may be given a group of sentences with the same parts of speech highlighted and asked to determine what the words have in common. If a deductive method is used, teachers might explicitly teach what each part of speech does and provide examples.

Mini-lessons can also be used. A **mini-lesson** on nouns, for example, might include listing nouns that fit into the categories of people, places, and things. It might also include finding examples of nouns in texts or sorting words according to whether or not they are nouns. Teachers can also use shared reading and writing activities as opportunities to discuss parts of speech in context.

Sentence diagrams are pictorial representations that show how parts of speech work together to form sentences. Although sentence diagramming can help some students visualize sentence structure, it can be frustrating and tedious for others. Therefore, it can be considered as one component of grammar instruction as long as it fits the needs of the learners.

Diagram format: Components of a sentence	**Diagram example:** Identify the components in the sentence
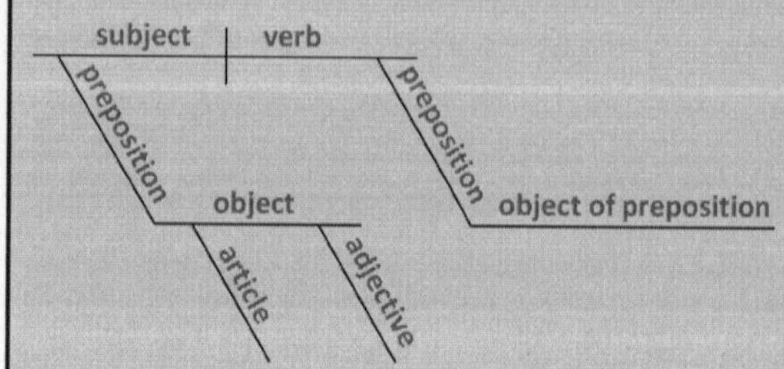	Sentence: Children in the preschool classroom nap after lunch. 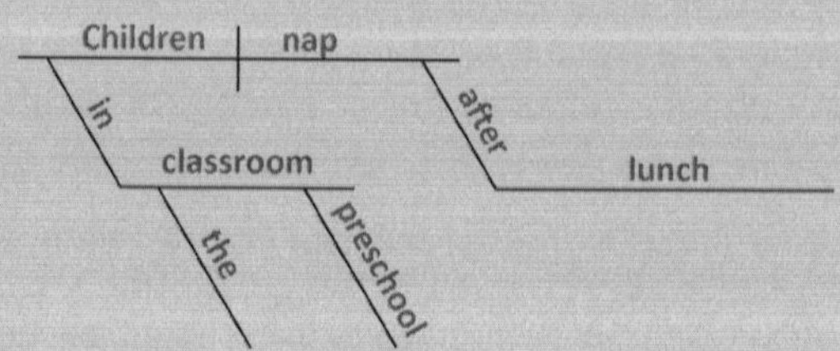

Chapter Quiz

Ready to see how well you retained what you just read? Scan the QR code to go directly to the chapter quiz interface for this study guide. If you're using a computer, simply visit the online resources page at **mometrix.com/resources719/aepafoundread** and click the Chapter Quizzes link.

Development of Reading Comprehension

Reading Development

TYPICAL PROGRESSION OF READING DEVELOPMENT

Readers typically progress through four stages of reading development. The first stage of reading development is known as **emergent reading**. It is the stage in which readers develop pre-reading behaviors and begin understanding concepts of print. The second stage is called **early reading**. Early readers begin to use a combination of reading strategies and cueing systems to decode and comprehend simple texts. The third stage is called **transitional reading**. Transitional readers use a wide range of reading strategies to support comprehension of more complex texts. Rapid word recognition combined with effective use of strategies allows readers to read at an increased pace. **Fluent reading** is the last stage of reading development. Fluent readers confidently read and comprehend a wide range of complex texts independently.

Students' individual differences and prior experiences can affect at what ages and rates they progress through the stages.

Review Video: Stages of Reading Development
Visit mometrix.com/academy and enter code: 121184

CHARACTERISTICS OF THE EMERGENT STAGE OF READING

Emergent reading skills are strong predictors of future reading success. In the emergent stage, readers display **pre-reading behaviors**. They begin interacting with texts without actually reading the words. They learn the concepts of print, such as learning how to correctly hold books and understanding that print holds meaning. They begin to identify capital and lowercase letters, and they understand the predictable relationships between letters and sounds. They begin to understand that letters are combined to form words and words are combined to form sentences.

Readers in the **emergent stage** also develop oral language skills. This includes phonological awareness skills, such as rhyming and alliteration. They develop phonemic awareness skills, including the ability to blend, segment, and manipulate phonemes within words.

Emergent readers enjoy having others read to them. They respond to texts that are read aloud by making predictions, retelling events, and other activities. They react to illustrations and use them to make sense of the texts.

INSTRUCTIONAL STRATEGIES USED IN THE EMERGENT STAGE

Teachers should read aloud to students in the emergent stage often, choosing from a range of genres. When reading, teachers should model concepts of print and how to make predictions, retell story events, and other reading strategies. Concepts of print should be explored in environmental print within the classrooms and the schools. Teachers should create print-rich environments containing several different types of texts for students to explore. Students should be given multiple opportunities to interact with different types of texts daily, both with others and independently.

Teachers should also plan **explicit instruction** on letter identification and letter-sound correspondence and give readers opportunities to practice recognizing and forming both capital and lowercase letters.

Additionally, teachers should plan classroom activities to build emergent readers' phonological awareness and phonemic awareness skills. This includes opportunities to practice rhyming, alliteration, onset and rime manipulation, and phoneme manipulation.

Characteristics of Texts Designed for Emergent Readers

Texts designed for emergent readers should have **pictures** or **illustrations** that strongly support the print. They should have a limited amount of text on each page and use **repetitive words** and phrases. They should include several high-frequency and easily decodable words, and the text should be placed in predictable places on each page. Simple sentence structure should be used.

Additionally, books for emergent readers should be focused on familiar objects and topics that will activate readers' prior knowledge. This assists readers with comprehension and making connections and allows them to focus on print concepts. The vocabulary should also be familiar. Print should be large and contain wide spaces between letters and lines of text.

Some emergent texts follow a pattern in which only the last word in each sentence changes. For example, each page of a text might say, "I like to ____." The missing word could be easily guessed based upon picture support.

Characteristics of the Early Reading Stage of Reading Development

In the early reading stage of development, readers increasingly use strategies to figure out unknown words and make meaning from texts. They begin to self-monitor their reading and self-correct if they realize that errors have been made. They expand their vocabularies and their automatic recognition of high-frequency words. They use picture clues, knowledge of letter-sound relationships, and repetition to decode unknown words in longer and more complex texts.

Early readers also continue developing comprehension strategies, such as predicting and summarizing. They use a combination of these comprehension strategies to make meaning from what they have read. They begin to read silently and no longer need to point to each word while reading.

Characteristics of Texts for Readers in the Early Reading Stage

Texts for **early readers** contain more print than those for emergent readers. They include longer sentences, more sentences per page, and more pages per book. The texts also contain more complex and **varied sentence structure**. There is less reliance on picture clues than in books for emergent readers, with the print carrying most of the meaning. More complex and content-specific vocabulary words are included. Multiple spelling patterns are used, requiring readers to use a combination of decoding strategies. There is less repetition, or longer and more complex phrases are repeated than those in emergent texts.

Texts for early readers also frequently focus on more complex story lines. Descriptive language is often included. The content of these books is still typically familiar to readers.

Readers in the early stage understand a variety of genres and purposes for reading. Therefore, texts for this stage are varied in genre and purpose.

Instructional Strategies Used with Readers in the Early Reading Stage

Students in the early reading stage are beginning to increase their reading rates and build fluency. Teachers need to provide systematic and explicit phonics instruction during this time. Teachers can provide decodable text based off phonics instruction that has already been taught. Teachers can also provide students with opportunities to frequently read and reread favorite books, which will help them build fluency. Teachers can prompt students to decode words using previously taught phonics instruction.

Early readers also benefit from activities that focus on advanced phonemic awareness skills, such as phoneme substitution. Additionally, students benefit from instruction on complex vocabulary words and spelling patterns. Teachers can also provide students with frequent opportunities to read varied text types and genres that incorporate more sophisticated vocabulary words and sentence structures than emergent texts.

Characteristics of Readers in the Transitional Stage of Reading Development

Readers in the transitional stage of reading development are able to engage in sustained, quiet reading for extended periods of time. They are able to read and comprehend longer, more advanced texts and can automatically identify a large number of high-frequency words. They have knowledge of complex spelling patterns, which they use to independently decode most unknown words, including multisyllabic words. They are also continuing to increase their fluency and reading rates.

Transitional readers utilize more strategies to assist with comprehension than early readers. They have an awareness of text structures and can gather and synthesize information from multiple text features, including print, graphs, charts, and sidebars. They rely more on the print than the pictures for meaning and can identify story elements, such as characters, setting, problem, and solution. Additionally, they develop higher-level comprehension skills, such as making inferences and drawing conclusions.

Characteristics of Texts for Readers in the Transitional Reading Stage

Students in the transitional reading phase are able to read more difficult texts than early readers. This includes both fiction and nonfiction texts covering a wide range of genres. It also includes both beginning chapter books and challenging picture books. Nonfiction texts may utilize multiple text structures and include features like graphs, charts, photographs, sidebars, and more. The topics may be either familiar or unfamiliar to readers. Some challenging and unknown vocabulary words may be included along with many high-frequency words. Story elements may be described in detail, using descriptive words and phrases. There are numerous chapter book series designed for transitional readers.

Books written for transitional readers have several lines of text per page. Some pages may be composed entirely of text, as in chapter books. The books have many pages with clearly defined spaces between lines of text.

Instructional Strategies Used with Readers in the Transitional Stage

Because **transitional readers** are beginning to read more complicated texts of different genres, it is helpful to teach about text structures. Understanding text structures and where to look for main ideas can assist transitional readers with comprehension. Teachers can also teach strategies to determine the meanings of **unknown vocabulary** words by analyzing word morphology. This includes recognizing and analyzing both affixes and roots.

Teachers can plan several opportunities for students to build reading fluency by rereading texts for meaningful purposes. They can also model advanced analysis and comprehension strategies during shared reading experiences, such as making inferences and drawing conclusions. They can provide students with tools like graphic organizers to assist with comprehension during independent reading. Additionally, they can encourage readers to support responses with text evidence.

Teachers can also assist transitional readers with selecting appropriately challenging texts for independent reading.

Characteristics of Readers in the Fluent Stage of Reading Development

Readers in the **fluent stage** of reading development read complex texts both **quickly** and **accurately**. They read with appropriate expression. They automatically recognize high-frequency words and efficiently use multiple strategies to determine unknown words they encounter. These strategies include using cueing systems, context clues, and substitutions.

Fluent readers are able to comprehend a wide range of complex fiction and nonfiction texts. They understand content-specific and technical vocabulary words or use strategies and tools to determine their meanings. They have a strong understanding of different types of text structures and know how to efficiently use text features to locate key information. They understand multiple purposes for reading and writing and are able to understand texts from multiple points of view. Additionally, fluent readers use **high-level thinking skills** to comprehend what they have read. They are able to evaluate texts and argue points using text evidence for support.

Characteristics of Texts for Readers in the Fluent Reading Stage

Texts for readers in the fluent reading stage are complex, varied, and sometimes abstract. Complex text structures are often used. For example, they may use flashbacks or weave back and forth while comparing and contrasting two things. Fictional texts for fluent readers contain highly developed plots and character development. They often use descriptive and figurative language. Additionally, these texts may have multiple themes or layers that require deep analysis. Content-specific and technical vocabulary words are commonly used. Topics may be either familiar or unfamiliar to readers.

Texts for fluent readers rely mostly on the print to convey meaning. Photos or illustrations are mainly included to convey important information that may be difficult to explain in print. For example, photographs of animals may be included in biology texts. Illustrations may be included in historical fiction texts where the settings or characters may be unfamiliar to readers.

Instructional Strategies Used with Readers in the Fluent Reading Stage

Readers in the fluent stage often read texts about new and **unfamiliar topics**. Therefore, teachers can instruct them to activate related prior knowledge that may assist them with making sense of the new texts. They can also model how to efficiently use **research tools** to learn more about unfamiliar topics.

Teachers can also model and encourage readers to use close reading techniques to deeply analyze texts. This process includes rereading texts multiple times to analyze different layers each time. It also includes evaluating, comparing and contrasting, making connections, and using other high-level comprehension strategies. Teachers can encourage readers to analyze texts from multiple perspectives, using text evidence to support their responses.

Because readers in this stage will frequently encounter content-specific and technical vocabulary words, teachers can continue to model word analysis skills, such as analyzing affixes and roots.

Academic Literacy

Academic literacy refers to the knowledge and skills necessary to communicate effectively in academic situations. It includes content-specific knowledge and vocabulary, such as mathematical terms. It also includes general knowledge and vocabulary used across all content areas, such as the terms *synthesize*, *summarize*, and *evaluate*. Additionally, it refers to the ability to communicate effectively in academic situations through reading, writing, listening, and speaking.

Academic literacy helps students flexibly adapt their use of reading strategies according to the types of text used and the purposes for reading. It helps them acquire content-specific vocabulary needed to comprehend academic texts and effectively communicate their learning using a variety of response types. It helps them summarize, evaluate, and make connections among content acquired from multiple sources and across content areas. Academic literacy also encourages students to effectively communicate and collaborate with others to construct meaning.

Types of Knowledge Commonly Used in Education

There are many types of knowledge commonly used in education.

- **Social** knowledge is knowledge about social conventions passed down within members of a community. It includes conventions related to expected greetings, manners, and conversational behavior.
- **Procedural** knowledge refers to the knowledge applied to carry out procedural tasks. An example is solving a complex math problem using a multistep algorithm.
- **Physical** knowledge refers to knowledge learned by observing the features of something. When students discuss the physical properties of rock samples, they are using physical knowledge.
- **Domain** knowledge refers to the knowledge and skills used by experts in a particular field. For example, a student explaining how she completed a division problem using the terms *dividend, divisor,* and *quotient* is using domain knowledge.
- **Empirical** knowledge refers to knowledge obtained from scientific experimentation and data collection. Determining the boiling points of different liquids as part of a science experiment is an example of empirical knowledge.

Role of Literacy in Different Types of Knowledge

Literacy plays a large role in the development and application of different types of knowledge in the classroom. Social knowledge is passed down through oral language and written texts. Students learn about social norms through the actions of characters in stories and through discussing texts with others. For example, children learn about solving conflict with friends by reading about characters who work through conflict. They also learn how to listen attentively and take turns through participation in literature circles.

- When students read nonfiction **procedural texts**, they develop procedural knowledge that can be used to accomplish tasks. Procedural texts also provide models of text structures students can use when explaining procedures to others.
- Reading texts containing **academic language** helps students develop and apply physical, domain, and empirical knowledge. Developing their academic vocabularies can assist students with expressing their observations and conclusions using academic language.

Academic Reading vs. Reading for Entertainment

- **Academic reading** refers to thoughtfully reading and analyzing academic texts as part of content area studies. Readers usually have specific purposes in mind before beginning academic reading. For example, an entomology student may consult a field guide to correctly classify an insect found during a nature hike. Another student may read a social studies textbook to identify some major causes of the Revolutionary War for an essay assignment.
- **Reading for entertainment** refers to reading for fun. A student may select a fictional book from a favorite series to read on a rainy day.

When completing academic reading, readers often pay special attention to text structures and features to efficiently **locate needed information**. They may skim or skip around in the texts. They may stop to look up the meanings of **unfamiliar vocabulary words**. They may also read more slowly or reread passages multiple times to make sense of unfamiliar content.

When reading for entertainment, proficient readers still self-monitor their comprehension, but they have more freedom about which text elements they wish to respond to and analyze. They may also read at a quicker pace and choose to reread favorite parts for fun.

Development of Reading Fluency

Components of Fluency

Reading fluency is made up of several elements including rate, accuracy, and prosody.

- **Rate** refers to reading speed. Proficient readers adjust their reading speed flexibly depending on their purposes for reading. For example, they may read scientific textbooks containing technical vocabulary more slowly than graphic novels they are reading for entertainment. Rate is important for comprehension. If readers read too slowly, they may forget what they have already read and lose the overall meanings of the texts. If readers read too quickly, important points may be overlooked.
- **Accuracy** is another component of fluency. It refers to decoding words correctly without errors. Fluent readers automatically recognize many high-frequency words and use multiple strategies to decode unknown words. Accuracy is important because frequent errors may affect comprehension, especially if errors are made on words central to the meaning of the text.
- **Prosody** is another component of fluency. It refers to reading expression, including phrasing and intonation. Prosody affects the ways texts are understood. For example, readers should pause appropriately at commas to emphasize certain phrases. Using the correct intonation associated with each punctuation mark affects the tone of the texts.

Progression of Fluency Development in Readers

- **Early readers** devote most of their mental energy to decoding words. In this stage of reading, the focus is on developing reading accuracy, which is one component of fluency. Early readers practice high-frequency words and learn strategies to decode words with simple spelling patterns. Rate and prosody play lesser roles but are still practiced with scaffolding.

- In the **transitional reading stage**, readers automatically recognize many high-frequency words and more efficiently use strategies to decode unknown words. There is still a focus on accuracy as readers encounter more complex vocabulary and spelling patterns. However, transitional readers increase their reading rates and begin to read independently with prosody. As readers gain confidence with familiar texts, their fluency increases.
- By the time they reach the **fluent stage**, readers are able to flexibly adapt their reading rates based upon their purposes for reading. Automatic recognition of most words results in reading accuracy. Fluent readers read with prosody, and they appropriately match their expressions to the texts.

Developing Fluency in Early Readers

When teaching early readers, the main focus is on developing **accuracy**. This is done through activities to develop automatic recognition of high-frequency sight words and explicit phonics instruction that teaches strategies to decode words with common spelling patterns.

To assist early readers with developing **speed and prosody**, teachers can encourage repeated readings of favorite texts. As readers develop more confidence with the texts through these repeated readings, their reading rates will increase. Because readers already know how to decode the words in these familiar texts, they have more energy available to focus on expression.

Teachers should frequently **model fluent reading**. This includes reading with appropriate speed, phrasing, and intonation. Teachers can also model disfluent reading, such as reading texts without expression, and ask students to explain the effects it has on comprehension. Choral reading of shared texts can also assist students with developing fluency.

Review Video: Fluency
Visit mometrix.com/academy and enter code: 531179

Maintaining Fluency in On-Level Readers

Like struggling readers, on-level readers can benefit from frequent teacher modeling of fluent reading, choral reading, and opportunities to reread familiar texts. Additionally, they can benefit from partner reading. Partner reading allows students to hear fluent reading modeled by classmates and reread texts repeatedly while receiving feedback. Students should first be taught procedures for how to listen attentively to their partners' reading and provide effective and encouraging feedback. Teachers should always be mindful of individual needs when pairing students.

Reader's theater is another strategy to assist on-level readers with fluency. In **reader's theater**, students read scripts from appropriately leveled texts to perform for classmates. Through rehearsing and performing, students have multiple opportunities to reread the scripts. They must also practice reading with appropriate expression for their characters and reading with appropriate speeds so they can be understood by their audiences. Additionally, reader's theater allows students in the audience to hear models of fluent reading. In reader's theater, the focus is on the reading, and few or no props are used.

Interventions to Use Assisting Readers Who Are Struggling with Fluency

Readers who are struggling with fluency can benefit from frequent modeling of fluent reading. As teachers reread familiar texts, students can join in and read chorally, matching their phrasing, speed, and expression to the teachers' reading. Students can also listen to audio recordings of texts.

Readers who struggle with fluency can also benefit from repeated readings of texts. After initial readings, teachers can give feedback to students and help them set goals for rereading. For example, they may encourage readers to pause at the periods between sentences. It is important that readers are given passages within their instructional reading levels. Reading texts far below their instructional levels will not challenge the readers. Reading texts that are too difficult will result in readers stopping frequently to decode unknown words, which interrupts fluency and causes frustration. Encouraging repeated readings of texts with rhyming and repetition, including poetry, can assist readers who are struggling with fluency.

Although teachers may monitor students' reading fluency over time, it is also important to create encouraging environments for readers. Continuously timing readers or forcing disfluent readers to read aloud in front of others may have negative effects.

Writing Development

Relationship Between Reading and Writing Development

Reading and writing are **interrelated** and should be taught together. Students who read a lot tend to have stronger writing skills, and students who write a lot tend to have stronger reading comprehension skills.

When students read varied types of texts, they learn how authors convey meaning differently through tone, language use, and sentence structure. They learn about different types of genres. They often use the texts as models and experiment with these elements in their own writing. Students also increase their vocabularies through reading, and they develop automatic recognition of high-frequency words. Students may then integrate the new vocabulary words into their own writing and remember how to spell words they have seen repeatedly in texts.

When students learn to write, they learn about and use different sentence and text structures. Awareness of these structures can help students recognize and make sense of them when encountered in other texts. Additionally, when students write about texts they have read, it facilitates additional analysis and comprehension. For example, writing about whether or not they would recommend books to others requires students to evaluate the texts and provide support for their reasoning.

Characteristics of Writers in the Preliterate Stage of Writing Development

The earliest stage of children's writing development is **scribbling**. Children begin scribbling at random places on the pages and do not proceed in any consistent direction. They typically hold writing utensils, such as pencils or crayons, with their fists. Scribbling helps children improve their fine motor skills and sets the stage for the understanding that writing carries meaning.

Over time, scribbling begins to follow a left-to-right directionality across the pages. Drawings may be included to help convey meaning.

Eventually, strings of pretend, letter-like symbols are used. They are sometimes mixed with numbers. Students are able to explain the meanings they are trying to convey through their writing. This phase demonstrates a beginning awareness of concepts of print. Spacing between words is not initially included but develops over time. There is no evidence of letter-sound relationships in the writing at this stage.

Characteristics of Writers in the Emergent Stage of Writing Development

In the **emergent stage,** writers begin to form letters correctly. Initially, they often write using all capital letters. They also begin to use their understandings of letter-sound relationships to write words. Some sounds are correctly represented in words, typically starting with the initial sounds.

In this stage, writers also begin spelling some words correctly. The first written words typically hold high personal meaning to students, such as their names and words like *mom* and *dad*. They may also write words found in environmental print, such as the names of popular restaurants frequently seen on signs. Some high-frequency sight words begin to be spelled correctly.

Students in the emergent stage write with left-to-right directionality and begin using spacing to separate words. They also begin to use common punctuation marks to split their writing into sentences, although this skill is still developing. Because it requires a lot of energy to encode words at this stage, writing pieces are typically short.

Characteristics of Writers in the Transitional Stage of Writing Development

In the **transitional stage** of writing development, students begin using a mixture of capital and lowercase letters appropriately. They also correctly use several different punctuation marks. Their writing includes a broader vocabulary than when they were in the emergent stage.

Transitional writers know how to automatically spell many high-frequency words, and they use multiple strategies to encode words they do not know how to spell. These strategies include considering letter-sound relationships to record the sounds they hear, considering known spelling patterns, and thinking of related, known words. Writing includes a mixture of conventionally spelled words and phonetically spelled words that are readable.

Because transitional writers are able to encode many words quickly, they have more available energy to focus on writing development. They focus more attention on developing story elements and including descriptive details. They write longer texts than they wrote in the emergent stage, and their writing includes a mixture of text structures and genres. Transitional writers also have the ability to reread and edit their work.

Characteristics of Writers in the Fluent Stage of Writing Development

Fluent writers spell most words correctly and use capitalization and punctuation marks conventionally throughout their writing. They are able to edit and evaluate their own writing and provide constructive feedback to others.

With the ability to spell most words quickly and automatically, fluent writers are able to focus more on writing craft, such as using descriptive language and developing story elements. Author's voice begins to develop. Writing may span several pages. Fluent writers consider their audiences and purposes for writing and consider them during the planning process. They use multiple strategies to plan their writing, such as brainstorming and using graphic organizers. They are able to write texts in a wide range of genres and select appropriate text structures to fit their purposes. Additionally, fluent writers are able to independently use tools like dictionaries and thesauri to improve their writing pieces.

Review Video: Sensory Language
Visit mometrix.com/academy and enter code: 177314

Oral Language and Nonverbal Language Development

Stages of First Language Acquisition

- Until about four to six months of age, babies are in the **cooing stage**. Babies in this stage commonly make vowel sounds, which represent their first attempts at oral language.
- From about four to six months until one year of age, babies are in the **babbling stage**. At first, they commonly make repeated consonant-vowel sounds, such as *ma-ma*. Over time, their babbling begins to show the expressive patterns they hear in the language around them. They repeat sounds that others respond to and reinforce.
- From about 12 to 24 months of age, children are in the **one-word stage**. In this stage, children begin referring to objects by consistent, one-word names. These words may be real or invented, and children begin to use language to convey meaning to others.
- From ages two to three, most children enter the **telegraphic stage**, when they string together words to convey meaning. The words that convey the most meaning in sentences are often included, whereas articles, conjunctions, and other words are omitted.
- After age three, most children enter the beginning **oral fluency stage**. They now use more complex sentences and begin using sentence structure and syntax appropriately. They use language for a variety of purposes.

Early milestones in language

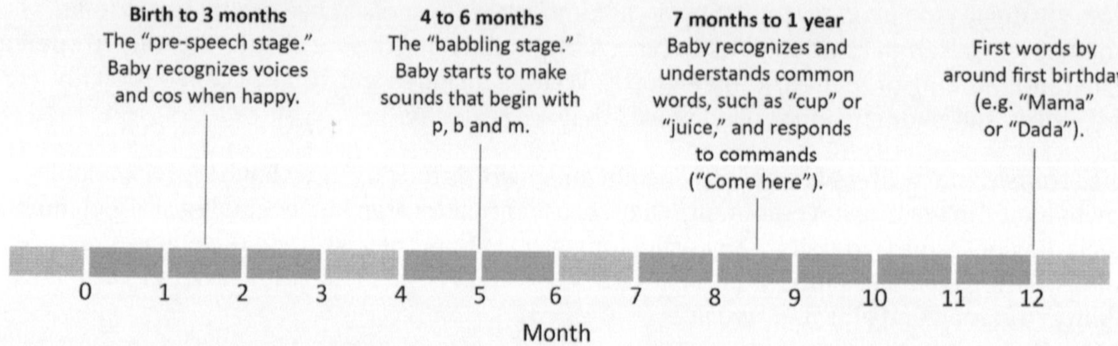

Stages of Second Language Acquisition

- In the **preproduction stage**, English language learners (ELLs) are listening and taking in the second language. Comprehension is minimal at this point. ELLs may not yet speak to others in the second language, and this stage is therefore sometimes referred to as the silent period. ELLs may communicate with gestures or single words.
- In the **early production stage**, comprehension is still limited. ELLs begin responding using one- or two-word answers. Vocabulary in the second language begins to grow.
- The **speech emergence stage** is marked by increased comprehension. ELLs begin speaking in longer sentences, but grammatical errors may be present. Vocabulary in the second language greatly increases.
- In the **intermediate proficiency stage**, ELLs are able to comprehend much of what they hear. They begin speaking in more complex sentences that contain fewer grammatical errors. They are able to fluently communicate with others in the second language for a variety of purposes.
- In the **advanced fluency stage**, ELLs understand academic vocabulary and need little support to participate actively in the classroom. Students in this stage speak with near-native English fluency.

Components of Oral Language Development

- **Phonological skills** are one component of oral language development. These skills include the ability to recognize and manipulate sounds in spoken words. Rhyming and identifying syllables are examples of phonological skills.
- **Syntactic skills** are another component. Syntactic skills (syntax) include understanding grammatical rules and how to correctly arrange words in sentences. Children begin by using simple syntax, such as combining two words to express needs and wants. Over time, their sentence structure becomes more complex.
- **Oral language** also includes a semantic component, which refers to the ability to understand the meanings of words, phrases, sentences, and longer texts. The semantic component is vital for comprehension.
- **Morphological skills** are another component of oral language development. Morphological skills include understanding the meanings of word parts.
- Finally, **pragmatics** refers to understanding the social rules of language. Examples of pragmatics include knowing how to adjust the formality of language depending on the audience and knowing how to respond in certain social situations.

Review Video: Components of Oral Language Development
Visit mometrix.com/academy and enter code: 480589

Relationship Between Oral Language Development and Literacy Development

Most children learn to speak through immersion in language-rich environments, with no formal speech instruction necessary. Starting at birth, these early language interactions help set the stage for later literacy development. Early language play, such as sharing songs, nursery rhymes, and poems, assists young children with the development of phonological awareness skills. Strong phonological awareness skills are a solid predictor of future reading success. Hearing spoken language also helps children understand syntax and how sounds and words are combined to form meaning.

- As children engage in frequent and varied oral language opportunities, they also increase their **vocabularies**. Opportunities to use both social and academic vocabulary during listening and speaking activities assists students with comprehending vocabulary words encountered in texts.
- **Oral language experiences** also help readers understand that language can be used for a variety of purposes, such as meeting needs, social interaction, and persuading others. This assists with recognizing an author's purpose. An understanding of cultural norms and nuances is also developed through oral language experiences.
- Additionally, comprehension requires the ability to combine literal meanings of words with prior knowledge and world experiences. Oral language activities, such as following directions, can assist with this.

Role That Oral Language Plays in the Development of Critical Thinking Skills

Oral language leads to the development of other communication skills. Babies first listen to their caregivers and later say their first words before they learn to read and write. Through listening, children learn to evaluate the messages of others and make sense of newly learned information. Through speaking, they learn to organize and communicate their thoughts to others. All of these skills assist with the development of critical thinking skills.

Teachers can ask students to explain their thinking to others. They can also teach students to defend their answers using support and evidence. Students can also be explicitly taught to use strategic questioning when interacting with classmates. Strategic questions require higher-level thinking to answer, and questions with yes-or-no answers should be limited. For example, students explaining the results of science experiments might be asked to evaluate their processes and explain what they might do differently in the future. Additionally, students can respond to high-level questions about texts during class discussions and literature circles. For example, they can be asked to evaluate the ways that authors use persuasive techniques.

Promoting Oral Language Skills

When engaging in listening and speaking activities with students, it is recommended to use vocabulary words in context to promote comprehension later. Research has shown that identifying vocabulary words on flash cards and other similar types activities has **little effect** on later reading comprehension, whereas the ability to recognize and use words **in context** does.

Students should also have many opportunities to listen and speak for a **variety of purposes** to both peers and adults. Friendly conversations, academic discussions, formal presentations, and social interactions are all examples of different types of oral language activities. Varied activities will help students learn to change their language structures to fit the purposes of the interactions. Teachers can change their language structures throughout the school day. For example, they might chat informally with students about their interests during a morning meeting and switch to academic language when discussing a novel.

Additionally, students of all ages can benefit from reading and listening to a large variety of texts containing different types of sentence structure, language, and vocabulary. Young children can also benefit from word play and phonological awareness activities.

Developing Listening and Speaking Skills

Like reading and writing, listening and speaking activities should be incorporated throughout all content areas rather than taught in isolation. Students should be given multiple opportunities each day to listen and speak for a variety of purposes.

Students can listen to texts in audio form, listen to teachers read aloud, or participate in paired reading activities in all content areas. Before beginning, they can be given specific purposes for listening to focus their attention. They can participate in role-playing scenarios to model common social situations and conflict resolution. They can be given frequent opportunities to present their learning to others using a variety of formats. Audience members can be instructed to ask specific and relevant questions, and presenters can be instructed to provide well-supported and evidence-based answers. Additionally, collaborative, problem-based learning activities can be planned, requiring all students to have roles within their groups.

For ELLs and students who struggle with speaking, partially completed scripts and/or sentence stems can be provided. These tools can assist students with outlining thoughts and organizing sentence structure before speaking.

Teaching Students Nonverbal Communication Skills

Nonverbal communication, sometimes known as body language, includes gestures, facial expressions, and posture. Verbal and nonverbal communication work together to convey desired messages. If nonverbal communication is inappropriate for the audiences or purposes used, the meaning of the verbal communication may be lost or misconstrued. For example, a child may thank a grandparent for a gift. However, if the child has a disappointed look on his or her face while speaking, the grandparent may believe the child does not like the gift.

Additionally, certain types of nonverbal communication can be interpreted differently depending on culture. What is socially acceptable in one culture may be considered rude in another. Students should be aware of the messages their nonverbal communication sends to different audiences.

Teachers can engage students in discussions about what messages are sent by different types of nonverbal communication. They can role-play common scenarios and have other students evaluate the messages conveyed through both verbal and nonverbal communication. Students can also watch video clips of realistic situations, such as job interviews, and evaluate the nonverbal language of the participants. When giving presentations, teachers also provide checklists outlining expected nonverbal communication, such as eye contact with others and strong posture.

Supporting the Development of Writing Skills

Stages of the Writing Process

- In the **prewriting stage**, writers brainstorm ideas, decide on topics, and plan the structure of their writing. This may include brainstorming, using webs or other graphic organizers to map out main ideas and details, and creating outlines. Writers consider who their audiences will be and what their purposes are for writing.
- In the **drafting stage**, writers create their rough drafts. The focus of this stage is recording thoughts. Students are encouraged not to worry about spelling, grammar, and punctuation errors, which will be corrected later.
- In the **revising stage**, writers consider if any portions of their writing lack clarity or if any parts should be added or removed. They examine word choice and consider if there are ways to make the writing more descriptive. They also seek feedback from others about ways their writing could be improved.
- In the **editing stage**, writers carefully check their writing for spelling, capitalization, punctuation, and grammatical errors. They also ask others to edit their writing to ensure no errors are overlooked.
- In the **publishing stage**, writers share their writing with others. This may involve creating illustrated books, reading aloud in authors' circles, putting on plays, or presenting in other ways.

Review Video: The Recursive Writing Process
Visit mometrix.com/academy and enter code: 951611

Teaching Students the Writing Process

Modeling is an important strategy to help students become familiar with the writing process. Teachers can lead their classes in creating shared pieces of writing, going through each step as a group. Teachers can also share examples of their personal writing as they introduce each step of the process. Multiple examples that represent writing from various genres should be included to show students how the process can be applied to different types of writing.

Teachers can post charts outlining the **steps of the writing process** in their classrooms. Regular time should be set aside to work on writing so that, at the beginning of each session, students can identify which steps of the writing process they will focus on that day. This will help them establish goals for each session and maintain focus.

Teachers should also schedule time for frequent conferring with students to provide feedback and ensure they are staying focused on the process. Additionally, teachers can provide opportunities for students to reflect on the process and the changes they have made to improve their writing.

Benefits of Conferring with Students During the Writing Process

There are several benefits of conferring with students during the writing process. When writers know they will be frequently meeting with teachers, it increases accountability for following the writing process. It also gives teachers opportunities to provide timely feedback to students and personalize instruction based on their individual needs.

It is important for teachers to model the conference process for students before beginning. Students should be aware of the purposes of the conferences and the expectations for their roles. Additionally, students should practice routines for what to do while their teachers are conferring with others. This modeling and practice will increase the likelihood that conferences can be conducted without interruptions.

There are multiple ways that conferences can be conducted, but they typically include students sharing the progress they have made since their last conference and discussing any questions or concerns they have. Teachers usually pick a few points to focus on with each student, showing specific ways that improvements can be made using examples or mentor texts. Teachers should use the academic language of writing in their conferences. Additionally, conferences should be positive and motivating in nature to help students develop positive feelings about writing.

Helping Students Write Effectively for Different Audiences

As part of the prewriting process, writers should be encouraged to identify their **intended audience**. Once they have identified their audience, they should consider several factors. One factor is how much **prior knowledge** their audience has about the topics. This will affect what level of background information and detail the writers should go into to meet the **audience members' needs**. For example, writers who are explaining how to use computer programs will focus on different program capabilities depending on whether the audience members are beginners or advanced users. Another factor to consider is what type of relationship the writers have to their audience. This will affect the level of **formality** used in the writing. For example, a friendly letter to a classmate will be less formal than a letter written to a government representative.

Teachers should give students frequent opportunities to complete **authentic writing activities** for varied audiences rather than only submitting assignments for teacher evaluation. They can also provide opportunities for students to compare and contrast texts that are written about the same topics but written for different audiences.

Helping Students Effectively Write in Various Forms and Genres

Genre studies are one way to help students learn to effectively write in different genres. In **genre studies**, classes study one genre at a time, in detail, over the course of a few weeks. They read many different mentor texts in the genre and discuss common characteristics. Students can then be encouraged to complete their own writing activities within the genre, using the mentor texts as models.

A similar approach can be used to teach students to effectively write in different forms. For example, when learning to write friendly letters, students can explore many different examples. They can discuss common characteristics and use the examples as models when writing their own friendly letters.

Another strategy is to provide a mixture of **strong and weak examples** of a genre or writing form and ask students to evaluate their effectiveness. They can discuss which examples they think are the most effective and what characteristics these examples display that make them more successful. Similarly, they can discuss which features the weak examples contain or lack that make them less successful. They can then be encouraged to consider these findings during their own writing activities.

Developing Writing Skills

Developing effective writing skills requires a multifaceted approach. Like reading, writing should be interwoven through the school day and all content areas rather than taught in isolation. It requires a combination of explicit skills instruction and opportunities to freely explore and experiment with writing. Skills instruction should include a wide range of topics, including spelling, grammar, language use, text structures, and more.

It is important to help students develop **positive attitudes** about writing. Building a community of writers where students can freely collaborate, share, and solicit feedback can help students feel safe and supported in the writing process. Students need to be explicitly taught how to solicit feedback from classmates and how to provide constructive and respectful feedback to others.

Because reading and writing are interrelated, students also need frequent opportunities to both read and write texts of different genres and purposes. They need to compare and contrast different texts and evaluate both their own writing and the writing of others. They should be explicitly taught how to participate in the five steps of the writing process, and they should receive frequent feedback on their writing. Feedback should provide specific suggestions for improvement in a positive and encouraging manner.

Helping Students Effectively Compose Written Texts

While teaching the writing process, teachers should help students understand that quality writing takes time. They can model their own writing processes and share stories about the writing processes of favorite authors. Writing stamina can be developed gradually in younger students, with writing workshop time increasing as the year goes on.

- Although students need models of **quality writing**, they also benefit from seeing **weak examples**. Students can evaluate a range of writing samples and contrast their effectiveness. Comparing both strong and weak examples will help writers identify the characteristics of quality texts and consider them in their own writing.
- Students should also be encouraged to engage in **multiple rounds of revision**. Revisions should be based on feedback from both peers and teachers as well as personal reflection. Students should also be explicitly taught how to consider feedback critically and decide which suggestions to implement and which to disregard.
- Additionally, teachers should monitor students' writing through observation and conferences and plan mini-lessons based on the issues they notice. For writing that will be evaluated, **rubrics** should be given in advance. Students should be encouraged to consult the rubrics and **self-evaluate** their own writing at multiple stages throughout the process.

Assisting Students with the Revision Process

Revising is often a difficult part of the writing process as students may struggle to see how they can improve their own writing pieces. First, it is important that students understand that the **focus of revision** is on improving clarity, detail, word choice, and other features rather than on the spelling and mechanical issues they will address during editing.

Modeling is often an effective way to help students understand the revision process. Teachers can share their own writing pieces and ask students to identify areas that do not make sense or could be explained in better detail. For example, teachers may ask students to close their eyes and visualize while they read one portion of their written pieces aloud. After asking students to share their visualizations, teachers may revise the writing to include more sensory details. Students can repeat the **visualization process** and note the differences. Teachers can also model writing sentences in multiple ways and ask which ways sound best. They may also help students identify descriptive words that can be used to replace commonly used words, such as replacing the word *nice* with *amiable*. These lists can be posted in classrooms for students to refer to when writing.

Helping Students Produce Quality Writing in the Content Areas

In preparation for the workforce and independent living, students must be able to successfully write for a variety of purposes and audiences. This is essential because effective writing is required in many professions. For example, scientists publish research studies, sales professionals write sales reports, and marketing specialists create advertisements.

Going through the steps of the writing process helps students organize, synthesize, analyze, and evaluate complex information. They must make judgments about what information is relevant and which text structures should be used to best convey meaning. Putting content into their own words helps students comprehend difficult information and vocabulary. Therefore, writing in the content areas supports comprehension in these areas as well.

Teachers can provide varied types of texts to support learning in the content areas. This may include fiction books, journal articles, diaries, field guides, research studies, maps, interview transcripts, and more. Students should interact with various quality texts and discuss the roles they play in different professions.

Helping Students Recognize and Use Abbreviations and Acronyms

Because there are numerous abbreviations and acronyms, teachers need to selectively choose which ones to focus on for instructional purposes. Therefore, teachers often address abbreviations and acronyms as they come up in students' reading and writing. For example, when writing letters, teachers can explain the abbreviations Dr., Mr., and Mrs. Teachers can also observe issues with abbreviations and acronyms as they occur in students' writing and address them through mini-lessons. Examples of abbreviations and acronyms can be pointed out in texts. Charts displaying common abbreviations and their long-form versions can also be displayed in classrooms to provide scaffolding before they are memorized.

In the age of digital communication and social media, it is also important to teach students when it is appropriate to use abbreviations and acronyms. Students need to consider their purpose for communication and their relationship with their audience. For example, informal acronyms may be appropriate for texts between friends but not for use in business letters.

Principles of Effective Writing

- **Clarity** and **brevity** are two related principles of effective writing. They require writers to include sufficient detail to convey their intended meanings while simultaneously omitting any extraneous or repetitive information. Students should be encouraged to consider the value that each word and sentence adds to their writing to determine whether or not it should be included. They should also consider the background knowledge of their intended audiences to ensure they go into the appropriate amount of detail to meet their needs.
- **Author's craft** and **voice** are also important principles of effective writing that draw readers in and compel them to read more. In fictional texts, they help readers identify with characters and make the stories seem realistic. These principles help maintain reader engagement with the texts.

- Additionally, careful **editing** is important for effective writing. If numerous errors are present, the meanings of the texts may be affected.

Helping Students Edit Their Writing to Correct Errors with Mechanics

Frequent modeling is helpful when teaching students to edit. Teachers can model using editing checklists or rubrics to check for errors in their own work. The class can edit writing pieces they have composed together during shared writing experiences or edit texts containing errors written by other authors.

Teachers can also instruct students to **follow routines** when editing. This may include completing editing checklists or recalling mnemonic devices to ensure that all areas have been checked. CUPS is one mnemonic device that can be used to remind young writers to check for capitalization, usage, punctuation, and spelling. Because it can be difficult for students to recognize errors in their own writing, teachers can also encourage students to edit their own work first and then ask other students to edit it as well.

Additionally, students benefit from frequent, shared reading experiences using large print books, projected digital texts, or other means that allow them to follow along as teachers read. Teachers can stop to point out how authors use capital letters, punctuation marks, and other conventions. Frequently seeing these conventions in use will help students understand their purposes and notice when they are used incorrectly in other texts.

Helping Students Use Correct Punctuation in Their Writing

Teachers can explicitly teach students about each punctuation mark by introducing it, discussing its purpose, and demonstrating how to use it correctly in writing.

Students should also have frequent opportunities to explore how punctuation is used in context. They can be asked to find examples of certain punctuation marks in texts and examine the roles they play in the sentences. They can try reading the sentences with the given punctuation marks. They can then reread them with the punctuation marks omitted or substituted and discuss the differences in meaning and tone. For example, students could read a sentence in a book ending with a period, using appropriate intonation and pausing. They could then substitute the period for an exclamation point, adjusting their intonation. They could discuss how the meaning and tone of the sentence changed. Students can also edit their own writing by reading it aloud, using the intonation and phrasing suggested by the punctuation marks they included. They can ask themselves if any areas sound unclear, such as if sentences seem to blend together. They can also use punctuation checklists and ask other classmates to edit their work to double-check for errors.

Review Video: Consistency in Punctuation
Visit mometrix.com/academy and enter code: 169489

Helping Students Use Correct Capitalization in Their Writing

One strategy to teach proper capitalization is to give students texts and ask them to circle all capital letters. Students can then be asked to identify what the words with capital letters have in common, leading to a discussion of capitalization rules. These rules can also be explicitly taught with examples provided.

- Posters can be displayed in classrooms as reminders of when to capitalize letters, such as at the beginnings of sentences, when using proper nouns, or when writing the word *I*.

- Additionally, students can be asked to edit texts, including their own writing pieces, to locate capitalization errors. Students should be reminded that errors may include both randomly capitalized letters and lowercase letters that should be capitalized.
- The ability to differentiate between common and proper nouns is needed to apply capitalization rules correctly. To assist with this skill, students can complete word sorts with common and proper nouns. They can also locate and circle examples of each type in texts.

Review Video: Capitalization in Grammar
Visit mometrix.com/academy and enter code: 369678

Types of Language Disorders

Language delays and disorders can fall into three categories. **Receptive disorders** make it difficult for people to understand the messages communicated by others. **Expressive disorders** make it difficult for people to communicate their thoughts and ideas to others. **Mixed receptive-expressive language disorders** involve difficulties in both areas. These disorders can either be developmental or acquired. Acquired disorders are caused by injury or illness.

Within each of these categories, there are many different types of disorders. Apraxia, stuttering, and articulation disorders are some examples of expressive disorders. Students with expressive disorders may find it difficult to produce certain sounds, organize their thoughts into sentences, or use language appropriately in social situations. Therefore, classroom activities that require speaking and/or writing may be difficult. Students with receptive disorders may find it difficult to remember details or follow spoken directions. For example, they may not remember multistep directions that are given verbally for assignments.

Meeting the Needs of Students with Language Delays and Disorders

Although students with **language delays** and disorders often receive professional speech therapy, there are many strategies teachers can use to support these students within the classroom.

Teachers should model treating students with language disorders respectfully. They should not interrupt students with expressive disorders or attempt to finish their sentences. Instead, adequate response time should be provided. Students can also be given advance notice of the questions they will be asked, allowing them time to formulate responses.

Students with **receptive disorders** who have difficulties processing or remembering speech may benefit from receiving information in multiple forms. When giving project directions, for example, teachers can provide written directions and explain them verbally. Multistep directions can be broken down into simple steps. Visuals can be used to help students comprehend vocabulary used in speech. Additionally, teachers can ensure that they have obtained students' attention before speaking, and they can monitor students for understanding.

For students who struggle with language pragmatics, role-playing activities can be used to practice appropriate responses for a variety of common social situations, such as asking for help or greeting people.

Review Video: Least Restrictive Environment
Visit mometrix.com/academy and enter code: 100354

Factors that Impact Student Learning

Home and Community Factors that Impact Student Learning

Students are exposed to multiple social and cultural factors from their homes and communities that significantly impact learning, so it is imperative that the teacher is conscious of these factors to effectively adapt instruction and assessment to enhance students' learning. Students are often held to different academic and behavioral expectations by their parents depending on their social and cultural backgrounds. These expectations affect self-motivation, engagement, and academic performance. When adapting instruction and assessment, teachers must ensure that all students are held to high expectations while providing individual students with the necessary supports for success. Teachers must also consider the availability of community resources that offer support and enhance learning, as this differs among social and cultural groups. Students from low sociocultural backgrounds may lack quality resources such as libraries, tutoring, or after-school activities, so teachers must adapt to include time outside of instruction for completing assignments, additional support, and use of school resources. Community problems pose obstacles that hinder students' motivation, self-concept, and attitude toward learning. It is important that teachers establish a safe, welcoming, and engaging classroom while providing the necessary academic and behavioral supports to foster equity and promote a growth mindset.

Self-Directed Learning

In a **self-directed learning** environment, students are given a sense of agency that enhances self-motivation and feelings of ownership and responsibility for their own learning. By choosing what and how they learn based on their individual interests, learning styles, and preferences, students have the ability to explore and inquire freely, thus increasing their natural curiosity and motivation to do so. In choosing their own learning, students determine their own learning goals, thus creating a sense of ownership and self-responsibility. This sentiment is also increased when students can tailor their learning according to their own needs and challenge themselves based on their skills and abilities. Furthermore, when students achieve self-decided goals, they develop a sense of ownership over their learning. In order to foster a self-guided environment in which students are fully engaged in their own learning, teachers must adopt a facilitator role in instruction and offer support when necessary. Instruction and assessment must allow multiple opportunities for student choice in how learning is determined and demonstrated. By providing opportunities for self-evaluation and reflection, teachers further facilitate self-motivation, ownership, and responsibility over students' own learning through encouraging them to make personal connections, reflect on accomplishments, and seek areas for self-improvement.

Teacher Roles in Student Learning

The teacher's role is multifaceted in nature, and teachers must often adopt multiple roles within a single lesson to effectively facilitate learning and accommodate individual students' needs. The role of the **lecturer**, **model**, and **facilitator** are applicable to different learning situations and have varying impacts on learning. As the lecturer, the teacher delivers direct instruction to students. This role is most appropriate when introducing a new concept, providing instructions for an upcoming activity, or reviewing material. In addition, teachers can effectively communicate new skills, ideas, and thought processes through modeling to students, as this is a highly influential method of instruction. When teachers serve as facilitators, they guide students in learning while offering support, scaffolding, and assistance when necessary. This role is effective in active and open-ended learning situations in which students are encouraged to explore, practice, and engage in creative problem solving. Through this method, teachers allow students to adopt a self-directed approach that encourages ownership over their own learning, thus creating an engaging, empowering learning experience.

IMPACT OF STUDENT ROLES ON LEARNING

Students adopt multiple roles in the learning process, and teachers must be cognizant of individual learning styles and specific learning situations to determine which role is most applicable and effective for enhancing learning. As **active learners**, students participate and interact throughout the learning process. In this role, students are encouraged to implement higher-order thinking skills through exploration, inquiry, and problem solving, thus creating an engaging learning environment that promotes the retainment of information. This role is particularly effective in learning situations in which students are practicing new skills, testing hypotheses, and exploring new concepts. The opportunity to actively participate in learning allows them to better internalize new information and formulate creative solutions to problems. Active learning also occurs in effectively designed collaborative learning situations. As **group participants**, students can build upon one another's skills, abilities, and experiences to solve problems, explore new information, and understand new perspectives to enhance the overall learning experience. When students are learning new skills, behaviors, or thought processes, they often adopt the role of the observer. Modeling is an influential instructional strategy. In **observing** the teacher or another more experienced individual, students learn to utilize and implement new information in learning situations.

GARDNER'S THEORY OF MULTIPLE INTELLIGENCES

When determining instruction, activities, and assessment, teachers must consider and incorporate students' various approaches to learning. Every student learns differently and has unique needs, so teachers must ensure that auditory, visual, kinesthetic, and tactile learning styles are addressed in all areas of curriculum to maximize students' learning potential. Through incorporating multiple modalities using Howard Gardner's **theory of multiple intelligences** as a framework, teachers can design content and activities that deliver instruction in a variety of ways simultaneously (visual-spatial, linguistic, musical, naturalistic, interpersonal, intrapersonal, logical-mathematical, bodily-kinesthetic). Through this approach, student understanding is reinforced, and each student is provided the opportunity to learn in the way that best suits their individual needs. By differentiating instruction with these modalities, teachers can incorporate several strategies simultaneously when teaching a concept, such as independent practice, cooperative learning, music, art, problem solving, and movement. Opportunities for student choice in learning further allows the integration of multiple modalities in instruction, as it lets students decide the method of learning that is best tailored to their individual learning style and needs.

> **Review Video: Teaching Through Multiple Modalities**
> Visit mometrix.com/academy and enter code: 100371

Howard Gardner's Theory of Multiple Intelligences

Visual/Spatial	Prefers visual representations, able to visualize with the mind's eye, excels in activities that incorporate drawing, building, creative expression, and manipulatives.
Logical-Mathematical	Prefers activities that require order, analysis, and problem-solving using logical reasoning. Excels in solving math equations, conducting science experiments, puzzles, and analyzing data.
Verbal-Linguistic	Prefers learning through reading, writing, speaking, and listening. Often skilled in acquiring foreign languages. Excels in activities that incorporate discussion, debate, oral presentations, and written assignments.
Bodily-Kinesthetic	Prefers hands-on learning experiences that involve movement and physical interaction with the learning environment. Excels in activities that involve sports, dance, building, and hands-on projects.
Interpersonal	Prefers learning opportunities that involve communicating and collaborating with others. Excels in partner, small group, and whole group learning activities.
Intrapersonal	Prefers to learn and work independently. Usually possesses a strong sense of self-awareness. Excels in activities that allow for independent, self-paced learning and self-reflection.
Musical	Learns best when music is incorporated into instruction. Prefers using songs, mnemonic devices, and rhythms to learn concepts and retain information.
Naturalistic	Learns best when opportunities to connect with nature are incorporated into instruction. Prefers activities such as nature walks, identifying and classifying elements of nature, and working outside.

MULTIPLE LITERACIES

Multiple literacies are part of modern learning and business. To be successful, people must effectively process and share different types of information using **multiple forms of media**. Teachers must devote instructional time to teaching students the skills they need to succeed in this technology-rich environment.

Teaching multiple literacies requires a mixture of explicit instruction, guided practice, and opportunities for application. For example, teachers need to teach students to find supporting details in digital texts. They may explicitly teach this skill during mini lessons by modeling how they highlight key phrases. Teachers may then ask students to highlight key phrases in digital texts independently while they observe and provide feedback. Students may then be given multiple opportunities to apply this skill throughout the year to complete projects and assignments.

Teachers should also provide opportunities for students to interact with texts of all types and communicate using different media. They can offer choices in projects and assignments as long as instructional objectives are met. This method allows students to pursue their own interests and leads to increased engagement and ownership over learning.

CHARACTERISTICS OF AUDITORY LEARNERS

Auditory learners easily gather and process information through listening. For example, they may determine main ideas from lectures, assess subtle details from speakers' tones during conversations, and follow oral directions to complete multistep tasks. Auditory learners often enjoy speaking as well, and they may frequently participate in class discussions and conversations.

Teachers can implement many instructional strategies to support auditory learners. They can incorporate read-alouds, discussions, and lectures into classroom activities. They can provide audio versions of textbooks and storybooks. They can also record lectures so that students can listen to them later to prepare for assignments and assessments. Teachers can allow students to interview others to gather information, and they can introduce songs, chants, and rhymes to assist with memorization. When designing projects and assessments, teachers can allow students to complete oral reports or presentations. Additionally, they can allow students to think through problems out loud and offer verbal feedback. Directions can also be given orally.

Characteristics of Visual Learners

Visual learners easily gather and process information by observing. They may learn by seeing written words, photographs, models, or any other visual representations of information. For example, they may locate words signaling the main ideas of written texts, summarize events detailed in illustrations, or complete new tasks after seeing the steps modeled.

Teachers can implement many instructional strategies to support visual learners. They can encourage visual learners to take notes when reading new texts or learning new concepts. Notes can consist of words, pictures, or combinations of both. Teachers can also provide written directions to complete tasks, or they can visually model the steps. Additionally, teachers can use photos, realistic objects, diagrams, and other visual materials when introducing new concepts to learners. They can provide graphic organizers to help learners visualize the connections among concepts. When reading aloud, teachers can also share and discuss the illustrations. When teachers are designing projects and assessments, they can allow students to present their learning through multimedia presentations, models, or other visual means.

Characteristics of Kinesthetic Learners

Kinesthetic learners learn best by doing. They benefit from watching people model how to do things and being given opportunities to do things themselves. They also benefit from opportunities to be active within the classroom.

Teachers can implement many instructional strategies to support kinesthetic learners. They can consider active ways for students to learn and practice new concepts. For example, first-grade students can trace sight words in chalk and hop along the letters, helping them memorize the spellings. Students of all ages can complete science experiments that allow them to mix, measure, and complete other scientific tasks. During math lessons on comparing and ordering numbers, students can form human number lines and discuss the processes they used.

Classroom arrangements and routines are also important for kinesthetic learners. Teachers can consider flexible seating arrangements and opportunities to move throughout the classroom to accommodate these students' needs.

Characteristics of Tactile Learners

Tactile learning is sometimes viewed as a synonym of kinesthetic learning, but there are some key differences. Kinesthetic learning refers to active learning by doing, and **tactile learning** refers to learning through **physical touch**. Tactile learners benefit from frequent opportunities to feel and manipulate items during instruction.

Teachers can implement many instructional strategies to support tactile learners. For example, early childhood students can trace letter cards made of different textures. Students can be given opportunities to spell words in rice, sand, or other textured materials. Manipulating letter tiles can also be used during word work activities. When completing science activities, students can feel objects and describe their textures. During math activities, students can use manipulatives to explore concepts and solve problems. When teachers are designing projects and assessments, they can also allow students to present their learning using models constructed from types of artistic materials.

Using Instructional Strategies That Address All Learning Modalities

Teachers should consider all learning modalities and accommodate auditory, visual, kinesthetic, and tactile learners within the classroom. This is important for several reasons, including the possibility that each student may display preferences for multiple modalities. Additionally, students can benefit from having information presented in multiple ways. For example, students may learn how to complete new tasks by watching their teachers model the steps; however, if given opportunities to practice the steps themselves, students may be better able to remember and apply them in the future.

Teachers need to consider the specifics of each concept they are teaching when determining which **modalities** to address during instruction. For example, it is difficult to teach letter formation using only oral directions. Students benefit from seeing the process teachers use to form each letter and from having opportunities to practice forming the letters independently. When teaching rhyming, auditory instruction is important. All modalities play a role in learning.

Classrooms are also made up of **diverse students** who prefer different modalities. To meet the needs of all learners, teachers can offer instructional choices and present information in multiple ways. For example, teachers can offer print and auditory versions of texts. Directions can be provided in written form and spoken verbally. Teachers can also offer project choices that allow students to present their learning in oral, written, or visual form.

Types of Literacies

Digital Literacy

Digital literacy refers to the ability to communicate effectively using digital sources. It involves many component skills, such as locating, processing, analyzing, evaluating, and creating information in digital form. Information can be communicated digitally through websites, social media, apps, digital textbooks, multimedia presentations, emails, texts, and more.

The continually evolving nature of digital communication presents challenges for teachers. Tools, software, and equipment should be selected carefully based upon the ability to help students achieve learning objectives.

Teachers also need to help students locate and synthesize information from multiple sources and evaluate the sources for reliability. Students must also learn to share information responsibly and adhere to acceptable use policies. Additionally, students need to be taught to consider their audiences and purposes for communicating in digital environments, just as they do when communicating through speaking and writing. For example, different language and sentence structure will likely be used in business websites than in text messages. With global business and distance education now common, students also need to be taught how to use modern tools to collaborate with others.

Media Literacy

Media literacy refers to the ability to comprehend, evaluate, and create media. Media includes methods of communication, such as newspapers, magazines, videos, television, radio, and books.

Students need to critically evaluate the authors' messages and points of view to determine what biases may exist. They also need to determine whether the information presented is supported by reliable sources. Advertisements and testimonials may contain unsubstantiated information, for example.

Because there are many different types of media, students also need the ability to flexibly apply different comprehension strategies. For example, they may skim through newspaper articles to locate and highlight key information, whereas they may take notes during videos. Teachers should incorporate forms of media into classroom instruction and teach strategies for comprehending and evaluating each type.

Teachers can also allow students opportunities to present their learning using different forms of media, such as creating podcasts, writing newspaper articles, filming videos, and more. Students should be taught to consider which types of media will best convey their messages and reach their intended audiences. In addition to helping students develop media literacy, these project options will also accommodate students who prefer different learning modalities.

Review Video: Different Types of Media
Visit mometrix.com/academy and enter code: 785859

VISUAL LITERACY

Visual literacy refers to the ability to comprehend, evaluate, and create visuals. It includes all types of visuals, such as cartoons, photographs, illustrations, graphs, infographics, and maps.

Visual literacy is important from an early age. Before students can read words, they "read the pictures" to tell stories and make predictions. They are later presented with other visuals, such as graphs to explain data in nonfiction texts and infographics on websites.

As with all forms of media, students need to evaluate author bias and verify the sources used to create visuals. For example, they can be taught to consider where the data used to create graphs comes from. Students also need to extract key information from visuals by looking for clues, such as bolded print or use of color. Additionally, students need to be taught about the legal issues involved in creating visuals, including copyright issues. They also need to consider design and aesthetics issues.

Teachers can assist students with visual literacy by presenting information using a combination of print and visual forms and allowing students choices when completing assignments. For example, students can create posters to convince other classmates to read favorite books.

DATA LITERACY

Data literacy refers to the ability to comprehend, evaluate, gather, and organize data. With the increasing reliance on data analytics to drive business and education-related decisions, data literacy must be addressed in the classroom.

Students need to learn how to read and interpret **different representations of data**, such as charts, graphs, and tables. They also need to draw informed conclusions from the data and recognize potential author bias and data misuse.

Additionally, students must decide which types of data will be **useful** to answer specific questions and convey certain information. They need to determine the most effective ways to gather data and present it to others.

Teachers should incorporate data gathering and analysis into classroom activities across all subject areas. Students can gather data when completing science experiments and create tables and graphs to represent their findings. Teachers can conduct surveys with students and record their responses using poll-generating tools on the web. Mini-lessons can be focused on interpreting and evaluating data found in nonfiction texts.

Financial Literacy

Financial literacy refers to making informed decisions about financial resources to prepare for a secure future. It includes skills such as saving and spending money, creating budgets, and paying bills. It also includes business-related terms like profit, expense, and revenue.

Although financial literacy is commonly linked to math skills like balancing checkbooks, it relates to traditional literacy as well. People must be able to read banking and billing statements and understand their terms and conditions. They must also critically evaluate financial offers, such as credit card deals, and consider authors' biases and underlying intentions. These skills are needed to make informed financial decisions.

While teaching about financial literacy, teachers should include a variety of realistic materials for students to read, analyze, and evaluate. They should be given opportunities to make and justify realistic financial decisions based on research and analysis.

Information Literacy

Information literacy refers to the ability to locate, analyze, and evaluate information. It also refers to the ability to responsibly share information with others. Information can be obtained from a variety of sources, including websites, interviews, newspapers, books, and more.

Students first need to recognize when more information is needed. Teachers can encourage students to self-monitor their thinking and recognize when they need to learn more about topics before drawing conclusions. When planning a school garden, for example, students may recognize that they need to learn more about which plants grow well in their area. They may then consult gardening guides to select plants that are well suited for their climate and soil type.

Once information is located, it needs to be critically analyzed so students can comprehend it. They also need to consider author bias and reliability of sources. When sharing information, students need to ensure that they are using reliable sources and not misleading their audiences.

Technology Literacy

Technology literacy involves the ability to use technological tools, equipment, and software to communicate effectively. It includes using technology to access, analyze, evaluate, and share information.

Technological tools are now commonly used in education, and teachers must dedicate instructional time to teaching students how to use them effectively and responsibly. Teachers can assist students with learning to use technology to locate information, such as teaching them to enter specific key words in search engines and skim the results for relevant matches. They can also teach students how to carefully select which technological tools they will use to accomplish specific tasks. For example, if students want to create visual representations of information for a class project, they may consider and evaluate the effectiveness of different infographic building tools.

Technology literacy also involves recognizing the possibilities and limitations of technology in accomplishing specific learning objectives. Additionally, it involves troubleshooting common technological problems and using technology in ethical and responsible ways.

Reading Various Types of Texts

Genres of Fiction

Realistic fiction stories are about events that could happen in real life. The characters and settings are realistic. **Historical** fiction stories also contain realistic characters, settings, and events, but they take place in the past—often during important times in history. **Mysteries** contain crimes or puzzling events that the characters must solve. **Fantasies** contain story elements that are unrealistic, such as talking animals or magic. **Science-fiction** stories focus on imagining life with advanced science or technological capabilities and other theorized situations, such as the existence of extraterrestrial life.

Folktales are another type of fiction. They are popular stories that are passed down from generation to generation, often by word of mouth. Fairy tales are one type of folktale. They often contain magical events and creatures, take place in enchanted places, have happy endings, and have good characters battling evil characters. There are often multiple versions of fairy tales. Cinderella is one example. Tall tales are folktales that are portrayed as if they were realistic but include characters with superhuman traits and exaggerated events. Paul Bunyan is an example of a tall tale.

> **Review Video:** Best Tips for Effectively Reading Fiction
> Visit mometrix.com/academy and enter code: 391411
>
> **Review Video:** Myths, Fables, Legends, and Fairy Tales
> Visit mometrix.com/academy and enter code: 347199

Importance of Being Able to Recognize Different Genres of Fiction

Understanding the characteristics of different genres and being able to correctly classify texts by type is beneficial to readers for many reasons. Knowledge of the typical text structures of each genre assists readers with making predictions. For example, knowing that fairy tales typically end with good overcoming evil can help readers predict how stories will end. It also helps readers analyze texts deeply and incorporate characteristics of the genres in their own writing.

There are different approaches that can be used to teach about genres. One approach is to complete genre studies in which genres are explored in detail one at a time. Teachers may begin by providing explicit instruction on the characteristics of each genre and then give students opportunities to analyze examples. Teachers may also begin by sharing multiple texts of the same genre and asking students to identify common characteristics on their own. Another approach is to present multiple genres at once using a compare-and-contrast approach. No matter which approach is used, readers should have opportunities to explore many texts of each type of genre to develop an understanding of their common characteristics and text structures.

Fictional Story Elements

Fictional texts contain characters. There are both **primary characters**, who are central to the conflicts and resolutions of the stories, and **secondary characters**, who play smaller roles. The settings of the stories are another feature. The **settings** include both the times in history and the geographical locations where the stories occur. Fictional stories also contain problems or conflicts. The **conflicts** are usually introduced early in the stories to hook readers and encourage them to continue reading. The **plots** contain the main events of the stories, when the characters work to resolve the problems. The **solutions** contain the resolutions to the problems, which typically occur toward the ends of the stories. Fictional texts also typically contain **themes**, which are the underlying messages the authors are trying to convey to readers.

It is important for readers to understand that not all fictional texts contain every element. However, recognizing the common features will assist readers with making predictions and comprehending the texts.

Review Video: Determining Relationships in a Story
Visit mometrix.com/academy and enter code: 929925

Review Video: How to Make a Story Map
Visit mometrix.com/academy and enter code: 261719

Teaching Students to Identify Fictional Story Elements

A common way for teachers to introduce students to fictional story elements is modeling their thinking during shared reading experiences. For example, teachers may pause their reading when evidence is provided about the story's settings. The teachers may explain what they have gathered about the settings and show students which textual clues they used to make these determinations.

Graphic organizers, including story maps, are commonly used tools that help students locate and record story elements. These story maps typically ask students to locate the characters, settings, problems, events, and solutions in stories. Foldables or flip books can also be used to record these elements. These elements can be recorded using a combination of pictures and text depending on the ages and needs of the students. Students can also fill out these graphic organizers as prewriting activities when outlining their own stories.

Teachers should ask guiding questions to focus students' attention on story elements before reading. For example, they can ask students to listen for the problem in the story before they begin reading.

Types of Characters Found in Fictional Stories

There are several common types of characters found in fictional stories. However, not all fictional stories contain all types of characters.

- **Protagonists** are the main characters in fictional stories that readers can relate to and want to succeed. Protagonists can be complex characters with both positive and negative traits. Although readers empathize with protagonists, these characters do not always demonstrate admirable behavior.
- **Antagonists** are characters who stand in the way of protagonists accomplishing their goals. Antagonists are not necessarily bad characters and can also have both positive and negative traits.
- **Flat characters** do not change over time. Their actions and personalities are consistent throughout the stories. They are sometimes known as static characters.
- **Dynamic characters** change over time, usually as a result of experiencing the events in the narrative. Readers can identify changes in these characters as the story progresses. Dynamic characters change over time, usually as a result of experiencing the events in the stories. Readers can identify changes in these characters as the stories progress.

Review Video: Definition of a Character in a Story
Visit mometrix.com/academy and enter code: 429493

Analyzing Character Development

Authors of fictional texts present a variety of information about their characters. They describe the characters' physical characteristics, personality traits, hobbies, dreams and goals, and approaches to solving problems. After reading the stories, readers get to know the characters and develop the ability to predict how the characters might react to different types of situations. They also identify the roles that the characters play in the stories, such as being the protagonists or antagonists. Additionally, they determine whether or not any characters have changed as the stories progressed, and they identify reasons for these changes. All of these steps are part of analyzing **character development**.

Students can be asked to discuss character traits and complete character maps using text evidence from the stories. They can be asked to predict how characters would likely react in other situations, based upon their actions in the stories. Students can also be asked to describe how characters have changed from the beginnings of the stories to the ends, using text clues for support. They can compare and contrast characters from different texts or the same characters during different periods of time.

Role That the Setting Plays in a Story

Setting plays an important role in a story. It describes both the geographical location where the story takes place and the time in history when it occurs. A well-described setting also has the power to set the mood for the story. It can help readers visualize the story's events and imagine that they are present. This can assist readers with comprehension and increase engagement with the text.

To recognize setting, readers can be asked to identify both where and when the story takes place as well as to locate key words within the story that signal the answers to these questions. To explore setting more deeply, readers can be asked to identify how the story evokes their five senses. Using a graphic organizer, they can explore what the characters see, hear, taste, smell, and feel in the story. They can discuss how the use of these details helps readers visualize the setting, and they can be encouraged to use similar details in their own writing.

Teachers can also find examples of mentor texts with detailed settings. Students can explore the ways that the authors describe the settings and discuss how these details affect readers.

Elements of Poetry

Discussing and analyzing poetry is a common part of literacy instruction. As part of this instruction, teachers can help students learn to recognize common elements in poetry and use the appropriate terminology to describe them.

There are several elements of poetry. A **verse** is a single line of poetry. Verses can be grouped together to form **stanzas**. The **rhythm** in a poem is developed from patterns of stressed and unstressed syllables. **Meter** refers to a poem's rhythmic structure. Some poems incorporate rhyme, which occurs when words end with the same sounds. **Rhymes** are often found at the ends of verses. Poetry can also use other literary elements, such as alliteration, similes, and metaphors.

Students can learn much about elements of poetry by exploring different types of poems. Students can be asked what they like or dislike about each poem, and these observations can be used to introduce the elements that are used. Students can also compare and contrast different types of poems to see how the elements can be used in different ways. While discussing these observations, teachers can also introduce the correct terminology and provide additional examples to explain how the elements are used by different poets.

Review Video: Structural Elements of Poetry
Visit mometrix.com/academy and enter code: 265216

Helping Students Develop an Appreciation of Poetry

There are many ways teachers can make learning about poetry fun and engaging for students. Early childhood and elementary students can be introduced to poetry during read-alouds and shared reading experiences. They can be encouraged to participate by clapping, making hand motions, and joining in the reading. As students get older, they can participate by highlighting and annotating poems and presenting them aloud to others.

Students can also be encouraged to explore different types of poetry to find styles that appeal to them. Free verse, sonnets, limericks, haikus, villanelles, and sestinas are just some examples of the many types of poetry. Students can also be encouraged to experiment with writing their own examples of different types of poetry.

Additionally, teachers can design poetry challenges for students. For example, students can be given magnetic words or print media that can be cut apart. Students can then explore rearranging the words into verses and stanzas to create different types of poems—seeing how the rhythm, meter, and other elements change. Students can also explore poetic elements in their favorite songs.

Encouraging Students to Locate and Use Evidence from Nonfiction Texts

Students can use T-charts while reading nonfiction texts. On the left side, they can record opinions, predictions, inferences, and similar thoughts made while reading. On the right side of the T-chart, students can record the **text evidence** used to support these thoughts.

Students can also complete scavenger hunts to find text evidence. Teachers can ask students **broad questions** that require higher-level thinking skills and instruct them to search nonfiction texts to find the answers. Information in the texts that are used to answer the questions can be highlighted or recorded on graphic organizers.

Teachers can also **model** this process for students. They can begin shared reading experiences by identifying what questions they want to answer by reading the texts. They can then model stopping when they reach evidence that answers the questions and making annotations as they go. Possible annotations include strong evidence presented by the author and additional questions that have arisen.

Promoting Close Reading of Nonfiction Texts

Close reading activities are designed to help students deeply analyze texts. In all close reading activities, students begin reading without first completing any pre-reading activities. They reread the text multiple times, analyzing different layers each time.

The first time that students read the text, they can be encouraged to determine the overall main idea and supporting details. The second time they read the text, they can be encouraged to analyze the author's craft and the text structure. This might include determining which text structure the author used, identifying the key vocabulary words and their meanings, locating nonfiction text features, and establishing the author's purpose for writing. The third time that students read, they can be encouraged to evaluate the text, draw conclusions, and make connections to other texts, personal experiences, or real-world events.

Teachers can model this process for students during shared reading experiences. They can also provide students with graphic organizers to help them record information during each reading. Additionally, they can encourage students to highlight or make notes in the text to label key information.

Role Reading Fluency Plays in the Comprehension of Nonfiction Texts

Fluency is important in comprehending any type of text. When readers are able to recognize words quickly and accurately, their working memories are available to focus on comprehension. Additionally, their thinking is not interrupted by stopping frequently to decode words.

Nonfiction texts present some special considerations for readers because they can utilize many types of structures. They also may contain several **content-specific vocabulary** words. Readers who are unfamiliar with these text structures and words may have difficulty locating key information and predicting what will come next, impeding comprehension.

Therefore, it is important to expose readers of all ages to a variety of text genres and structures. When practicing fluency passages, a combination of fiction and nonfiction texts should be included. Teachers should also model reading nonfiction texts so students will recognize what fluent reading sounds like.

Promoting Comprehension of Nonfiction Texts with Writing Activities

Writing can assist students with comprehension of nonfiction texts in many ways. Students often read nonfiction texts to learn new information or figure out how to accomplish tasks. They can create lists of questions they would like to have answered by the texts and record their answers as they read. They can also add additional questions that are generated by reading the texts.

Readers can **take notes** to record the main ideas and supporting details of nonfiction texts. There are many note-taking formats that can be used, such as outlining. Readers can also write text summaries or record the main concepts on semantic maps.

Additionally, there are many written response activities that can be used to encourage the use of **higher-level thinking skills**. Readers can write evaluations, compare and contrast essays, alternate endings, recommendations, and other similar responses.

Applying Comprehension Strategies to Digital Texts

Digital literacy includes the ability to make meaning from **digital texts**. Because the use of digital texts is now commonplace, teachers should give students opportunities to interact with both digital and print-based texts frequently.

Readers need to develop the ability to search **efficiently**. This includes generating lists of questions they want to have answered before they begin searching. It also includes selecting relevant search key words. Once search results are displayed, readers need to be able to scan the options and identify the links most likely to be relevant to their needs.

Digital texts are often nonlinear and contain multiple hyperlinks, so readers need the ability to break down the texts and **locate key information**. They can be taught to use note-taking strategies. This may involve using digital tools, like highlighting and annotation tools, or using graphic organizers.

Readers also need to develop the ability to identify author **bias** in digital sources. They should be encouraged to verify the sources and the validity of authors' claims.

Digital communications vary in **formality**. Readers should develop the ability to identify the **main points** in formal texts, like research articles, and informal texts, like blog posts.

Promoting Comprehension by Building Students' Academic Language

Academic language is language used in textbooks, class discussions, tests, and other school-related situations. It includes both vocabulary and syntax that differs from social language, which is less formal and structured.

Understanding the **vocabulary** of academic language is vital to understanding the authors' messages. If readers do not know the meanings of several key words, they will not understand the meanings of the texts and will be unable to analyze them deeply. Understanding academic syntax is also important because it helps students break down complex sentence structure to locate key information.

Students need **frequent exposure** to academic language and opportunities to use it across all content areas. For example, rather than asking students how texts are arranged, teachers can ask them to describe the *text structures*. Using these terms builds familiarity over time. Additionally, teachers can provide partial scripts that students can use to incorporate academic language when making presentations. To help students see the differences between social and academic language, teachers can also help students translate texts from one type to the other.

Types of Informational Texts

- **Literary nonfiction** texts contain true information about topics but are presented using structures similar to fictional texts.They often include clear beginnings and endings and contain literary elements such as figurative language and imagery. Biographies, memoirs, and travel writing are examples of literary nonfiction.
- **Expository** texts are written to explain things using facts. They are structured differently than literary nonfiction texts.They often contain headings, tables of contents, glossaries, charts, graphs, and similar features. These text structures help readers navigate expository texts and locate specific information quickly. A science book explaining the water cycle is an example of an expository text.
- **Persuasive** texts are written to influence readers. They contain evidence to support the authors' claims. An advertisement urging readers to vote for a specific candidate is an example of a persuasive text.
- **Procedural** texts provide step-by-step directions for how to complete tasks. A manual describing how to complete office tasks using specific software is an example of a procedural text.

Review Video: Informational Text
Visit mometrix.com/academy and enter code: 924964

Teaching Readers to Identify Different Types of Informational Texts

Readers can look for specific features to identify types of informational texts. These features can be explicitly taught using example texts, and charts outlining each type of informational text and its features can be displayed in the classrooms.

- To identify **literary nonfiction** texts, readers can look for accurate and factual texts that are written using text structures commonly used in fiction. Although true, these texts read more like stories, with clear beginnings and endings. Literary elements such as figurative language and symbolism may also be included.

- To identify **expository texts**, readers can look for common expository text structures, including tables of contents, headings, sidebars, glossaries, charts, and other similar features. Readers should also be encouraged to check that the texts are factual because some fictional texts may contain these text features as well.
- To identify **persuasive texts**, readers can look for key phrases that signal opinions. These phrases include *I believe, you should*, and *in my opinion*. Readers can also look for details provided by the authors to support their viewpoints.
- To identify **procedural texts**, readers can look for clues that indicate sequence. This might include numbered steps or key words like *first, next*, and *finally*.

Purposes of Nonfiction Texts

- One purpose of nonfiction texts is to **persuade**. In this type of text, authors try to convince readers to adopt their points of view using supporting statements. An article written by a doctor urging parents to limit their children's soda consumption is an example of a persuasive text.
- Another purpose is to **compare and contrast** two things. An essay comparing and contrasting the forms of government in two different countries is an example of this type.
- Other nonfiction texts are written to **inform**. These texts describe and explain topics using facts. A nonfiction book about characteristics of reptiles is an example of a text written to inform.
- Some nonfiction texts are written to **instruct**. These texts explain how to do something. A text about how to change a tire is an example of this type.
- Other nonfiction texts are written to **narrate** real-world events. These texts convey real information in entertaining and/or engaging ways. A personal narrative describing a funny event that occurred on a family vacation is an example of a text written for this purpose.

Adjusting Reading Strategies When Reading Different Types of Texts

It is important for students to self-monitor their reading and adjust their use of strategies depending upon the situation. This will help them focus their attention on key information. It will also ensure that they are comprehending the text and meeting their expected purposes for reading.

When students are reading fiction, they typically read from beginning to end rather than skipping around. This helps them understand the plot and correctly sequence story events. When reading nonfiction texts to answer specific questions, readers may utilize text features like the table of contents to jump to specific sections. This helps readers locate the desired information quickly.

When students are reading for entertainment, they may read the text at a faster rate than when they are reading to analyze specific literary elements or answer comprehension questions. Slowing the reading rate or rereading passages may allow for deeper interaction with the text.

Features of Expository Texts

Expository texts often contain some common features. These features help readers locate and organize key information, and they also provide additional information about the content of the text.

The **table of contents** and **index** help readers know what information is presented in the text and on which pages to find certain topics. **Titles** and **headings** are used to separate content into sections of related information. Enlarged and/or **bolded print** is often used to draw attention to these titles and headings. Important vocabulary words are often highlighted or written in bold print to catch readers' attention. A **glossary** or set of sidebars is often included to provide definitions for these vocabulary words. Photographs or **illustrations** are used to convey information visually, and captions are used to explain their content. Charts, graphs, and tables are frequently used to present relevant data. Maps are also included to provide additional information about places discussed in the text.

Helping Readers Locate and Identify Features of Expository Texts

There are many instructional strategies that can be used to help readers locate and identify features of expository texts. Leading students in feature walks is one common strategy. Using this strategy, teachers share informational and expository texts with students, previewing each section of the texts together. They point out each of the text's features, such as the titles, headings, table of contents, captions, and charts, and discuss the purposes of each. When reading the texts out loud, they model how to use the features to locate and make sense of key information.

To help readers locate and use these text features independently, charts listing the features and their functions can be posted in classrooms. Students can also be given blank charts they can use to record text features found while reading independently. Additionally, students can be given comprehension questions that require the use of text features to answer.

Nonfiction Text Structures

Some nonfiction texts use a **compare-and-contrast** structure. In this type of structure, both similarities and differences between two or more topics are explained. Sometimes the author presents each topic separately and then includes a discussion of similarities and differences. Other times, the author weaves back and forth between the two topics, comparing and contrasting different features along the way.

- **Cause and effect** is another nonfiction text structure. In this structure, the author describes an event and provides reasons why it happened.
- Another nonfiction text structure is **chronological order**. An author who retells the details of an event or period of time in the order that they happened is using this text structure.
- In the **problem/solution** text structure, a problem is introduced by the author. Possible solutions to the problem are then discussed.
- A **description** or **list** structure can also be used. In this type of structure, a topic is introduced. Descriptive details about the topic are then listed.

Review Video: Organizations of Texts: Chronological and Cause and Effect
Visit mometrix.com/academy and enter code: 804598

Faulty Reasoning in Nonfiction Texts

Faulty reasoning occurs when conclusions are not supported by facts and evidence. The ability to recognize faulty reasoning is important because it helps readers evaluate the claims made in texts to determine if they are factual or not. It also helps readers identify potential author bias.

To assist readers with recognizing faulty reasoning, teachers can explicitly teach several different types and provide examples of how they are used in real texts. **Overgeneralizations** occur when authors draw conclusions based upon insufficient data. An example is stating that all fourth graders must like pizza because one fourth grader likes pizza. **Personal bias** occurs when authors base conclusions on personal opinions rather than factors or data. **Illogical conclusions** occur when authors draw conclusions about the relationships between things without data supporting the relationships. An example is stating that because someone was outside in the rain and later got a cold, the rain must have caused the cold.

Students can be encouraged to locate and share examples of faulty reasoning found during their independent reading experiences. They can also be encouraged to verify the sources used by authors to validate their claims and be wary of unsubstantiated online sources.

Reading Comprehension Tools and Strategies

Graphic Organizers That Promote Reading Comprehension and Analysis

Know, want, and learn (KWL) **charts** can be filled out before and after reading to identify what readers know, want to know, and learned about a topic. These charts help activate prior knowledge and give readers a purpose for reading.

KWL Chart

Name: ____________

Date: ____________

Topic: ____________

Know	Want	Learned
What do you think you already know about this topic?	What do you want to know about this topic? Write your questions below.	After you complete your project, write what you learned.

Story maps can be used to help readers identify the main elements of a story, such as characters, setting, problem, events, and solutions. **Character maps** can be used to describe traits of characters in the story.

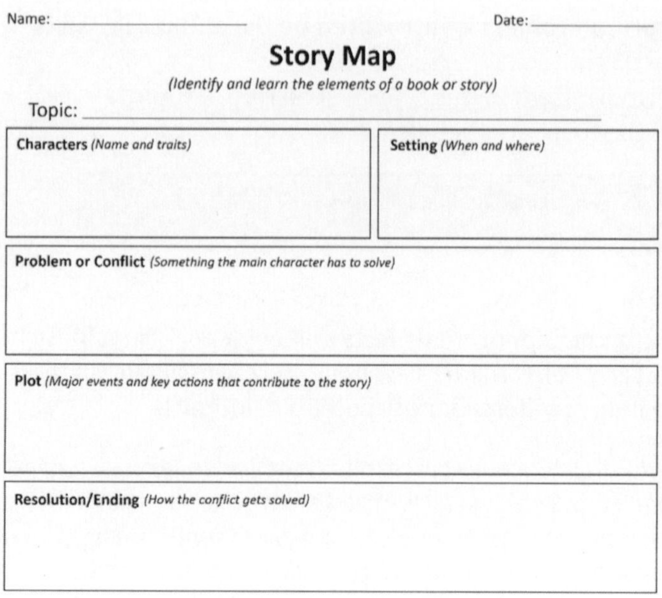

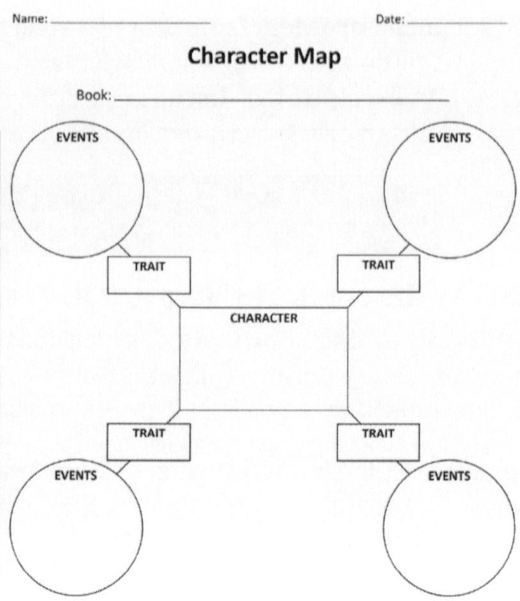

Other graphic organizers can be used to help readers explain the relationships among events or ideas in a story. **Graphic organizers** can be used to help readers identify the problem and solution in a story, along with the events that led to the solution. Other graphic organizers can be used to record inferences and the text evidence used to make them. Graphic organizers like webs can be used to record the main idea and supporting details of a story. Venn diagrams can also be used to compare and contrast two stories, characters, or other elements.

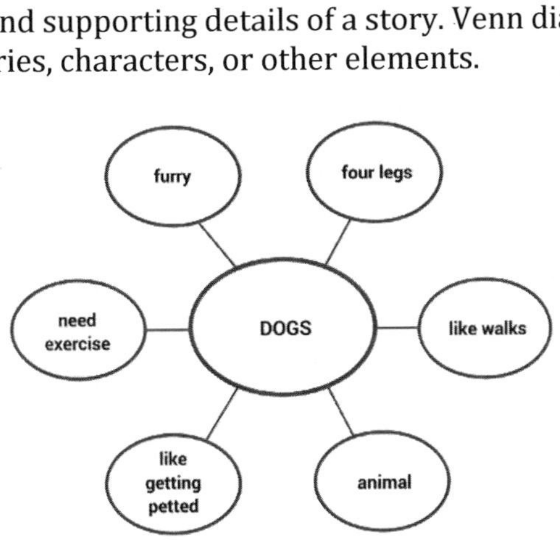

SQ3R Reading Strategy

SQ3R is a strategy used to help students comprehend textbooks. The S stands for **survey**. In this step, students preview the text and note features like headings, graphs, and charts. They use this information to predict what the text is about. In the Q or **question** step, students reread the headings and convert them into questions. They then predict the answers to these questions. The first R stands for **reading**. In this step, students read the text and attempt to answer the questions they listed. They may also make annotations to note important points or additional questions. The second R stands for **recite**, and this step involves summarizing each section of the text immediately after it is read. The last R stands for **review**. Students attempt to answer their original questions without using the text. If they are unable to answer any questions from memory, they review the text and their notes for assistance.

The SQ3R strategy has several benefits. By surveying the text, students activate prior knowledge and set purposes for reading. Listing questions helps focus students' attention during reading.

Annotating helps students analyze and make meaning from the text. Summarizing and reviewing help students remember key information.

Name: ____________________ Date: ____________

SQ3R Chart

Title of Work: ________________________________

Survey: Record important titles and subtitles from work.

____

____

Question: Write "Who, What, When, Where, and Why" questions from main topics.

____

____

Read: Write answers to questions from above.

____

____

Recite: Record key facts and phrases as needed for each question.

____

____

Review: Create a summary paragraph for each question.

____

____

Instructional Strategies to Support Reading Skills

Supporting Reading Comprehension in ELLs and Struggling Readers

It is helpful to build background knowledge before introducing new texts to English language learners (ELLs) and struggling readers. Readers can then draw upon this background knowledge to make meaning from the new texts. After assessing what students already know about the topics, background knowledge can be developed using other texts, charts, graphs, photographs, videos, discussions, and additional methods.

- ELLs and struggling readers can benefit from **previewing** new texts before reading them independently. This may include picture walks or receiving text outlines that identify the **main ideas** covered in each section.
- **Pre-teaching vocabulary** can also help ELLs and struggling readers comprehend new texts. Teachers can introduce the vocabulary words and use photos or real objects to help explain their meanings. The vocabulary words can be frequently incorporated into class discussions to familiarize students with them.
- Additionally, **graphic organizers** can be used to help ELLs and struggling readers identify and organize key parts of texts that assist with comprehension. To offer scaffolding, partially completed graphic organizers and/or sentence stems can be provided initially, and support can be gradually withdrawn over time.

Supporting Reading Comprehension in Proficient Readers

Proficient readers can be encouraged to comprehend at the inferential and evaluative levels in addition to the literal level. They can analyze texts deeply and make inferences, draw conclusions, and form evaluations. They can also be encouraged to complete activities that require higher-level thinking skills. Rather than listing the main characters, for example, proficient readers can be asked to retell the stories from each character's point of view or evaluate the choices the characters made.

To **challenge proficient readers** and encourage them to be enthusiastic about reading, they can also be given choices about book selection. Teachers can guide students in expanding their text selections to include different topics and genres but allow them to make their own selections. Teachers can also encourage students to choose texts that are appropriately challenging. Proficient readers can benefit from ownership in reading-related activities. Teachers can create menus of challenging questions or projects that readers can choose from based on their interests.

Engaging in Collaborative Discussions About Print and Digital Texts

Engaging in **collaborative discussions** can have several benefits for readers. It allows them to learn from other people's experiences and perspectives, which may differ from their own. Readers may hear additional evidence that strengthens their own initial understandings and conclusions. Conversely, they may hear evidence that challenges their initial thoughts and requires them to make revisions. Readers also have to support their points with text evidence to explain their thoughts to classmates. Locating and analyzing text evidence can assist with comprehension.

Discussing texts with others also has broader social benefits. It gives students opportunities to be **active and social learners**. Sharing ideas and collaborating helps build a community of learners who are able to communicate and respect different points of view. It also allows students to experience different social roles within the group and develop conflict resolution skills.

Influence of Culture on Reading Comprehension

Culture affects the ways people view and interact with the world around them. As a result, readers of different cultural backgrounds may comprehend the same texts differently. Readers rely on prior knowledge and existing schemata to make sense of what was read. Texts that are culturally familiar and related to readers' existing cultural schemata are more easily comprehended than those that are unfamiliar. When reading culturally familiar topics, readers are better able to make predictions, inferences, and conclusions based on existing schemata.

Therefore, it is important for teachers to activate both students' content knowledge and cultural knowledge prior to reading. For example, students may read a text describing a birthday celebration. The teacher can activate students' knowledge about how birthdays are celebrated in different cultures.

Research has indicated that cultural differences in syntactic complexity are less likely to affect comprehension.

Structuring Collaborative Discussions About Print and Digital Texts

Literature circles are one way to structure collaborative discussions about print. **Literature circles** consist of small groups of students who lead discussions about shared texts, which may or may not have been self-selected. Students collaboratively analyze the texts, discussing topics such as character development and theme. In some classrooms, guiding questions are provided by the teachers, whereas discussion questions are student-generated in others. Sometimes students are assigned roles within the group, such as summarizer and discussion leader.

Other times, there may be whole-class collaborative discussions. These types of discussions may occur when the whole class is completing an author study, for example, and are comparing and contrasting the events of different texts. These discussions are typically teacher-led.

There may also be small-group, teacher-led, collaborative discussions about teacher-selected texts. For example, discussion time may be included during guided reading groups.

Reciprocal Teaching Strategy

Reciprocal teaching is a strategy designed to assist students with reading comprehension. In reciprocal teaching, students and teachers **share the responsibilities** of leading small-group discussions about texts. Teachers initially take the lead and model using four main comprehension strategies, including generating questions, summarizing, clarifying, and predicting. They gradually share more responsibility with students, who eventually take over leading the groups in applying these strategies to analyze texts.

Reciprocal teaching has several benefits. It requires students to be actively engaged in the reading process, as they must understand and apply the reading strategies to guide their classmates. It encourages the use of higher-level reading strategies that can then be applied to other texts. It also encourages discussion and collaboration among class members. Additionally, reciprocal teaching can help build students' confidence in their abilities to independently read and analyze challenging texts.

Activities Promoting Reading Comprehension

Before reading, teachers can set the purposes for reading and activate students' prior knowledge by making connections to what they already know. They can **preview** the texts and important vocabulary words and encourage students to make **predictions**.

During reading, teachers can model thinking aloud to demonstrate how they **monitor** their own understanding. They can check and revise predictions, make inferences, and form connections. They can provide students with guiding questions or graphic organizers to use as they read independently to encourage the same reading behaviors.

After reading, teachers can **model** summarizing, drawing conclusions, and evaluating the texts. They can also discuss how their thinking changed as they read and were presented with new evidence. They can encourage students to use the same strategies after reading independently by setting up literature circles, creating written response activities, and designing other reading response projects.

Types of Connections Readers Can Make to Texts

- Readers can make **text-to-text connections**. These are connections made between two or more different texts that have been read. Readers might make connections between the texts' events, characters, themes, or any other features. An example is when a reader identifies that characters in two different books both persisted to overcome challenges.
- **Text-to-self connections** refer to connections readers make between texts and their own personal experiences. An example is when a reader understands the sadness a character feels when losing a pet after having personally experienced the same thing.
- **Text-to-world connections** refer to connections readers make between events in texts and events that have happened in the real world. An example is when a reader makes connections between a text about an astronaut and news about a recent space launch.

To encourage readers to make these connections, teachers can model their own thinking during shared reading experiences. They can model thinking deeply about similarities rather than making surface connections. For example, rather than pointing out that two characters are both girls, they can compare their character traits. Teachers can also encourage the use of Venn diagrams to show the similarities and differences between two texts, people, or events.

Benefits of Comparing Different Books by the Same Author

When students read and compare multiple books by the same author, they use several reading strategies important for comprehension. They compare and contrast story elements between texts, such as characters, settings, problems, and solutions; they make text-to-text connections. They also consider how the author's life experiences may impact his or her writing style and content.

After completing multiple author studies, readers may also begin to identify favorite authors. These authors can serve as **mentors** for students, providing models of how to use language and incorporate story elements in their own writing. The connections readers feel to their favorite authors can boost engagement with reading and encourage them to seek out additional texts. Students can learn about the authors' lives and the paths they have taken as writers. They may be inspired by learning that people similar to themselves have become published authors.

Benefits of Learning About Topics Using Different Texts and/or Genres

Reading different texts on the same topic can give readers a more comprehensive understanding of the topic. Each text reflects the personal writing style and bias of the author. Reading multiple texts allows readers to hear different perspectives and form their own judgments.

Reading texts from **multiple genres** about the same topic is also beneficial. Each genre presents the information differently and serves unique purposes. Reading an **informational text** about the Civil War may provide readers with an understanding of the war's causes, events, and major figures. Reading a **historical fiction** book written from the perspective of a soldier may give readers a more personalized account of this period in time, engaging the readers and helping them form personal connections.

When reading multiple texts, readers also need to identify the important points from each and synthesize the information. They need to consider the authors' purposes for writing. These skills assist with reading comprehension.

Chapter Quiz

Ready to see how well you retained what you just read? Scan the QR code to go directly to the chapter quiz interface for this study guide. If you're using a computer, simply visit the online resources page at **mometrix.com/resources719/aepafoundread** and click the Chapter Quizzes link.

Reading Assessment and Instruction

Spelling Development

Stages of Spelling Development

Students typically progress through a series of stages of spelling development. Researchers name the stages differently, but they contain common characteristics.

In the **pre-phonetic stage**, students spell using random letter and number strings. There are no letter-sound relationships evident in words. In the **semi-phonetic stage**, some letter-sound relationships are used to spell words. Students typically learn to correctly spell the beginning and ending sounds in words first, followed later by the medial sounds. In the **phonetic stage**, some simple words begin to be spelled correctly, such as CVC words. In addition to initial, medial, and final sounds, some more complex sounds are accurately represented. This includes some consonant blends and digraphs. In the transitional, or **word extension stage**, students learn to use syllable patterns to spell more complex words. Most words are spelled correctly in this stage. In the **derivational constancy stage**, students use knowledge of roots and affixes to spell related words. Most or all words in students' writing pieces are spelled correctly in this stage.

Orthography

Orthography refers to the conventional spelling of words in a language. Because many words are spelled using the same patterns, studying orthography helps students increase the number of words they can spell correctly. Learning to apply orthographic patterns is an important part of any literacy program.

Word studies, or word work, should be regularly included in the school day. Word work should be sequential and built upon the knowledge of orthographic patterns that students already possess.

There are three layers of orthography that students can explore during word work. The **alphabet layer** refers to letter-sound relationships. Activities in which students combine letters or letter groups to form words will help them explore the alphabet layer. When students explore the **pattern layer**, they look for larger patterns that guide the spellings of words. Activities in which students build words within word families, such as CVCe words, help them explore the pattern layer. The **meaning layer** explores the relationships between word meanings and spellings. Sorting and writing words that contain the same Latin roots will help students explore the meaning layer of orthography.

Layers of English Orthography

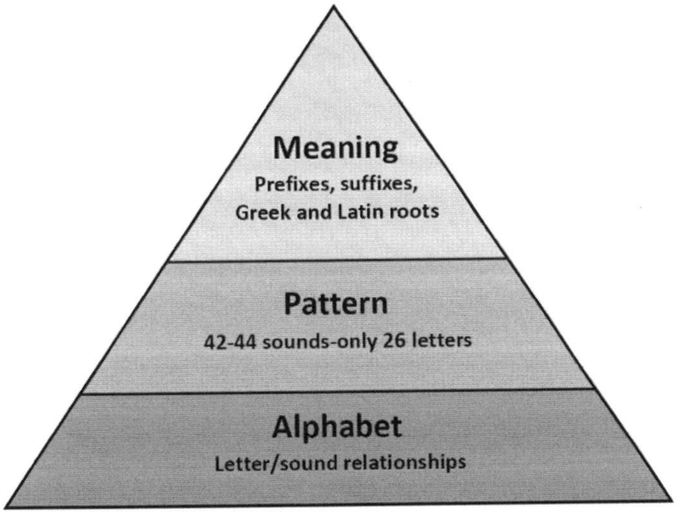

PHONETIC SPELLING

Phonetic spelling is common in the early stages of writing development. When writing words, students consider what sounds they hear. They use knowledge of phonics rules to select letters or groups of letters to represent those sounds. For example, a student who is familiar with CVC words might write *love* as *luv*.

Parents are sometimes concerned with the amount of misspelled words in their children's writing. However, phonetic spelling plays a role in reading and writing development and is a stepping stone to conventional spelling.

At this stage, students know how to automatically spell a limited number of words. Using known phonics rules helps them efficiently encode words they do not know how to spell. If students are worried about spelling every word conventionally, they must continuously ask others for help. This slows the writing process and puts more emphasis on spelling than on recording ideas. Therefore, teachers typically tell students in this stage to write the sounds they hear and move on. This process also allows students to apply the phonics skills they use while reading.

Over time, students learn more complex spelling patterns and automatically remember how to spell more words. At this point, spelling becomes more conventional.

ROLE OF MEMORIZATION IN SPELLING DEVELOPMENT AND INSTRUCTION

There are some words that students cannot learn to spell by learning spelling patterns. These include many high-frequency words with irregular spelling patterns, such as the word *the*. Students should have frequent and repeated exposure to these words to memorize their spellings. Practice activities are helpful, such as building these words with letter tiles.

Some academic vocabulary words are also difficult for students to spell using knowledge of spelling patterns. For example, second graders may learn about camouflage as part of a science unit on animal adaptations. However, it would be difficult for students of this age to spell the word *camouflage* using knowledge of spelling patterns. Frequent exposure to these academic words in print will help students learn to spell them over time. Adding these words to word walls or classroom charts can serve as tools to assist with spelling initially. Being given numerous opportunities to write these words with scaffolding will assist with memorization.

Although memorization plays a role in spelling some words, its use as an instructional strategy should be balanced with explicit instruction in spelling patterns. When choosing weekly spelling lists, teachers should focus on patterns that can be applied to multiple words.

Different Approaches to Teaching Students to Spell

There are many methods and commercial programs available to teach spelling. Although they vary in approach, the methods that are most effective share some common characteristics.

Effective spelling instruction should be explicit. Although students naturally learn to spell many words through frequent reading experiences, some explicit spelling instruction is still helpful to teach common spelling patterns and relationships among words. The instruction should be both incremental and sequential.

Teachers can introduce weekly spelling patterns, and students can complete activities to familiarize themselves with the patterns. Depending on the ages of the students, this may include word sorts, word hunts, and tracing. Multisensory activities are also helpful, such as building words with letter tiles and writing words in sand. Teachers may assess students' applications of the spelling patterns at the end of each week. Some teachers give students lists of words to study ahead of time. Other teachers assess students by asking them to spell new words that follow the patterns they have been studying.

Instructional Activities that Support Reading and Writing Skills

Activities That Support Reading, Writing, Listening, and Speaking Development

Reading, writing, listening, and speaking are the four main components of English language development. All of these components are important and interdependent. They all play roles in making and conveying meaning, which are goals of literacy instruction.

These skills are sometimes practiced in isolation, such as when students listen to audio texts without any follow-up activities. However, when solving real-world problems, these skills are often used together. For example, doctors must listen to their patients' symptoms, make notes on the patients' charts, and then explain their treatment plans. Therefore, it is important for teachers to plan activities that integrate these four skills.

Project-based learning activities and performance assessments are useful for integrating these four skills. As an example, students could read about the benefits of recycling. They could then speak to the school principal to recommend implementing a school-wide recycling plan, listening and responding to the principal's concerns. They could then create posters to advertise the new program to other students.

Cloze Reading Procedure

Cloze reading is an instructional strategy in which students read brief passages containing omitted words. They rely on background knowledge, semantic clues, and/or syntactic clues to determine the unknown words.

When designing cloze reading passages, teachers should consider a few key factors. The passages should be at the appropriate reading levels for the students. Students should be able to guess the omitted words by using reading strategies. If students need additional scaffolding to determine the missing words, word banks can be provided.

Cloze reading activities can be done independently or with partners. They can also be done as whole-class activities, with teachers reading the main passages and students supplying the missing words.

Cloze reading has several benefits. It requires students to use a variety of reading strategies, including using context clues, to determine the missing words. Students also cross-check their use of cueing systems to determine unknown words in cloze passages. If students read the passages multiple times to determine the missing words, it builds fluency as well.

Language Experience Approach to Reading Instruction

The **language experience approach** focuses on using students' own experiences as the topics of literacy experiences. Students think about experiences they would like to share. They dictate the experiences to teachers, who write the students' words down in front of them. The teachers then read the texts aloud while pointing to each word, modeling appropriate fluency. Students are then invited to join the teachers in rereading the texts.

The language experience approach can also be done as a whole-class activity, with classes writing about shared experiences together. For example, they could write about projects recently completed at school. Teachers help students generate ideas for what to include and list relevant vocabulary words that may be used. Students then dictate sentences to their teachers, who record them on chart paper. The classes then reread the texts multiple times.

A benefit of the language experience approach is that it involves reading, writing, listening, and speaking. It also builds upon students' prior knowledge and interests. If students are given multiple opportunities to reread the texts they have created, it also assists with fluency.

Guided Reading and Small Group Reading Instruction

Guided reading is a term closely related to balanced literacy programs. Even though these programs are not considered to be best practice anymore, small groups should still be implemented in reading instruction. In guided reading, teachers arrange students in flexible groups and meet with each group separately. While meeting with each group, teachers provide leveled texts to each student, conduct picture walks, and focus on strategies that might be helpful when reading the texts. Instead of this, teachers should provide students with their own copies of decodable texts that are based off previously taught phonics skills. Before reading, teachers should review any irregular sight words that may appear and review previously taught phonics rules that will be helpful when reading the given texts. Teachers also should encourage the students to apply the rules they have learned to decode unknown words. Similarly to guided reading, students then read the texts independently in whisper voices while the teachers observe and make notes about students' reading. After students have read the texts independently, the teacher should conduct mini-lessons on skills that are targeted in the texts, such as specific phonics rules that are used a lot through the text. Students then take the texts to reread later, helping build fluency.

The flexible nature of reading groups ensures that students are always reading books within their instructional reading levels. Because the groups are small, teachers can target phonics skills that students within that specific group may still be struggling with. Teachers also have frequent opportunities to observe students' progress and determine which skills need additional practice.

Shared Reading Experiences

During **shared reading experiences**, teachers read aloud to students using materials like large print books, texts written on chart paper, and projected texts. Students follow along as teachers read and point to each word. Shared reading is an interactive experience, and teachers stop frequently to ask questions and model use of strategies. Depending on the ages and reading levels of the students, teachers focus on different teaching points. For example, kindergarten teachers may model and discuss concepts of print, whereas teachers of students in older grades may model and discuss comprehension strategies. Students may join the teachers in reading the texts as well.

Shared reading can be used across all subject areas and has several benefits. It allows students to see teachers modeling the use of reading strategies and practice using these strategies with scaffolding. It also allows students to participate in reading and discussing quality texts that they may not yet be able to read independently. Students learn about text features like punctuation marks and spelling patterns that they can incorporate into their own writing. They also have opportunities to hear examples of fluent reading.

Read-Alouds

During **read-alouds**, teachers read texts aloud to students. Depending on their purposes for reading, they may or may not pause to model the use of strategies or ask questions. Some read-alouds may be done strictly for entertainment purposes, whereas others may be done to provide background knowledge in content areas or allow for the modeling of reading strategies.

The key difference between read-alouds and shared reading experiences is that students do not have access to the texts during read-alouds. They listen as teachers read aloud, and they are sometimes shown the pictures. The focus is on listening to the texts and the teachers' use of strategies; students do not join in reading.

Benefits of Independent Daily Reading Time

Independent daily reading has several benefits. Reading self-selected books can boost engagement with reading and help students develop a love of reading. When given opportunities to reread favorite texts, fluency may also increase. Independent reading also gives students opportunities to apply reading strategies to new texts autonomously.

Books for independent reading are usually self-selected. Students in the early stages of reading development who cannot read texts independently can be encouraged to "read the pictures." Teachers can model how to use prior knowledge and picture clues to tell the stories in their own words. Students who are able to read the words can be encouraged to select appropriate texts for independent reading time. Depending on the ages of the students, teachers may need to help readers build reading stamina. They can schedule a few minutes of daily independent reading time early in the school year and gradually add additional minutes. Teachers may schedule whole-class independent reading time or establish it as one station for students to complete during literacy stations.

Students can also be encouraged to have book boxes that contain several texts at the appropriate reading levels for use during independent reading time.

Role of Flexible Groupings in Effective Reading Instruction

Flexible groupings are one way that teachers can differentiate instruction. When using **flexible grouping**, teachers strategically group students together to accomplish specific instructional goals. The groups may be large or small, and they vary depending on the activity. For example, a teacher may work with a small group of students who are all having difficulties with cause-and-effect relationships. The teacher is able to target instruction in this skill area to only the students who need extra practice. Guided reading groups are also flexible because students typically progress through instructional reading levels at different rates. Teachers can use both formal and informal assessment data to group students.

Flexible groupings have several benefits. They allow students to receive targeted instruction, often in small-group settings that allow for more teacher interaction. Students who have mastered these skills are able to work on other things, preventing them from becoming bored or frustrated. Additionally, students may feel more comfortable participating in small groups of their peers. Flexible groupings also mean that students will have opportunities to work with many other students throughout the year.

Review Video: Differentiated Instruction
Visit mometrix.com/academy and enter code: 100342

Considerations When Grouping Students for Instructional Purposes

When determining when and how to group students for instructional purposes, teachers should take many factors into consideration. They should consider what instructional goals they want to accomplish. These goals are often based upon specific learning objectives.

Once teachers know what goals they want to accomplish, they can consider what types of groupings to use. Possibilities include partner learning as well as small or large group instruction. Teachers also need to consider the characteristics of the students in each group. For example, teachers may group students who need to practice specific skills together to target instruction. Other times, they may group students who have differing perspectives on topics to facilitate active discussion and sharing of viewpoints. These decisions should support the learning objectives. Teachers also need to consider what types of learning activities to use within the groups. Additionally, they need to consider what roles students will be assigned within their groups, if any. It is common for classrooms to use a variety of grouping arrangements throughout the year to accomplish different instructional goals.

Classroom Management Strategies for Effective Reading Groups

Reading groups are important components of literacy instruction because they allow students to receive differentiated, small-group instruction on a routine basis. However, they may be ineffective if frequent interruptions or classroom management issues occur. Clearly established and practiced routines can prevent these issues from occurring.

Students who are not working with their teachers in reading groups should be engaged in activities that they are able to successfully complete either independently or with the help of their peers. If center rotations are being used, students should know in what order to proceed through the centers and what the expectations are for each rotation.

Additionally, routines should be in place for how to solve problems without interrupting the reading groups. There should be clear criteria in place for when the teachers can be interrupted, such as in the case of emergencies. Students should be taught how to independently access any materials they may need to complete their activities. Hand signals or sign-out sheets may be utilized to minimize interruptions when students need permission to leave the classroom. Students can also be taught to ask a set number of classmates for assistance with problems before asking their teachers.

Characteristics of Shared Writing Experiences

During **shared writing experiences**, teachers and students collaboratively plan the content of shared writing pieces. Teachers assist their students with choosing topics, deciding which details to include, selecting words, and organizing text structure. Students are asked to share their ideas, and teachers help students organize their thoughts and put them into writing. Teachers control the writing instruments and put the words down on paper. Along the way, they may ask students for assistance with spelling words, determining how to punctuate, and other issues. Teachers model their thinking and use of writing strategies throughout the process. Once the drafting is finished, students may assist with revising, editing, and reading the texts aloud.

Shared writing experiences give students opportunities to be active participants in scaffolded versions of the writing process and work collaboratively to develop quality writing pieces. Additionally, they benefit from observing their teachers as they model the use of writing strategies.

Characteristics of Interactive Writing Experiences

During **interactive writing experiences**, teachers and students work together to create shared writing pieces. With teacher guidance, students help plan writing topics, determine which details to include, and organize text structure. Students share the writing utensils with teachers and contribute to recording the words on paper. Teachers provide guidance along the way. For example, they may remind students of recently learned spelling patterns while students are spelling the words on paper. Classes may also work together to revise, edit, and read the writing pieces.

Giving students control over the writing utensils is what differentiates interactive writing from shared writing. In shared writing, teachers record the words on paper.

Interactive writing allows students to be active participants in the writing process while receiving scaffolding from teachers. It also allows students to collaboratively create quality writing pieces they are unable to produce independently at their current stages of writing development. Additionally, teachers can build targeted mini-lessons into the interactive writing process.

Assessment Methodology

Assessment Methods

Effective teaching requires multiple methods of assessment to evaluate student comprehension and instructional effectiveness. Assessments are typically categorized as diagnostic, formative, summative, and benchmark and are applicable at varying stages of instruction. **Diagnostic** assessments are administered before instruction and indicate students' prior knowledge and areas of misunderstanding to determine the path of instruction. **Formative** assessments occur continuously to measure student engagement, comprehension, and instructional effectiveness. These assessments indicate instructional strategies that require adjustment to meet students' needs in facilitating successful learning and include strategies like checking for understanding, observations, total participation activities, and exit tickets. **Summative** assessments are given at the end of a lesson or unit to evaluate student progress in reaching learning targets and identify areas of misconception for reteaching. Such assessments can be given in the form of exams and quizzes or be project-based activities in which students demonstrate their learning through hands-on, personalized methods. Additionally, portfolios serve as valuable summative assessments in allowing students to demonstrate their progress over time and provide insight regarding individual achievement. **Benchmark** assessments occur less frequently and encompass large portions of curriculum. These assessments are intended to evaluate the progress of groups of students in achieving state and district academic standards.

Assessment Types

- **Diagnostic:** These assessments can either be formal or informal and are intended to provide teachers with information regarding students' level of understanding prior to beginning a unit of instruction. Examples include pretests, KWL charts, anticipation guides, and brainstorming activities. Digital resources, such as online polls, surveys, and quizzes are also valuable resources for gathering diagnostic feedback.
- **Formative:** These assessments occur throughout instruction to provide the teacher with feedback regarding student understanding. Examples include warm-up and closure activities, checking frequently for understanding, student reflection activities, and providing students with color-coded cards to indicate their level of understanding. Short quizzes and total participation activities, such as four corners, are also valuable formative assessments. Numerous digital resources, including polls, surveys, and review games, are also beneficial in providing teachers with formative feedback to indicate instructional effectiveness.
- **Summative:** Summative assessments are intended to indicate students' levels of mastery and progress toward reaching academic learning standards. These assessments may take the form of written or digital exams and include multiple choice, short answer, or long answer questions. Examples also include projects, final essays, presentations, or portfolios to demonstrate student progress over time.
- **Benchmark:** Benchmark assessments measure students' progress in achieving academic standards. These assessments are typically standardized to ensure uniformity, objectivity, and accuracy. Benchmark assessments are typically given as a written multiple choice or short answer exam, or as a digital exam in which students answer questions on the computer.

Review Video: Formative and Summative Assessments
Visit mometrix.com/academy and enter code: 804991

Determining Appropriate Assessment Strategies

As varying assessment methods provide different information regarding student performance and achievement, the teacher must consider the most applicable and effective assessment strategy in each stage of instruction. This includes determining the **desired outcomes** of assessment as well as the information the teacher intends to ascertain and how they will apply the results to further instruction. **Age-** and **grade-level**-appropriateness must be considered when selecting which assessment strategies will enable students to successfully demonstrate their learning. Additionally, the teacher must be cognizant of students' individual differences and learning needs to determine which assessment model is most **accommodating** and reflective of their progress. It is also important that teachers consider the practicality of assessment strategies and methods they will use to implement the assessment for maximized feedback regarding individual and whole-class progress in achieving learning goals.

Assessments That Reflect Real-World Applications

Assessments that reflect **real-world applications** enhance relevancy and students' ability to establish personal connections to learning that deepen understanding. Implementing such assessments provides authenticity and enhances engagement by defining a clear and practical purpose for learning. These assessments often allow for hands-on opportunities for demonstrating learning and can be adjusted to accommodate students' varying learning styles and needs while measuring individual progress; however, assessments that focus on real-world applications can be subjective, thus making it difficult to extract concrete data and quantify student progress to guide future instructional decisions. In addition, teachers may have difficulty analyzing assessment results on a large scale and comparing student performance with other schools and districts, as individual assessments may vary.

Diagnostic Tests

Diagnostic tests are integral to planning and delivering effective instruction. These tests are typically administered prior to beginning a unit or lesson and provide valuable feedback for guiding and planning instruction. Diagnostic tests provide **preliminary information** regarding students' levels of understanding and prior knowledge. This serves as a baseline for instructional planning that connects and builds upon students' background knowledge and experiences to enhance success in learning. Diagnostic tests allow the teacher to identify and clarify areas of student misconception prior to engaging in instruction to ensure continued comprehension and avoid the need for remediation. They indicate areas of student strength and need as well as individual instructional aids that may need to be incorporated into lessons to support student achievement. In addition, these tests enable the teacher to determine which instructional strategies, activities, groupings, and materials will be most valuable in maximizing engagement and learning. Diagnostic tests can be **formal** or **informal** and include pre-tests, pre-reading activities, surveys, vocabulary inventories, and graphic organizers (such as KWL charts). These tests are used to assess student understanding prior to engaging in learning. Diagnostic tests are generally not graded, as there is little expectation that all students in a class possess the same baseline of proficiency at the start of a unit.

Formative Assessments

Formative assessments are any assessments that take place in the **middle of a unit of instruction**. The goals of formative assessments are to help teachers understand where a student is in his or her progress toward **mastering** the current unit's content and to provide the students with **ongoing feedback** throughout the unit. The advantage of relying heavily on formative assessments in instruction is that it allows the teacher to continuously **check for comprehension** and adjust instruction as needed to ensure that the whole class is adequately prepared to proceed at the end of the unit. To understand formative assessments well, teachers need to understand that any interaction that can provide information about the student's comprehension is a type of formative assessment which can be used to inform future instruction.

Formative assessments are often a mixture of formal and informal assessments. **Formal formative assessments** often include classwork, homework, and quizzes. Examples of **informal formative assessments** include simple comprehension checks during instruction, class-wide discussions of the current topic, and exit slips, which are written questions posed by teachers at the end of class, which helps the teacher quickly review which students are struggling with the concepts.

Summative Assessments

Summative assessment refers to an evaluation at the end of a discrete unit of instruction, such as the end of a course, unit, or semester. Classic examples of summative assessments include end-of-course assessments, final exams, or even qualifying standardized tests such as the SAT or ACT. Most summative assessments are created to measure student mastery of particular **academic standards**. Whereas formative assessment generally informs current instruction, summative assessments are used to objectively demonstrate that each individual has achieved adequate mastery of the standards in question. If a student has not met the benchmark, he or she may need extra instruction or may need to repeat the course.

These assessments usually take the form of **tests** or formal portfolios with rubrics and clearly defined goals. Summative assessments are usually high-stakes, heavily-weighted, and they should always be formally graded. These types of assessments often feature a narrower range of question types, such as multiple choice, short answer, and essay questions to help with systematic grading.

Project-based assessments are beneficial in evaluating achievement, as they incorporate several elements of instruction and highlight real-world applications of learning. This allows students to demonstrate understanding through a hands-on, individualized approach that reinforces connections to learning and increases retainment. **Portfolios** of student work over time serve as a valuable method for assessing individual progress toward reaching learning targets. Summative assessments provide insight regarding overall instructional effectiveness and are necessary for guiding future instruction in subsequent years but are not usually used to modify current instruction.

Review Video: Assessment Reliability and Validity
Visit mometrix.com/academy and enter code: 424680

Benchmark Assessments

Benchmark assessments are intended to quantify, evaluate, and compare individual and groups of students' achievement of school-wide, district, and state **academic standards.** They are typically administered in specific intervals throughout the school year and encompass entire or large units of curriculum to determine student mastery and readiness for academic advancement. Benchmark assessments provide data that enable the teacher to determine students' progress toward reaching academic goals to guide current and continued instruction. This data can be utilized by the school and individual teachers to create learning goals and objectives aligned with academic standards. It can also be used to plan instructional strategies, activities, and assessments to support students in achieving these academic standards. In addition, benchmark assessments provide feedback regarding understanding and the potential need for remediation to allow the teacher to instill necessary supports in future instruction that prepare students for success in achieving learning targets.

Alignment of Assessments with Instructional Goals and Objectives

To effectively monitor student progress, assessments must align with **instructional goals** and **objectives**. This allows the teacher to determine whether students are advancing at an appropriate pace to achieve state and district academic standards. When assessments are aligned with specific learning targets, the teacher ensures that students are learning relevant material to establish a foundation of knowledge necessary for growth and academic achievement. To achieve this, teachers must determine which instructional goals and objectives their students must achieve and derive instruction, content, and activities from these specifications. Instruction must reflect and reinforce learning targets, and the teacher must select the most effective strategies for addressing students' needs as they work to achieve them. Assessments must be reflective of content instruction to ensure they are aligned with learning goals and objectives, as well as to enable the teacher to evaluate student progress in mastering them. The teacher must clearly communicate learning goals and objectives throughout all stages of instruction to provide students with clarity on expectations. This establishes a clear purpose and focus for learning that enhances relevancy and strengthens connections to support student achievement.

Clearly Communicating Assessment Criteria and Standards

Students must be clear on the purpose of learning throughout all stages of instruction to enhance understanding and facilitate success. When assessment **criteria** and **standards** are clearly communicated, the purpose of learning is established, and students are able to effectively connect instructional activities to learning goals and criteria for assessment. Communicating assessment criteria and standards provides students with clarity on tasks and learning goals they are expected to accomplish as they prepare themselves for assessment. This allows for more **focused instruction** and engagement in learning, as it enhances relevancy and student motivation. Utilizing appropriate forms of **rubrics** is an effective strategy in specifying assessment criteria and standards, as it informs students about learning goals they are working toward, the quality of work they are expected to achieve, and skills they must master to succeed on the assessment. Rubrics indicate to students exactly how they will be evaluated, thus supporting their understanding and focus as they engage in learning to promote academic success.

Rubrics for Communicating Standards

The following are varying styles of rubrics that can be used to communicate criteria and standards:

- **Analytic:** Analytic rubrics break down criteria for an assignment into several categories and provide an explanation of the varying levels of performance in each one. This style of rubric is beneficial for detailing the characteristics of quality work as well as providing students with feedback regarding specific components of their performance. Analytic rubrics are most effective when used for summative assessments, such as long-term projects or essays.
- **Holistic:** Holistic rubrics evaluate the quality of the student's assignment as a whole rather than scoring individual components. Students' scores are determined based upon their performance across multiple performance indicators. This style of rubric is beneficial for providing a comprehensive evaluation but limits the amount of feedback that students receive regarding their performance in specific areas.
- **Single-point:** Single-point rubrics outline criteria for assignments into several categories. Rather than providing a numeric score to each category, however, the teacher provides written feedback regarding the students' strengths and ways in which they can improve their performance. This style of rubric is beneficial in providing student-centered feedback that focuses on their overall progress.
- **Checklist:** Checklists typically outline a set of criteria that is scored using a binary approach based upon completion of each component. This style increases the efficiency of grading assignments and is often easy for students to comprehend but does not provide detailed feedback. This method of grading should generally be reserved for shorter assignments.

Communicating High Academic Expectations in Assessments

The attitudes and behaviors exhibited by the teacher are highly influential on students' attitudes toward learning. Teachers demonstrate belief in students' abilities to be successful in learning when they communicate **high academic expectations**. This promotes students' **self-concept** and establishes a **growth mindset** to create confident, empowered learners that are motivated to achieve. High expectations for assessments and reaching academic standards communicates to students the quality of work that is expected of them and encourages them to overcome obstacles as they engage in learning. When communicating expectations for student achievement, it is important that the teacher is aware of students' individual learning needs to provide the necessary support that establishes equitable opportunities for success in meeting assessment criteria and standards. Setting high expectations through assessment criteria and standards while supporting students in their learning enhances overall achievement and establishes a foundation for continuous academic success.

Effective Communication and Impact on Student Learning

Communicating high academic expectations enhances students' self-concept and increases personal motivation for success in learning. To maximize student achievement, it is important that the teacher set high academic expectations that are **clearly** communicated through **age-appropriate** terms and consistently reinforced. Expectations must be reflected through learning goals and objectives and must be **visible** at all times to ensure student awareness. Teachers must be **specific** in communicating what they want students to accomplish and clearly detail necessary steps for achievement while assuming the role of facilitator to guide learning and provide support. Providing constructive **feedback** throughout instruction is integral in reminding students of academic expectations and ensuring they are making adequate progress toward reaching learning goals. When high academic expectations are communicated and reinforced, students are empowered with a sense of confidence and self-responsibility for their own learning that promotes their desire to learn. This ultimately enhances achievement and equips them with the tools necessary for future academic success.

Analyzing and Interpreting Assessment Data

Teachers can utilize multiple techniques to effectively analyze and interpret assessment data. This typically involves creating charts and graphs outlining different data subsets. They can list each learning standard that was assessed, determine how many students overall demonstrated proficiency on the standard, and identify individual students who did not demonstrate proficiency on each standard. This information can be used to differentiate instruction. Additionally, they can track individual student performance and progress on each standard over time.

Teachers can take note of overall patterns and trends in assessment data. For example, they can determine if any subgroups of students did not meet expectations. They can consider whether the data confirms or challenges any existing beliefs, implications this may have on instructional planning and what, if any, conclusions can be drawn from this data.

Analyzing and interpreting assessment data may raise new questions for educators, so they can also determine if additional data collection is needed.

Using Assessment Data to Differentiate Instruction for Individual Learners

By analyzing and interpreting assessment data, teachers can determine if there are any specific learning standards that need to be retaught to their entire classes. This may be necessary if the data shows that all students struggled in these specific areas. Teachers may consider reteaching these standards using different methods if the initial methods were unsuccessful.

Teachers can also form groups of students who did not demonstrate proficiency on the same learning standards. Targeted instruction can be planned for these groups to help them make progress in these areas. Interventions can also be planned for individual students who did not show proficiency in certain areas. If interventions have already been in place and have not led to increased learning outcomes, the interventions may be redesigned. If interventions have been in place and assessment data now shows proficiency, the interventions may be discontinued.

If assessment data shows that certain students have met or exceeded expectations in certain areas, enrichment activities can be planned to challenge these students and meet their learning needs.

Aligning Assessments with Instructional Goals and Objectives

Assessments that are congruent to instructional goals and objectives provide a **clear purpose** for learning that enhances student understanding and motivation. When learning targets are reflected in assessments, instructional activities and materials become more **relevant**, as they are derived from these specifications. Such clarity in purpose allows for more focus and productivity as students engage in instruction and fosters connections that strengthen overall understanding for maximized success in learning. Aligning assessments with instructional goals and objectives ensures that students are learning material that is relevant to the curriculum and academic standards to ensure **preparedness** as they advance in their academic careers. In addition, it enables the teacher to evaluate and monitor student progress to determine whether they are progressing at an ideal pace for achieving academic standards. With this information, the teacher can effectively modify instruction as necessary to support students' needs in reaching desired learning outcomes.

Norm-Referenced Tests

On **norm-referenced tests**, students' performances are compared to the performances of sample groups of similar students. Norm-referenced tests identify students who score above and below the average. To ensure reliability, the tests must be given in a standardized manner to all students.

Norm-referenced tests usually cover a broad range of skills, such as the entire grade-level curriculum for a subject. They typically contain a few questions per skill. Whereas scores in component areas of the tests may be calculated, usually overall test scores are reported. Scores are often reported using percentile ranks, which indicate what percentage of test takers scored lower than the student being assessed. For example, a student's score in the 75th percentile means the student scored better than 75% of other test takers. Other times, scores may be reported using grade-level equivalency.

One advantage of norm-referenced tests is their objectivity. They also allow educators to compare large groups of students at once. This may be helpful for making decisions regarding class placements and groupings. A disadvantage of norm-referenced tests is that they only indicate how well students perform in comparison to one another. They do not indicate whether or not students have mastered certain skills.

Criterion-Referenced Tests

Criterion-referenced tests measure how well students perform on certain skills or standards. The goal of these tests is to indicate whether or not students have mastered certain skills and which skills require additional instruction. Scores are typically reported using the percentage of questions answered correctly or students' performance levels. Performance levels are outlined using terms such as *below expectations*, *met expectations*, and *exceeded expectations*.

One advantage of criterion-referenced tests is that they provide teachers with useful information to guide instruction. They can identify which specific skills students have mastered and which skills need additional practice. Teachers can use this information to plan whole-class, small-group, and individualized instruction. Analyzing results of criterion-referenced tests over time can also help teachers track student progress on certain skills. A disadvantage of criterion-referenced tests is that they do not allow educators to compare students' performances to samples of their peers.

Ways That Standardized Test Results Are Reported

- **Raw scores** are sometimes reported and indicate how many questions students answered correctly on a test. By themselves, they do not provide much useful information. They do not indicate how students performed in comparison to other students or to grade-level expectations.
- **Grade-level equivalents** are also sometimes reported. A grade-level equivalent score of 3.4 indicates that a student performed as well as an average third grader in the fourth month of school. It can indicate whether a student is performing above or below grade-level expectations, but it does not indicate that the student should be moved to a different grade level.

- **Standard scores** are used to compare students' performances on tests to standardized samples of their peers. Standard deviation refers to the amount that a set of scores differs from the mean score on a test.
- **Percentile ranks** are used on criterion-referenced tests to indicate what percentage of test takers scored lower than the student whose score is being reported.
- **Cutoff scores** refer to predetermined scores students must obtain in order to be considered proficient in certain areas. Scores below the cutoff level indicate improvement is needed and may result in interventions or instructional changes.

Formal and Informal Assessments

Assessments are any method a teacher uses to gather information about student comprehension of curriculum, including improvised questions for the class and highly-structured tests. **Formal assessments** are assessments that have **clearly defined standards and methodology** and which are applied consistently to all students. Formal tests should be objective and scrutinized for validity and reliability since they tend to carry higher weight for the student. Summative assessments, such as end-of-unit tests, lend themselves to being formal tests because it is necessary that a teacher test the comprehension of all students in a consistent and thorough way.

Although formal assessments can provide useful data about student performance and progress, they can be costly and time-consuming to implement. Administering formal assessments often interrupts classroom instruction and may cause testing anxiety.

Informal assessments are assessments that do not adhere to formal objectives, and they do not have to be administered consistently to all students. As a result, they do not have to be scored or recorded as a grade and generally act as a **subjective measure** of class comprehension. Informal assessments can be as simple as asking the students to raise their hands if they are ready to proceed to the next step or asking a particular question of an individual student.

Informal assessments do not provide objective data for analysis, but they can be implemented quickly and inexpensively. Informal assessments can also be incorporated into regular classroom instruction and activities, making them more authentic and less stressful for students.

Using Various Assessments

The goal of **assessment** in education is to gather data that, when evaluated, can be used to further student learning and achievement. **Standardized tests** are helpful for placement purposes and to reflect student progress toward goals set by a school district or state. If a textbook is chosen to align with district learning standards, the textbook assessments can provide teachers with convenient, small-scale, regular checks of student knowledge against the target standard.

In order be effective, teachers must know where their students are in the learning process. Teachers use a multitude of **formal and informal assessment methods** to do this. Posing differentiated discussion questions is an example of an informal assessment method that allows teachers to gauge individual student progress rather than their standing in relation to a universal benchmark.

Effective teachers employ a variety of assessments, as different formats assess different skills, promote different learning experiences, and appeal to different learners. A portfolio is an example of an assessment that gauges student progress in multiple skills and through multiple media. Teachers can use authentic or performance-based assessments to stimulate student interest and provide visible connections between language-learning and the real world.

Assessment Reliability

Assessment reliability refers to how well an assessment is constructed and is made up of a variety of measures. An assessment is generally considered **reliable** if it yields similar results across multiple administrations of the assessment. A test should perform similarly with different test administrators, graders, test-takers, and over multiple iterations. Factors that affect reliability include the day-to-day wellbeing of the student (students can sometimes underperform), the physical environment of the test, the way it is administered, and the subjectivity of the scorer (with written-response assessments).

Perhaps the most important threat to assessment reliability is the nature of the **exam questions** themselves. An assessment question is designed to test knowledge of a certain construct. A question is reliable in this sense if students who understand the content answer the question correctly. Statisticians look for patterns in student marks, both within the single test and over multiple tests, as a way of measuring reliability. Teachers should watch out for circumstances in which a student or students answer correctly a series of questions about a given concept (demonstrating their understanding) but then answer a related question incorrectly. The latter question may be an unreliable indicator of concept knowledge.

Measures of Assessment Reliability

- **Test-retest reliability** refers to an assessment's consistency of results with the same test-taker over multiple retests. If one student shows inconsistent results over time, the test is not considered to have test-retest reliability.
- **Intertester reliability** refers to an assessment's consistency of results between multiple test-takers at the same level. Students at similar levels of proficiency should show similar results.
- **Inter-rater reliability** refers to an assessment's consistency of results between different administrators of the test. This plays an especially critical role in tests with interactive or subjective responses, such as Likert-scales, cloze tests, and short answer tests. Different raters of the same test need to have a consistent means of evaluating the test-takers' performance. Clear rubrics can help keep two or more raters consistent in scoring.
- **Intra-rater reliability** refers to an assessment's consistency of results with one rater over time. One test rater should be able to score different students objectively to rate subjective test formats fairly.
- **Parallel-forms reliability** refers to an assessment's consistency between multiple different forms. For instance, end-of-course assessments may have many distinctive test forms, with different questions or question orders. If the different forms of a test do not provide the same results, the test is said to be lacking in parallel-forms reliability.
- **Internal consistency reliability** refers to the consistency of results of similar questions on a particular assessment. If there are two or more questions targeted at the same standard and at the same level, they should show the same results across each question.

Assessment Validity

Assessment validity is a measure of the relevancy that an assessment has to the skill or ability being evaluated and the degree to which students' performance is representative of their mastery of the topic of assessment. In other words, a teacher should ask how well an assessment's results correlate to what it is looking to assess. Assessments should be evaluated for validity on both the **individual question** level and as a **test overall**. This can be especially helpful in refining tests for future classes. The overall validity of an assessment is determined by several types of validity measures.

An assessment is considered **valid** if it measures what it is intended to measure. One common error that can reduce the validity of a test (or a question on a test) occurs if the instructions are written at a reading level the students can't understand. In this case, it is not valid to take the student's failed answer as a true indication of his or her knowledge of the subject. Factors internal to the student might also affect exam validity: anxiety and a lack of self-esteem often lower assessments results, reducing their validity as a measure of student knowledge.

An assessment has content validity if it includes all the **relevant aspects** of the subject being tested—if it is comprehensive, in other words. An assessment has **predictive validity** if a score on the test is an accurate predictor of future success in the same domain. For example, SAT exams purport to have validity in predicting student success in a college. An assessment has construct validity if it accurately measures student knowledge of the subject being tested.

Measures of Assessment Validity

- **Face validity** refers to the initial impression of whether an assessment seems to be fit for the task. As this method is subjective to interpretation and unquantifiable, it should not be used singularly as a measurement of validity.
- **Construct validity** asks if an assessment actually assesses what it is intended to assess. Some topics are more straightforward, such as assessing if a student can perform two-digit multiplication. This can be directly tested, which gives the assessment a strong content validity. Other measures, such as a person's overall happiness, must be measured indirectly. If an assessment asserted that a person is generally happy if he or she smiles frequently, it would be fair to question the construct validity of that assessment because smiling is unlikely to be a consistent measure of all peoples' general happiness.
- **Content validity** indicates whether the assessment is comprehensive of all aspects of the content being assessed. If a test leaves out an important topic, then the teacher will not have a full picture as a result of the assessment.
- **Criterion validity** refers to whether the results of an assessment can be used to **predict** a related value, known as **criterion**. An example of this is the hypothesis that IQ tests would predict a person's success later in life, but many critics believe that IQ tests are not valid predictors of success because intelligence is not the only predictor of success in life. IQ tests have shown validity toward predicting academic success, however. The measure of an assessment's criterion validity depends on how closely related the criterion is.
- **Discriminant validity** refers to how well an assessment tests only that which it is intended to test and successfully discriminates one piece of information from another. For instance, a student who is exceptional in mathematics should not be able to put that information into use on a science test and gain an unfair advantage. If the student is able to score well due to his or her mathematics knowledge, the science test did not adequately discriminate science knowledge from mathematics knowledge.
- **Convergent validity** is related to discriminant validity, but takes into account that two measures may be distinct but correlated. For instance, a personality test should distinguish self-esteem from extraversion so that they can be measured independently, but if an assessment has convergent validity, it should show a correlation between related measures.

Practicality

An assessment is **practical** if it uses an appropriate amount of human and budgetary resources. A practical exam doesn't take very long to design or score, nor does it take students very long to complete in relation to other learning objectives and priorities. Teachers often need to balance a desire to construct comprehensive or content-valid tests with a need for practicality: lengthy exams consume large amounts of instruction time and may return unreliable results if students become tired and lose focus.

Assessment Bias

An assessment is considered biased if it disadvantages a certain group of students, such as students of a certain gender, race, cultural background, or socioeconomic class. A **content bias** exists when the subject matter of a question or assessment is familiar to one group and not another. For example, a reading comprehension passage that discusses an event in American history would be biased against students new to the country. An **attitudinal bias** exists when a teacher has a pre-conceived idea about the likely success of an assessment of a particular individual or group. A **method bias** arises when the format of an assessment is unfamiliar to a given group of students. **Language bias** occurs when an assessment utilizes idioms, collocations, or cultural references unfamiliar to a group of students. Finally, **translation bias** may arise when educators attempt to translate content-area assessments into a student's native language—rough or hurried translations often result in a loss of nuance important for accurate assessment.

Authentic Assessments

An authentic assessment is an assessment designed to closely resemble something that a student does, or will do, in the real world. For example, students will never encounter a multiple-choice test requiring them to choose the right tense of a verb, but they will encounter contexts in which they have to write a narration of an event that has antecedents and consequents spread out in time—like narrating their version of what caused a traffic accident. The latter is an example of a potential **authentic assessment**.

Well-designed authentic assessments require a student to exercise **advanced cognitive skills** (e.g., solving problems, integrating information, performing deductions), integrate **background knowledge**, and confront **ambiguity**. Research has demonstrated that mere language proficiency is not predictive of future language success—learning how to utilize knowledge in a complex context is an essential additional skill.

The terms "authentic" and "performance-based" are often used interchangeably when describing assessments; however, a performance-based assessment doesn't necessarily have to be grounded in a possible authentic experience.

Performance-Based Assessments

A performance-based assessment is one in which students demonstrate their learning by performing a **task** rather than by answering questions in a traditional test format. Proponents of **performance-based assessments** argue that they lead students to use **high-level cognitive skills** since they focus on how to put their knowledge to use and plan a sequence of stages in an activity or presentation. They also allow students more opportunities to individualize their presentations or responses based on preferred learning styles. Research suggests that students welcome the chance to put their knowledge to use in real-world scenarios.

Advocates of performance-based assessments suggest that they avoid many of the problems of language or cultural bias present in traditional assessments, allowing more accurate assessment of how well students learned the underlying concepts. In discussions regarding English as a second language, they argue that performance assessments come closer to replicating what should be the true goal of language learning—the effective use of language in real contexts—than do more traditional exams. Critics point out that performance assessments are difficult and time-consuming for teachers to construct and for students to perform. Finally, performative assessments are difficult to grade in the absence of a well-constructed and detailed rubric.

Technology-Based Assessments

Technology-based assessments provide teachers with multiple resources for evaluating student progress to guide instruction. They are applicable in most formal and informal instructional settings and can be utilized as formative and summative assessments. Technology-based assessments simplify and enhance the efficiency of determining comprehension and instructional effectiveness, as they quickly present the teacher with information regarding student progress. This data enables the teacher to make necessary adjustments to facilitate student learning and growth. Implementing this assessment format simplifies the process of aligning them to school and district academic standards. This establishes objectivity and uniformity for comparing results and progress among students. It also helps ensure that all students are held to the same academic expectations. While technology-based assessments are beneficial, there are some shortcomings to consider. This format may not be entirely effective for all learning styles in demonstrating understanding, as individualization in technology-based assessment can be limited. These assessments may not illustrate individual students' growth over time but rather their mastery of an academic standard, thus hindering the ability to evaluate overall achievement. As technology-based evaluation limits hands-on opportunities, the real-world application and relevancy of the assessment may be unapparent to students.

Advantages and Disadvantages of Technology-Based Assessments

Technology-based assessments can have many advantages. They can be given to large numbers of students at once, limited only by the amounts of technological equipment schools possess. Many types of technology-based assessments are instantly scored, and feedback is provided quickly. Students are sometimes able to view their results and feedback at the conclusion of their testing sessions. Data can be quickly compiled and reported in easy-to-understand formats. Technology-based assessments can also often track student progress over time.

Technology-based assessments can have some disadvantages as well. Glitches and system errors can interfere with the assessment process or score reporting. Students must also have the necessary prerequisite technological skills to take the assessments, or the results may not measure the content they are designed to measure. For example, if students take timed, computer-based writing tests, they should have proficient typing skills. Otherwise, they may perform poorly on the tests despite strong writing abilities. Other prerequisite skills include knowing how to use a keyboard and mouse and understanding how to locate necessary information on the screen.

Portfolio Assessments

A **portfolio** is a collection of student work in multiple forms and media gathered over time. Teachers may assess the portfolio both for evidence of progress over time or in its end state as a demonstration of the achievement of certain proficiency levels.

One advantage of **portfolio assessments** is their breadth. Unlike traditional assessments, which focus on one or two language skills, portfolios may contain work in multiple forms, such as writing samples, pictures, and graphs designed for content courses, video and audio clips, student reflections, teacher observations, and student exams. A second advantage is that they allow a student to develop work in authentic contexts, including in other classrooms and at home.

In order for portfolios to function as an objective assessment tool, teachers should negotiate with students in advance of what genres of work will be included and outline a grading rubric that makes clear what will be assessed, such as linguistic proficiency, use of English in academic contexts, and demonstrated use of target cognitive skills.

Curriculum-Based Assessments

Curriculum-based assessments, also known as **curriculum-based measurements (CBM)**, are short, frequent assessments designed to measure student progress toward meeting curriculum **benchmarks**.

Teachers implement CBMs by designing **probes**, or short assessments that target specific skills. For example, a teacher might design a spelling probe, administered weekly, that requires students to spell 10 unfamiliar but level-appropriate words. The data from these assessments can be tracked over time to measure student progress toward defined grade-level goals.

CBM has several clear advantages. If structured well, the probes have high reliability and validity. Furthermore, they provide clear and objective evidence of student progress—a welcome outcome for students and parents who often grapple with less-clear and subjective evidence. Used correctly, CBMs also motivate students and provide them with evidence of their own progress; however, while CBMs are helpful in identifying areas of student weaknesses, they do not identify the causes of those weaknesses or provide teachers with strategies for improving instruction.

Textbook Assessments

Textbook assessments are the assessments provided at the end of a chapter or unit in an approved textbook. **Textbook assessments** present several advantages for a teacher: they are already made; they are likely to be accurate representations of the chapter or unit materials; and, if the textbook has been prescribed or recommended by the state, it is likely to correspond closely to Common Core or other tested standards.

Textbook assessments can be limiting for students who lag in the comprehension of academic English or whose preferred learning style is not verbal. While textbooks may come with DVDs or recommended audio links, ESOL teachers will likely need to supplement these assessment materials with some of their own findings. Finally, textbook assessments are unlikely to represent the range of assessment types used in the modern classroom, such as a portfolio or performance-based assessments.

Peer Assessment

A peer assessment is when students grade one another's work based on a teacher-provided framework. **Peer assessments** are promoted as a means of saving teacher time and building student metacognitive skills. They are typically used as **formative** rather than summative assessments, given concerns about the reliability of student scoring and the tensions that can result if student scores contribute to overall grades. Peer assessments are used most often to grade essay-type written work or presentations. Proponents point out that peer assessments require students to apply metacognition, build cooperative work and interpersonal skills, and broaden the sense that the student is accountable to peers and not just the teacher. Even advocates of the practice agree that students need detailed rubrics in order to succeed. Critics often argue that low-performing students have little to offer high-performing students in terms of valuable feedback—and this disparity may be more pronounced in ESOL classrooms or special education environments than in mainstream ones. One way to overcome this weakness is for the teacher to lead the evaluation exercise, guiding the students through a point-by-point framework of evaluation.

Selecting Appropriately-Leveled Texts

Selecting Appropriate Texts to Support Diverse Learners

When selecting appropriate texts to support diverse learners, teachers should take several factors into consideration. First, they should consider students' reading levels and stages of reading development to determine how much text support is needed. For emergent and early readers, teachers should consider how much picture support is present, how many words are printed on each page, and the predictability of the text. They should also consider how easily students will be able to decode the words based on spelling patterns, text clues, and use of high-frequency words.

For transitional and fluent readers, teachers should consider text complexity. This includes the vocabulary, language use, and sentence structure used in the texts. They should also consider how the texts relate to students' prior knowledge and interests and whether the content supports learning objectives. If topics are unfamiliar to students, some scaffolding or pre-teaching may be needed.

Determining If Texts Are at Students' Independent Reading Levels

When determining reading levels, teachers typically consider both accuracy rate and comprehension. Different reading programs vary slightly in their cutoff levels, but texts are generally considered to be at the independent level if they are read with 95% to 100% accuracy. Additionally, responding correctly to 90% to 100% of comprehension questions may indicate that texts are at students' independent levels. Texts at the independent reading level can be read by students with no assistance.

Texts that students can read independently are good candidates for free choice reading time. They also can be used when practicing comprehension strategies, such as inferring and drawing conclusions. Because students do not struggle to decode words in these texts, they have the mental energy available to do more complex analysis. Additionally, students can repeatedly read favorite books at their independent reading levels for fluency practice. They can also read these books to partners or family members.

Determining If Texts Are at Students' Instructional Reading Levels

Different reading programs vary slightly in their cutoff levels, but texts are generally considered to be at the instructional level if they are read with 90% to 94% accuracy. Additionally, responding correctly to 70% to 89% of comprehension questions may indicate that texts are at students' instructional levels. These books present some challenges for readers, but they can still be read without frustration.

Texts at the instructional level are appropriate for use in guided reading groups. Students are able to decode most words, yet a few miscues may occur that can be used as teaching points. Teachers may analyze student errors and use this information to plan mini-lessons. Additionally, students are able to apply comprehension strategies to analyze and discuss these texts. Texts at the instructional level allow students to have successful and positive experiences with reading while learning from their challenges.

Determining If Texts Are at Students' Frustration Levels

Different reading programs vary slightly in their cutoff levels, but texts are generally considered to be at the frustration level if they are read with less than 90% accuracy. Additionally, responding correctly to less than 70% of comprehension questions may indicate that texts are at students' frustration levels. These books are considered difficult for students to read.

Texts at the frustration level are not good candidates for students to read independently during guided reading groups, when teachers need to observe students' reading and help them apply strategies. Students may become frustrated with too many unknown words or lose the meanings of the texts.

However, these texts can be used in other beneficial ways. Students may enjoy exploring difficult texts on topics of interest, which may help them develop a love of reading. Because these texts can provide valuable information that students cannot access independently, teachers can also read these texts aloud or provide digital versions with audio. Teachers can model using reading strategies with these difficult texts during shared reading experiences. Additionally, students can be encouraged to read these texts with family members.

Systems Used to Level Books

There are several different systems that are used to level books. **Lexile** measures consider both text complexity and word frequency to level books. Specialized assessments are used to determine students' Lexile levels, which can then be used to select appropriate books.

Irene Fountas and Gay Su Pinnell developed another system for leveling books based on their recommendations for guided reading groups. Their system, sometimes known as **guided reading levels**, considers several factors to assign book levels. These factors include word frequency, sentence complexity, vocabulary, and text features. Running records can help identify guided reading levels.

The **Developmental Reading Assessment (DRA)**, also provides a system for leveling books. Students can take the DRA to determine their instructional reading levels. Results can then be used to select books using the DRA system.

Because there are many different leveling systems, conversion charts are available online to help teachers and parents identify book levels using their preferred systems.

Assessment Methodology for Language Skills

Purposes of Literacy Assessment

Literacy assessments can serve many purposes. Assessments can be used to monitor the progress of students toward achieving district and state benchmarks as well as individualized goals. They can identify specific skills that students have mastered as well as those that need additional practice. They can also identify if students are making adequate yearly progress.

Additionally, assessments can be used to guide teacher instruction. By analyzing assessment results, teachers can determine which topics they should focus on for whole-class, small-group, and individualized instruction. This helps ensure that too much instructional time is not spent on topics students have already mastered while ignoring topics that need additional practice.

Assessments can also be used to evaluate the effectiveness of reading programs. By analyzing students' assessment data over time, districts can look for trends in student achievement and progress toward closing achievement gaps.

Advantages and Disadvantages of Group and Individual Literacy Assessments

Group literacy assessments are administered to groups of students at one time. Teachers explain the directions and then instruct all students to begin working, while they observe and answer questions. Assessments are scored after students finish and submit them. Examples of group literacy assessments include state-mandated standardized reading and writing tests. Using the group approach to literacy assessments is more efficient than individualized assessment, freeing up more time for classroom instruction. It also assists teachers with classroom management because all students are being assessed at once.

Individualized assessments are given to one student at a time. Teachers may listen to students read, observe strategy usage, or ask students to retell stories they have read. Dynamic Indicators of Basic Early Literacy Skills (DIBELS) and Developmental Reading Assessment (DRA) are examples of individual assessments. This approach allows teachers to closely observe the strategies each student uses. However, it is more time intensive, and the remaining students in the class must be engaged in other activities.

Using Progress Monitoring to Assess Students and Guide Instruction

Progress monitoring is used to track students' progress toward achieving certain performance goals over time. Teachers first identify students who may benefit from progress monitoring. This usually occurs as a result of assessment data. Students who score below expectations on certain components of criterion-referenced tests may be progressively monitored in those areas.

Teachers then set performance goals that can be measured and tracked over time. For example, if students are currently decoding five CVC words correctly in one minute, the goal may be for them to decode 15 words per minute. Interventions are put in place to help students with these skills. Teachers then repeat testing in these targeted areas on a regular basis, such as weekly or biweekly. Results are recorded, and teachers look for progress over time. Once students have mastered the initial goals, new goals are set, or progress monitoring is discontinued, depending on students' needs.

Progress monitoring can help teachers identify whether or not current interventions are successful or whether changes are needed. It can also help teachers identify when students have mastered certain skills.

Types of Formal Assessments Used to Assess Oral Language and Reading Skills

There are several types of formal assessments designed to assess readers. Some assessments assess knowledge of concepts of print. These are typically performance assessments. Students are asked to locate titles and authors' names, identify letters and words, track the direction of print, and more. Teachers observe students and mark their responses on recording sheets containing scoring criteria. Other formal assessments ask students to identify letter names, apply phonological and phonemic awareness skills, and decode words. Portions of the DIBELS assessment are examples of this type. Data gained from these assessments can be used to group students, plan differentiated instruction, and develop interventions.

Other formal assessments evaluate students' decoding abilities and reading fluency. Students may be asked to read short texts while being timed. They may also be asked to retell stories or answer comprehension questions. Both DIBELS and DRA are two examples of this type of assessment. State standardized tests often require students to read passages and answer comprehension questions. In addition to helping teachers group students and differentiate instruction, these assessments can also help teachers select appropriately leveled texts. There are also formal assessments that specifically assess students' vocabulary knowledge.

Formally Assessing Written Language

Students' writing is often formally assessed using teacher-created, district-mandated, and state-mandated assessments. These assessments typically provide students with specific writing prompts indicating the topics and text structures they are expected to use. Sometimes prompts are based on reading passages that are also contained in the assessments. For example, students may be asked to read two related texts and write responses that explain the common theme they share.

Students' written responses on formal assessments are usually scored using either analytic or holistic rubrics. These rubrics should contain clear criteria that reflect the performance expectations for students. Common criteria include development, organization, language use, conventions, and following the writing process. By analyzing students' performances on different rubric criteria, teachers can plan individualized instruction and develop interventions for struggling students. For example, if students are struggling with language use, teachers can help students analyze mentor texts that contain strong examples.

Informally Assessing Literacy Development

One type of informal assessment is **miscue analysis**, which occurs when teachers listen to students as they read and analyze their miscues. By looking for patterns in the miscues, teachers can determine which strategies students are using and which are lacking. This information can be used to guide instruction.

- **Informal reading inventories** require students to read leveled texts while teachers note errors and fluency. Students then respond to comprehension questions about the texts. Information gained from informal reading inventories can be used to select leveled texts, group students, and plan appropriate instruction.
- **Portfolios** are another type of informal assessment. Portfolios consist of collections of student work, which can be used to show progress over time.
- **Performance assessments** can also be used to assess students' literacy development while allowing students to complete authentic tasks. For example, students may research nutritional guidelines and read food labels to create healthy weekly meal plans.
- **Informal assessment** can also occur when teachers observe students engaged in literacy activities, ask them to explain their thinking, and note performance on assignments and homework. These methods can provide valuable information about students' knowledge and skills, which can be used to guide instruction.

Rubrics

Rubrics are evaluation tools used to assign scores to students' work. They explain the criteria used to assign scores for different levels of mastery. Rubrics can be given to students when projects are assigned to ensure they understand expectations. They can make evaluation more consistent because all students are evaluated using the same criteria. Rubrics can also be easily adapted to reflect different types of activities and assignments.

There are many ways rubrics can be used to evaluate literacy development. They can be used to assess students' reading fluency, with categories relating to speed, accuracy, and prosody. They can also be used to evaluate projects relating to analysis and comprehension.

Additionally, rubrics can be used to assess students' writing. Categories relating to development, use of language, conventions, and other topics can be included. The rubrics can be adapted to reflect the genres or text structures used.

Analytic vs. Holistic Rubrics

Analytic rubrics assign separate scores for each criterion being evaluated. For example, if a writing rubric has criteria for development, use of language, and conventions, each of these areas receives its own score. These scores are then added together to determine the overall score for the assignment. Analytic rubrics provide targeted feedback and help students understand their strengths and weaknesses. However, they can be time-consuming to create and adapt.

Holistic rubrics provide one overall score for the assignment rather than evaluating each criterion separately. They list varying levels of performance, and each level describes the characteristics of assignments earning that score. For example, a writing assignment might be assigned a score ranging from 1 to 4. Assignments earning a score of 4 would be well developed, have effective use of language, and have few or no errors with conventions. Holistic rubrics can be faster for teachers to create and adapt for different assignments. However, the feedback is less targeted than it is when using analytic rubrics, which evaluate each criterion separately.

RUNNING RECORDS

Running records are tools used to record students' behaviors and use of strategies during reading. To administer running records, teachers provide students with books in their developmental reading levels and ask them to read the books aloud. While students are reading, teachers record the words read correctly with check marks. They also note errors by recording the actual words in the texts and the words students substituted for them. Word repetitions, omissions, and self-corrections are also noted using special symbols.

While running records used to be considered best practice, new research has since denounced this tool. Running records are not efficient, and they do not act as a reliable indication of fundamental literacy skills. Educators are encouraged to use universal screenings to gather data to compose homogeneous skill-based groups. Another useful tool is a **decodable running record**. This defers from a normal running record because it assesses phonic and phonemic skills using a decodable text; whereas, a running record based off level generally assess reading behaviors and the use of cueing systems.

Behavior	Notation	Example
Correct response	Mark every word read correctly with a check mark.	✓ ✓ ✓ ✓ ✓ Can you see my eyes?
Substitution	Write the spoken word above the word in the text.	✓ ✓ the ✓ ✓ Can you see my eyes?
Omission	Place a dash above the word left out.	✓ ✓ ✓ – ✓ Can you see my eyes?
Insertion	Insert the added word and place a dash below it (or use a caret).	✓ ✓ ✓ ✓ big ✓ Can you see my eyes?
Attempt	Write each attempt above the word in the text.	✓ ✓ ✓ ✓ e-ey Can you see my eyes?
Repetition	Write R after the repeated word/phrase and draw an arrow back to the beginning of the repetition.	✓ ✓ ✓ ✓R ✓ Can you see my eyes?
Appeal* (asks for help)	Write A above the appealed word.	✓ ✓ ✓ A ✓ Can you see my eyes?
Told word	Write T beside the word supplied for the reader.	✓ ✓ ✓ T ✓ Can you see myTeyes?
Self-correction	Write SC after the corrected word.	✓ ✓ ✓ the/sc ✓ Can you see my eyes?

Role of Performance-Based Assessments in Literacy Assessment

Performance-based assessments require students to solve real-world problems and accomplish authentic tasks by applying literacy skills and strategies. An example of a performance-based assessment is writing a letter to a government official in support of a new law, citing evidence-based reasons for the position. Depending on the types of tasks involved, performance-based assessments may require students to synthesize information from multiple sources, defend positions with text evidence, write texts following the writing process, and create materials to convey information to others.

Performance-based assessments are open ended and do not contain right or wrong answers. Typically, there are multiple ways that students can approach the tasks. The assessments are evaluated using rubrics, with clear criteria determined and shared with students in advance.

An advantage of performance-based assessments is that they allow students opportunities to solve real-world problems, thereby increasing learner engagement. They also require higher-level thinking skills, such as analysis, application, synthesis, and creation. Additionally, they often allow students some choices in how they present their learning. A disadvantage is that performance-based assessments may be time-consuming to create and implement. Grading can also be subjective.

Role of Portfolios in Literacy Assessment

Portfolios are collections of students' projects and work gathered over time. They can serve many purposes in assessing literacy development. They can be used to track students' progress over time and check for mastery of certain skills, which is useful for planning differentiated instruction. Portfolios can also be passed along to students' future teachers, helping them determine students' instructional levels. Additionally, portfolios can be used to help students self-evaluate their own progress and set future goals.

If using portfolios, teachers must make several decisions. They must determine how the portfolios will be used, which will influence the criteria used to select portfolio entries. They also need to determine how entries will be selected. Will teachers or students select the entries, or will both play roles in the process? Teachers also need to decide if the portfolios will be graded. Checklists and rubrics are possible tools that can be used to grade portfolios.

Some advantages of portfolios include the ability to see concrete evidence of student progress over time and the possibility of having students actively involved in assessing their own progress. However, evaluating portfolios is subjective, and teachers may be unsure of how to use them to guide instruction.

Determining When to Respond to Student Miscues in Reading

Even proficient readers make errors at times. Fluent readers often read texts rapidly and may occasionally omit or substitute words without changing the meanings of the texts. For example, they may substitute "her house" for "the house" in a text. These types of errors do not impact meaning and, if occasional, can be ignored. Stopping to correct these types of minor errors can interrupt fluency and comprehension.

Readers in the emergent and early stages of development may make frequent errors and become frustrated if corrected each time. Overcorrection may interfere with confidence and reading enjoyment. Teachers should strategically choose which types of errors to respond to during each reading session. One approach is to focus on a single type of error each time, such as errors where syntax cues are ignored. Another approach is to intervene only when errors affect the meaning of the text. Minor errors can be ignored to build fluency and confidence.

Screening for Reading and Language Delays

Screening vs. Diagnostic Assessments

Screening assessments are used to identify students who may be at risk for future academic difficulties. Information gained from these assessments can be used to determine which students would likely benefit from specialized interventions to help prevent academic difficulties in the future.

Adequate literacy screening is important in young children. Studies have shown that literacy difficulties are harder to remedy through intervention after third grade. By identifying these students early and providing appropriate interventions, these difficulties can be prevented or lessened. For example, phonemic awareness screenings are frequently given to early childhood students because phonemic awareness is a key indicator of future reading success.

Review Video: Developmental Screening Strategies
Visit mometrix.com/academy and enter code: 100353

Diagnostic assessments are used to identify students' existing knowledge and skills before beginning instruction. For example, students may complete diagnostic assessments focused on using comprehension strategies to understand nonfiction texts. Data from diagnostic assessments can be used to help teachers plan differentiated instruction to meet students' individual needs.

Identifying Students Who Have Not Met Standards

It is important to identify concerns with literacy development early to prevent future academic difficulties. Reading, writing, listening, and speaking affect performance across all content areas. Therefore, students who struggle with literacy may struggle in all academic areas.

- **Early screening** is one way to identify students who are not meeting standards and may have literacy difficulties. Depending on the ages of the students, screening can be given on a range of topics, including alphabetic principle, phonological and phonemic awareness, decoding strategies, fluency, and comprehension.
- The results of **criterion** and **norm-referenced formal assessments** can also be used to identify students who have not met standards. Teachers can look for specific skills and standard areas that students struggled with on these formal assessments. They can also look for indications that students are not meeting their adequate yearly progress goals.
- Additionally, **informal assessments** can be used to identify students who are not meeting standards. Classroom observations, running records, responses during literature circles, and other informal assessments are helpful tools for teachers to use.

All of these data points can be considered when determining which students may benefit from targeted interventions.

Determining Whether Students Have Reading or Language Delays

Generally, teachers should collect multiple data points over time before requesting that students be evaluated for potential delays or disabilities. Students may perform below expectations on assessments for a variety of reasons, including illness and fatigue. Therefore, no one assessment score should be used as the basis for an evaluation. However, if students perform similarly on multiple assessments over time, further investigation may be warranted. Assessment data can also be combined with classroom observations for supplementary information. Additionally, interventions can be attempted first to determine if achievement gaps can be closed through targeted instruction.

Parents sometimes request that their children be evaluated. Parents are often the first to notice potential issues because they observe their children's progress from year to year and witness the challenges firsthand. Parents can submit their requests for evaluations in writing to classroom teachers, reading specialists, administrators, or other school officials for consideration.

Signs of Dyslexia

Dyslexia is a common disorder that affects reading. Students with **dyslexia** often have difficulties with phonological awareness, accurate word recognition, decoding, and reading fluency. As a result, they may also have difficulties comprehending what they have read. Spelling may also be affected. Teachers may notice that students struggle to decode words and read fluently, and students may become anxious or frustrated when asked to read. Dyslexia does not affect intelligence and is marked by a gap between students' abilities and achievements.

Although there is no cure for dyslexia, targeted interventions are often successful. A multisensory approach to reading instruction is often helpful, along with systematic and explicit instruction in reading skills and sight word recognition. The Orton-Gillingham method is one commonly used approach. Teachers should also maintain supportive classroom environments and not rush students or force them to read aloud. Students with dyslexia may also benefit from some accommodations, such as extra time on tests, increased wait time when responding to questions, and access to audio versions of texts.

Review Video: Understanding Learning Disability Needs of Students
Visit mometrix.com/academy and enter code: 662775

Review Video: Disorders that Impair Reading Comprehension
Visit mometrix.com/academy and enter code: 306758

Signs of Dysgraphia

Dysgraphia is a disorder that affects written expression. Students with dysgraphia may have difficulties holding pencils correctly, forming letters, writing on lines, putting thoughts into written words, and organizing writing in meaningful ways. Handwriting and spelling are also commonly difficult for students. Students with dysgraphia may become frustrated or anxious if asked to write, and they may try to avoid writing when possible.

There are many ways teachers can assist students with dysgraphia. To assist with spelling, explicit instruction on sound-symbol relationships and spelling patterns may be helpful. Graphic organizers can be provided to assist students with written organization. Additionally, students may qualify for occupational therapy to assist with developing coordination and motor skills. Students with dysgraphia may also benefit from some accommodations, such as being allowed to type responses or answer questions orally. They may benefit from receiving extra time to complete assignments and tests.

Signs of Dyspraxia

Dyspraxia is a disorder that makes it difficult for the body to coordinate movement. Students with dyspraxia may have difficulties with balance and coordination, and they may have trouble performing tasks that require motor skills. Students with dyspraxia may also be sensitive to noise or touch in addition to spatial or perceptual difficulties, all of which might affect reading and writing. Some types of dyspraxia may also affect language, especially enunciation.

In the classroom, teachers can break large, multistep tasks into smaller chunks. If activities require movement, teachers can begin with simple movements first, and gradually increase the difficulty.

Teachers can also provide extra processing time when giving directions and extra wait time when asking questions. Some students with dyspraxia may qualify for occupational therapy services. Students with dyspraxia may benefit from certain accommodations, such as seating that is free from noise and distractions.

Characteristics of Reading Comprehension Deficiencies

Students with **reading comprehension deficiencies** have difficulty understanding and responding to what they have read. They may have difficulty summarizing texts, making inferences, differentiating between main ideas and supporting details, and more. They often have issues with reading fluency as well, especially with phrasing and prosody. Students with comprehension deficiencies can often decode words efficiently, yet they struggle with comprehending the texts' meanings. However, some students may struggle with both decoding and comprehension.

To assist students with comprehension deficiencies, teachers can provide advance organizers that offer overviews of the text structures and story events. They can also preview texts or conduct picture walks to familiarize students with the topics. Before reading, they can instruct students to pay attention to specific key information within the texts. Additionally, teachers can model their use of comprehension strategies during think-alouds and shared reading experiences.

Characteristics of Reading Retention Deficiencies

Students with **reading retention deficiencies** have difficulties remembering what they have read. This may include difficulties summarizing texts, ordering story events, and making text connections after reading. Retention deficiencies may occur due to difficulties transferring information to short- or long-term memory or with difficulties retrieving information that has been previously stored in long-term memory.

To assist students with retention difficulties, teachers can provide students with graphic organizers that they can complete while reading. Story maps and sequencing charts are examples of graphic organizers that may be helpful. Teachers can also provide notes and text summaries to assist students with remembering important concepts and details. Additionally, students can be taught to use specific strategies to activate memory, such as visualizing as they read. They can also be taught to annotate texts by highlighting key phrases and taking notes, making it easier to locate important information in the future.

Motivating Students to Read

Creating School Environments That Promote a Love of Reading

Helping students develop a lifelong love of reading is an important goal of literacy instruction. Teachers can model their own love of reading by talking about their favorite books and authors and modeling their own use of reading strategies. They can share stories of how reading has positively affected their own lives and opened up new opportunities.

- Teachers can also help develop **communities of readers** within their classrooms, making reading a social experience. Fun and interactive read-alouds and shared reading experiences can help create communities of readers, along with organizing literature circles and reader's theater activities. Favorite books can be reread multiple times, with students participating in the reading.
- Teachers can give students frequent opportunities to read **books of choice**. They can create classroom libraries containing multiple types of texts that students can access easily.

Comfortable reading spaces, such as reading chairs and pillows, are also beneficial. Students should also have opportunities to visit their school libraries regularly.
- Additionally, teachers can guide students in completing **author studies**. Students may form connections to favorite authors and seek additional books they have written.

Review Video: Literacy-Rich Content-Area Classrooms
Visit mometrix.com/academy and enter code: 571455

Promoting Successful Independent Reading Experiences at School

Independent reading is beneficial for students' reading development and is sometimes necessary when teachers are working with other students. Therefore, some strategies can be used to make independent reading experiences successful.

It is important to teach students to select appropriate texts that will not lead to boredom or frustration. Some teachers instruct students to apply the five-finger rule. In this approach, students randomly select a single page of text to read. If they struggle to decode five or more words, the book is too difficult. Other teachers inform students of their reading levels and keep labeled boxes of leveled texts available. Students can also be encouraged to maintain personal book boxes that contain several appropriate books so that they are ready for independent reading time.

To remind students of decoding and comprehension strategies they can use during independent reading time, teachers can display posters in their classrooms. Students can also be given small, personalized copies of these strategies to use.

Additionally, students can be encouraged to analyze and discuss what they have read to build interest and engagement. They can maintain reader-response logs or join literature circles with others who have read the same texts.

Motivating Students to Read

One technique to motivate students to read is to make reading an enjoyable part of the daily routine. This includes designating daily time for reading, providing a comfortable, relaxed atmosphere, helping students select texts of interest, and showing genuine interest in discussing the texts together. This technique is easy to implement, and students who look forward to this reading time as children may continue reading for enjoyment in adulthood. A disadvantage is that some students may not respond to this approach.

Another technique is to use rewards and incentives for reading. Some programs reward students after they have read a certain number of books or for a certain number of minutes. Sometimes students are tested on the books they have read to assess comprehension. Read-athons are one example of this approach. Peer participation, competition, and opportunities to earn rewards may increase short-term motivation to read. Disadvantages include the costs of the incentives and the possibility that motivation will decrease once the rewards are removed.

Teachers frequently use a combination of these techniques by providing daily reading time while also incorporating some incentives for reading.

Print-Rich Learning Environments

Characteristics of Literacy-Rich, Content-Area Classrooms

Literacy-rich, content-area classrooms include frequent teacher modeling of academic behaviors. This includes teacher modeling of thinking aloud, use of reading and writing strategies, and incorporation of academic vocabulary into regular activities.

These classrooms also include daily reading, writing, listening, and speaking activities. Students are engaged in reading, writing, and discussing a range of different texts and media in both print in digital form. Depending on the content area, this may include lab reports, journal articles, maps, historical fiction, diaries, graphic organizers, narratives, and more.

Students in literacy-rich classrooms are encouraged to make connections between different sources and content areas. For example, readers may make connections between a historical fiction text about the Dust Bowl and what they have learned in science about weather patterns.

Additionally, teachers in literacy-rich classrooms encourage the respectful sharing of information and ideas among classmates.

Creating Environments Supportive of Cultural and Linguistic Differences

Classrooms should incorporate **culturally** and **linguistically diverse materials**, including those that represent the cultures of students. Reading materials, artwork, classroom labels, and posters are all examples of diverse materials that can be included. Students should also have opportunities to share items that are meaningful to them with other classmates.

Additionally, ELLs should not be punished for reluctance to participate in discussions. Instead, they should be offered **support** and **scaffolding** when needed. When ELLs are in the early stages of English language acquisition, teachers can also use simple sentence structures and provide visual clues to support students' comprehension.

Teachers should also work to create nonthreatening and supportive classroom environments by modeling accepting attitudes. They can model and explicitly teach how to compare and contrast different cultures respectfully. When studying historical and current events, teachers can help students explore the events from different perspectives and discuss how culture can affect people's experiences.

Review Video: Importance of Promoting Literacy in the Home
Visit mometrix.com/academy and enter code: 862347

Using Word Walls to Support Reading and Writing Development

Word walls are collections of words that are prominently displayed in classrooms. Words selected for display on word walls should be meaningful for students. They might include high-frequency words that students need to read and write often or academic vocabulary words related to units of study. Word walls are flexible, and words may be added or removed throughout the year based on students' needs.

Teachers should model how to use word walls to locate and spell high-frequency words. Words may be attached using Velcro, magnets, or other methods that allow them to be removed. This allows students to take the words down while using them and return them to the wall when finished.

There are many ways to organize word walls. Words can be listed alphabetically under letter headings, helping young writers quickly locate them for spelling assistance. If focused on academic vocabulary, the words can be grouped by topic. Visuals can be included with vocabulary words to assist students with remembering meanings.

Leveled Book Rooms

Leveled book rooms are consolidated collections of leveled readers that can be checked out by all teachers within a school. Reading specialists often help organize and maintain leveled book rooms as part of their responsibilities. Because teachers frequently have students who read both well above and well below grade level, these types of book rooms ensure that all students have access to books within their instructional reading levels.

To implement successful leveled book rooms, books should be clearly organized and labeled according to level. The same leveling system used by classroom teachers should be used in the leveled book rooms for consistency. Books may also be organized in additional ways, such as by genre, topic, or author. Teachers should be taught the procedures for checking out and returning books. Records should be maintained in order to keep track of where all books are located.

Instructional Technologies Supporting Literacy Development

There are many ways that instructional technologies can be used to create classroom environments that support literacy development. Computer programs and apps can be used to practice and assess literacy skills, and there are many options that differentiate instruction based on students' existing skills. Many of these programs and apps also save and track students' progress, helping both students and teachers track progress toward goals.

- Projectors, document cameras, and interactive whiteboards can also be used to **magnify texts** so students can follow along during instruction. Interactive whiteboards also allow students to actively participate in literacy activities with classmates.
- **Digital texts** can be used to support listening development and assist students with reading texts that are too difficult for them to read independently. Interactive storybooks that display and track text for emergent and beginning readers can also be used.
- There are many **digital tools** and **software options** that can be used to create forms of media such as slideshow presentations, infographics, digital storybooks, and newsletters. Modern tools can also be used to help students collaborate on projects, even if they are working remotely.

Print-Rich Environments for Early Childhood

Print-Rich Classrooms

In early childhood classrooms, print-rich environments contain books and texts of different genres and topics, including both audio and digital texts. Walls and shelves have signs and labels to help with classroom procedures and organization. Posters display information related to content students have been studying. Reading, writing, and listening centers are available for students to explore during center time. Puppet theaters and flannel boards are present to encourage oral language and storytelling. There are also many literacy-related materials, such as letter tiles and sight word cards. Word walls are posted.

In **print-rich environments**, students are encouraged to share and display texts they have created. They may add their own stories to the classroom libraries or hang up signs they have made. Materials created during shared and interactive reading and writing experiences may also be displayed.

In classrooms for older students, signs and posters are displayed containing academic vocabulary, content students have been studying, and classroom procedures. Written and digital texts from a range of genres are present. There are also ample resources available for students to use to locate and share information, such as computers, tablets, dictionaries, and thesauri.

Promoting Literacy Development with Dramatic Play Centers

Dramatic play centers are common in early childhood classrooms. These centers allow children to act out realistic situations through play. Examples include pretend restaurants, homes, veterinary clinics, and grocery stores. While engaging in dramatic play, children read, write, listen, and speak for authentic purposes.

As children role-play and interact with other children in dramatic play centers, they develop oral language skills. They engage in conversations and practice using language to accomplish tasks, such as ordering in restaurants. They also listen to peers and follow directions, such as when they are pretending to be restaurant servers.

Children also engage in reading activities in dramatic play centers. Labels and realistic print materials can be included. For example, pretend restaurants may include labeled cabinets and menus. Children can practice writing through dramatic play. For example, children who are pretending to be servers may write down orders on notepads.

Building Literacy Activities into Daily Routines and Activities

Teachers can plan reading, writing, listening, and speaking activities across all subject areas. This can include a mixture of independent literacy activities and shared and interactive reading and writing experiences. Texts focusing on topics that are being studied in all content areas can be accessible in the classroom. Students can also write in all subject areas. For example, they can write the processes used to solve problems in math and create travel brochures in social studies.

Teachers of early childhood and elementary students can plan morning meetings in which daily written messages are read and discussed. Students can share current events and topics of interest with their classmates during these meetings, while other students listen and ask questions.

Early childhood and elementary teachers can also incorporate oral language and listening into daily routines. For example, they may recite specific chants or songs during transitions.

Print-Rich Home and Community Environments

Print-Rich Homes

An important component of print-rich homes is easy access to developmentally appropriate texts in a range of genres. Although favorite texts can be kept and reread repeatedly, children should also have access to new and changing texts over time as their interests and skills develop. Both digital and print-based texts are commonly found in print-rich homes. This may include books, magazines, newspapers, online literacy games, and digital stories.

In addition to books, print-rich homes also contain a lot of environmental print that children can read. This may include cereal boxes, board game directions, recipes, mail, and more. Exploring this environmental print helps children understand different purposes for reading and writing.

Children in print-rich homes have easy access to a variety of writing materials, such as paper, pencils, and crayons. Computers can also be available to type texts. Children should be encouraged to write for a variety of purposes and audiences.

Family Members' Promoting Reading

Family members can help children make reading a part of everyday activities both at home and while out in the community. Helping children explore environmental print and its purposes is one important step family members can take. They can point out business and road signs while driving, for example. At home, they can help children explore environmental print like food labels, posters, and mail.

Family members can also help children understand how reading is used to accomplish daily tasks. They can ask children to help create and read lists at the grocery store and select meal choices from restaurant menus. While driving, they can ask children to help read road signs to determine which routes they will take. At home, they can read directions together to assemble new toys and follow recipes to prepare shared meals.

There are many benefits to reading with children for authentic purposes; it helps children understand that reading is part of daily life and learn that it can be used for many practical purposes. This approach also blends learning with daily life and real-world tasks, helping engage children in the learning process.

Family Members' Encouraging Oral Language Development

Parents and family members should talk to children frequently from the moment they are born. Children learn how to use language by listening to those around them. Family members can respond to their children's initial sounds and beginning attempts at speech by making eye contact and replying. When children begin speaking words and sentences, family members can respond by repeating what they have said and adding additional information. They can encourage children to imitate their words and actions, using games like peekaboo. Family members can talk about what they are doing and ask their children open-ended questions. They can use varied vocabulary and sentence structure in their speech.

Family members can also engage in wordplay with children. They can read rhyming and repetitive texts, songs, and poems together, encouraging their children to participate. Additionally, they can retell favorite stories orally and make up stories of their own.

Family Members' Promoting a Love of Reading at Home

Family members can incorporate reading time into their children's daily routines to promote a love of reading at home. This can include a variety of types of reading experiences. Sometimes family members can read aloud to their children, sometimes children can read aloud to their family members, and sometimes they can take turns reading. Each of these experiences has its own benefits. Children benefit from hearing their family members reading fluently and using reading strategies, and they also benefit from practicing their own reading skills in safe environments.

While reading together at home, families can read a mixture of new and favorite texts. The experiences should be fun and relaxing, with opportunities to talk about the stories and characters. They can also listen to audio texts together at various times, such as when they are in the car.

Children can benefit from seeing family members reading frequently and for a variety of purposes. Family members can talk about their favorite books and authors. They can also take children to the library regularly to find new books to read together.

Promoting Community Involvement in Literacy Activities

Teachers can share information with parents about free public story time events to promote parent involvement in community literacy activities. These events are commonly held at public libraries and bookstores. Teachers can also forge partnerships with their local public libraries. They can inquire about programs that issue library cards to students. Local librarians can be invited to visit classrooms to read aloud to students and share information about upcoming events.

Teachers can set up **community volunteer programs**. Community members can be invited to visit classrooms to read with students. Students can also potentially visit senior centers or other locations to read to adults. Local authors and business people who use reading and writing in their jobs can also be invited to visit classrooms to discuss the role that literacy plays in their lives.

Additionally, teachers can encourage students to communicate with community members for **authentic purposes**. For example, students can send thank-you letters to businesses that hosted field trips or sponsored school events. With parents' permission, student work can also be displayed during community events.

Using Instructional Technologies to Promote Literacy Development at Home

There are many free and inexpensive online games and apps that students of all ages can use to practice literacy skills. These include letter recognition activities, phonics skills practice, digital texts with comprehension questions, and more. School districts that subscribe to certain online programs may provide parents with links and passwords so students can practice at home.

Students can also listen to digital storybooks. Online versions are available that track the text for students and show pictures. Audio versions can be downloaded or checked out from public libraries. Family members can listen to and discuss these stories with their children to practice comprehension strategies.

With guidance and supervision, students can communicate with others using digital tools. They can create presentations and written texts using word processing and presentation tools. They can communicate with family members using emails, texts, and videoconferencing tools. They can also use free online tools to create and publish their own digital stories.

Review Video: Collaborating with Families
Visit mometrix.com/academy and enter code: 679996

Increasing Family Involvement in Reading Development

Teachers should communicate with caregivers frequently to increase family involvement in reading development. They should convey to caregivers that they are viewed as partners and assure them that they welcome questions and concerns. Teachers should frequently communicate positive information to caregivers in addition to sharing reading concerns. Teachers should also recognize that different families have different resources available, so they should try communicating through multiple channels. This may include phone calls, texts, classroom websites, paper newsletters, emails, and more. Teachers should also be aware of scheduling, cultural, and linguistic differences. Information can be sent home in multiple languages, if possible.

Teachers can share links to reading activities and strategies using classroom websites and newsletters. They can also send home reproducible books and texts from classroom libraries, that students can read with their families. Consumable supplies can also be sent home, such as cardstock letter tiles that can be used to practice spelling and building words.

Parent and family nights can also be scheduled to share strategies and display student work. These events can be recorded and shared with parents who are unable to attend.

Cultural Influences on Language Development and Use

Role of Social Context in Language Development and Usage

Members of a group have a shared social identity that is formed by reading, writing, listening, and speaking with one another. Group members develop common expressions, mannerisms, and favorite stories that are understood by other members. For example, members of a professional group may use academic language specific to their field at conferences and work events. However, they will not likely use these terms while talking with people outside the field.

Additionally, **social context** plays a role in how people select the appropriate language to use. When asking a stranger for directions, a person would likely consider social norms and begin with an expression like "Excuse me." When talking with a good friend on the phone, a person might use an informal, joking tone. It is important for people to consider each situation and determine which approach to use.

Teachers can provide frequent opportunities for students to communicate with others for a variety of authentic purposes. This can include communicating with classmates, other students and adults within the school, family members, and community members.

Role of Cultural Context in Language Development and Use

Language involves not only the words people say but also the ways in which these words are interpreted by recipients. Differing backgrounds and cultures can affect how messages are received, so it is important for people to consider that others may view communications differently. For example, in some cultures, students are encouraged to ask questions and initiate discussions in class. In others, students are expected to defer to their instructors and not speak unless they are directly questioned. A student who tells an instructor that something doesn't make sense may be praised for using metacognitive strategies in one class while perceived as being rude in another.

Cultural context also affects how nonverbal communications are interpreted. For example, different cultures have their own norms about making eye contact while speaking or the use of gestures during greetings.

Teachers should be sensitive to these cultural differences and consider the roles they may play in student participation and communication. Additionally, teachers should help students view situations from multiple perspectives and consider how their attempts at communication may be perceived by others in various situations.

Interdependent Relationship Between Culture and Language

The ways that people use language and interpret language directed toward them is related to their cultures. Additionally, as cultures change over time, so do languages. Existing words can take on new meanings, and new words may be added to languages. These changes sometimes occur as a result of popular culture, including television, video games, and music. As people with different cultural backgrounds interact, they must negotiate these differences to make meaning.

Because culture and language are so intertwined, understanding the cultural contexts in which language is used is an important part of learning any new language. English language learners should be taught English skills in context, helping them understand how the language is used in realistic social interactions. Additionally, it is important for teachers to understand the cultural backgrounds of ELLs and the roles their cultures may play in their language interactions and expectations. Teachers should incorporate a variety of teaching strategies and methods into their classrooms to meet the needs of all students.

Supporting Advanced Readers

Characteristics of Advanced Readers

Advanced readers can display many different characteristics. They are sometimes identified by above-average scores on standardized reading assessments. Other times, observed reading behaviors and performances on classroom assignments can provide clues.

Advanced readers typically read fluently and have strong word recognition and decoding abilities. They are also able to flexibly apply a variety of reading strategies to figure out unknown words and meanings.

Advanced readers may also have well-developed vocabularies and incorporate varied words into their speech and writing. They may show a strong interest in reading and get deeply immersed in the texts they have selected. Advanced readers often love to talk with others about the books they have read, and they may make connections between the texts and themselves, other texts, and real-world events. Additionally, they are often able to analyze texts using high-level comprehension skills, such as evaluating and drawing conclusions.

Challenging/Engaging High-Achieving Readers

Collaborative Learning Opportunities

High-achieving readers can often benefit from participating in collaborative, project-based learning opportunities that allow them to apply higher-level reading and writing skills with others. Collaborative projects draw upon the strengths and unique problem-solving abilities of all group members and allow high-achieving readers to work with others to solve realistic problems. The projects allow students to share ideas and receive feedback from others of all skill levels, including other high-achieving students who may enjoy analyzing and discussing the same types of complex texts that they do.

High-achieving readers can benefit from forming collaborative relationships with teachers. They can be taught to use metacognitive strategies to self-monitor their own reading and set realistic but challenging goals for their own reading and writing development. They can collaborate with teachers to select literacy projects that pertain to their interests. This involvement in the learning process can help high-achieving readers stay interested and engaged in literacy instruction.

Open-Ended Assignments and Projects

High-achieving readers often benefit from having some choices about what and how they learn. This can include choices about the types and topics of texts they explore. For example, if classes are learning about persuasive writing, students may choose the texts they will analyze from a range of genres and topics.

Students can also have some choices about the complexity of the projects they complete, with options to delve deeper into topics if desired. For example, if students in a class are identifying characteristics of fairy tales, some students may choose to compare and contrast multiple versions of the same tale and note identifying features.

High-achieving readers may also benefit from having choices about the formats of their projects. Possible project ideas include creating multimedia presentations, writing alternative endings to texts, creating three-dimensional artistic representations of story events, and more. These options also accommodate different learning modalities. Teachers may create a menu of options for students to choose from or encourage them to come up with their own ideas.

Although students may be directing some of their own learning, teachers should still conference with high-achieving readers frequently to assess progress and collaborate on ideas.

Issues and Frustrations of High-Achieving Readers

High-achieving readers are sometimes required to read the same texts as the other students in their classes during reading instruction and in other content areas. Because these texts are often designed for on-level readers, they may be easy for high-achieving readers to decode and comprehend. Without any challenges in the texts, high-achieving readers may **finish quick**ly and possibly become bored.

High-achieving readers are also sometimes given extra work to complete when they finish their on-level work early. They may view this extra work as a punishment, and the new work may not be challenging for these students either. **Boredom** and **frustration** may then occur.

Additionally, high-achieving readers may become bored during whole-class lessons on concepts they have already mastered. For example, readers who are successfully decoding complex multisyllabic words will likely become bored during lessons on CVCe spelling patterns.

These high-achieving readers may sometimes appear disengaged, resist coming to school, or have behavior issues within the classroom. To prevent these issues from occurring, teachers can **differentiate instruction** and provide high-achieving readers with opportunities to read texts within their **instructional levels**. These students can also be encouraged to complete alternate assignments that are more challenging.

Effective Literacy Interventions

Components of Effective Literacy Interventions

Literacy interventions should be targeted to students' individual needs and based upon assessment data. Interventions can be delivered either individually or in small groups, if multiple students can benefit from the same interventions.

If commercial intervention programs are used, they should be carefully evaluated to ensure they are research-based. Interventions should be based upon clear objectives. They should also incorporate ways to measure students' progress to evaluate if the interventions are successful. Pre-tests are commonly given when interventions are implemented, and the results are used to set goals. Student progress is then monitored regularly to determine if progress is being made toward the performance goals.

Research has shown that frequent interventions are more effective than infrequent interventions, even if they occur for shorter blocks of time. For example, teachers may conduct small-group interventions daily, for 15 minutes each time. Students need frequent opportunities to practice and apply new skills. Interventions should include a mixture of systematic and explicit instruction and guided practice with feedback.

Although students benefit from interventions with classroom teachers and literacy specialists, some carefully selected computer-based interventions may also be used.

Evaluating the Effectiveness of Literacy Interventions

Literacy interventions are planned for students based upon assessment data. This initial data is used to set performance goals, and progress toward goals is measured using progress monitoring and intervention post-tests. If students make regular progress and achieve their performance goals within the expected time frames, the interventions are usually considered effective. If students make minimal or no progress toward their goals despite receiving interventions, the interventions may be considered ineffective, unless additional factors are impeding success.

However, interventions must be implemented with fidelity to determine their effectiveness. Teachers must use the agreed-upon strategies and instructional methods and meet with students consistently according to their intervention schedules. They must also ensure that the interventions are not interrupted. If issues occur in these areas, lack of student progress may not be the result of ineffective intervention planning. The interventions may have the potential to be successful, but the implementation and delivery methods may need improvement.

Reading Strategies vs. Reading Interventions

Reading strategies and reading interventions are often used interchangeably, but there are some key differences between the two. Reading strategies are methods teachers use to help students learn reading skills. To teach students to comprehend texts, teachers may encourage them to make predictions and inferences. Strategies are taught during regular classroom instruction and may be reinforced individually or in small groups. Meeting informally with a student to review and practice how to make predictions during one class session is not a formal intervention as no set improvement plan, regular meeting schedule, or progress monitoring assessment is involved.

Interventions are specific plans to help students make progress in targeted areas. They are based on assessment data, and they are scheduled for regular, set periods of time. Students' progress is monitored through frequent assessments to look for improvement. Reading strategies may be taught and practiced as part of formal intervention plans.

Reading Specialist's Role in Professional Development

Reading Specialists Support of Classroom Teachers

Reading specialists often play a variety of roles within their schools. Some reading specialists serve as intervention teachers. These specialists directly provide targeted intervention services to students who are struggling with reading, often in areas including phonemic awareness, decoding, sight word recognition, and comprehension. They may go into students' classrooms to provide intervention services, or they may pull students out for a set number of minutes each week.

Reading specialists can also provide professional development opportunities for classroom teachers. In small or large-group sessions, they often model how to use instructional strategies that are supported by research. They compile literature and resources related to literacy instruction and make these resources available to teachers. They may also work with individual teachers to develop instructional plans or overcome difficulties with literacy instruction.

Reading specialists may also oversee standardized literacy assessments for their schools and train teachers in testing procedures. They work with teachers to analyze assessment data, track students' progress over time, and use the results to plan or change appropriate interventions.

Professional Development Opportunities

Reading specialists provide professional development opportunities for teachers on a wide range of topics. For early childhood teachers, reading specialists may offer training about modeling concepts of print, planning phonological and phonemic awareness activities, creating print-rich environments, and designing effective literacy centers. Other topics may include types of reading and writing experiences and using multisensory approaches to reading and writing instruction.

- Professional development for elementary teachers may include topics such as incorporating reading and writing across content areas, using interactive word walls, using assessment data to guide instruction, modeling comprehension strategies, and designing effective literature circles.
- For middle and high school teachers, professional development topics may include teaching academic vocabulary, incorporating reading and writing across content areas, teaching text structures, and using higher-level comprehension strategies.

Reading specialists may also provide professional development opportunities on specialized topics, such as meeting the needs of students with disabilities and teaching reading strategies to ELLs.

Role of the Reading Specialist

The Goals of Schools' Reading Programs to Parents and Family Members

Although it is common for classroom teachers to communicate with family members about reading development, reading specialists also play important roles in promoting literacy at home. Reading specialists may conduct family surveys to learn more about home literacy behaviors and to assess parents' literacy-related needs and concerns. They may help organize school- or district-wide family literacy events. These events offer hands-on literacy activities appropriate for different grade levels that family members can complete with their children and take home for additional practice. They also feature interactive read-alouds that model ways parents can encourage reading behaviors with their children at home.

Additionally, reading specialists might be involved in organizing book fairs or lending libraries that supplement their schools' traditional libraries. They may provide families with information about reading goals and interventions or summer reading programs.

Promoting Collaboration Among Teachers and Other Colleagues

One role of a reading specialist is to promote collaboration among colleagues. A collaborative approach allows colleagues to develop and work toward shared goals. It can increase motivation to implement reading programs with fidelity and help colleagues share strategies to address common problems and concerns.

In addition to attending staff meetings, reading specialists can attend grade-level team meetings. Reading specialists can help grade-level teams analyze assessment data to identify areas in need of improvement. Together, the teams can create performance goals that will be used to drive reading instruction. They can collaboratively develop instructional plans and activities to help reach the shared goals. This type of collaborative approach can encourage motivation and accountability.

Reading specialists may also look for each colleague's strengths and note strong examples of research-based reading instruction. They can encourage these colleagues to share their strategies and allow others to observe their teaching. Teachers may also be encouraged to share problems they are having with reading instruction, and colleagues can work together to develop solutions to these problems.

Role in Improving Schools' Reading Curricula

Reading specialists typically have access to assessment data from multiple grade levels and time periods. They can lead data analysis teams that look for trends that may indicate gaps in their schools' reading curricula. Once these gaps are identified, reading specialists can work with teachers to revise curricula and instructional methods to better address these needs and improve student performance. Reading specialists often also serve on committees to evaluate and select potential reading programs to supplement or replace existing ones. Reading specialists can share their knowledge of research-based approaches to literacy instruction and use this knowledge to evaluate the potential reading programs.

Reading specialists also identify external professional development opportunities that may be beneficial for teachers based on their schools' instructional gaps. They advocate for opportunities for teachers to attend these sessions and share what they have learned with colleagues.

Additionally, reading specialists can recruit teachers who are willing to apply and model specific research-based instructional strategies while receiving coaching and support. For example, reading specialists can recruit teachers willing to try interactive word walls or literature circles.

BUILDING CONSENSUS AMONG COLLEAGUES WHEN MAKING INSTRUCTIONAL DECISIONS

Reading specialists often deal with conflict in their roles. **Conflict** may occur when introducing new reading programs or helping teachers decide upon new instructional strategies and goals. One role of a reading specialist is to help establish a **consensus among the different stakeholders** involved, including teachers, administrators, board members, and other school staff.

To do so, reading specialists need to be seen as leaders who are respected in their area of expertise but also **flexible** and willing to listen to new ideas. By listening to suggestions and concerns while also explaining literacy-related research and best practices, reading specialists can help their teams develop shared visions for school reading instruction. They can help other stakeholders understand their roles in achieving these visions by outlining specific but attainable goals and defining the responsibilities of everyone involved. Other stakeholders will be more likely to cooperate with the plans if they understand the role they will play in accomplishing the shared goals.

RESOLVING CONFLICT AMONG COLLEAGUES REGARDING READING INSTRUCTION

Instructional decisions have lasting effects on teachers and students. This is especially true when major decisions are made, such as selecting new reading programs. Conflict about instructional strategies and ways to implement change can lead to interpersonal conflict. Therefore, reading specialists who are facilitating these changes must often assist with conflict resolution.

- Reading specialists can first acknowledge the issues rather than ignore them, recognizing that conflict can be healthy when it leads to open discussions and sharing of ideas. They can then look for the root causes of the conflict. Although the conflicts may be based on personality differences, they may also be based on other issues, such as concerns about adequate time or resources and differing prior experiences. Helping highlight the true issues may lead to discussions about how the concerns can be alleviated.
- Reading specialists can also bring the discussions back to shared performance goals. Colleagues can be asked to restate the shared goals and the reasons behind them, reminding everyone involved that student success is the focus. Colleagues can then collaborate to find solutions that incorporate the ideas while still addressing the concerns of all parties involved.

ADVOCATING FOR PUBLIC SUPPORT OF READING EDUCATION

It is important for reading specialists to be aware of policies that affect literacy education at the local, state, and national levels. This includes awareness of school board, state government, and US Department of Education policies. Attending local school board meetings and joining professional organizations that track impending legislation are two ways to assist with this goal. Reading specialists can share their knowledge with colleagues and community members and advocate for legislation and policies that support effective reading instruction. Additionally, they can interpret existing legislation for their colleagues and ensure that they understand the implications it has on their classroom instruction.

Reading specialists can assist their school districts with writing grants and educational proposals that can positively impact literacy instruction. This may include proposals for funding that can be used to purchase new materials or hire additional reading specialists.

Historical and Theoretical Background of Reading Programs

History of Reading Education in America

In colonial and early America, reading education focused on **memorization**. Students were expected to memorize the alphabet, syllables, words, verses, and poems. The poems and verses were recited in front of others for fluency practice.

In the 1800s, a more systematic approach to reading instruction was introduced. This included systematic phonics, sight word instruction, and reading across content areas. McGuffey Readers were a series of leveled primers commonly used for reading instruction. In the late 1800s, the idea of reading for meaning began to be promoted.

In the early 1900s, the focus continued to be on reading for **meaning** and **purpose**. Explicit and systematic phonics instruction was common. In the mid-1900s, basal readers became commonplace in schools. Basal readers contained leveled stories that were followed by comprehension questions, with separate phonics skill and drill activities.

In the 1980s, whole language was promoted. Proponents believed children would learn to read by being **immersed** in reading and writing experiences rather than using explicit phonics instruction. By the mid-1990s, a balanced approach to literacy instruction was common. **Balanced literacy** includes a combination of explicit and systematic phonics instruction and immersion in authentic reading and writing experiences.

Currently, best practices are connected to the **Science of Reading**. This term was first used in educational literature in the mid-20th century, but it was not until the beginning of the 21st century that the term reemerged. It took close to two decades before the Science of Reading began to be implemented across the nation. Based on this research, the five main components that make up effective teaching of reading are: **phonemic awareness, phonics, fluency, vocabulary, and comprehension**. The term **structured literacy** also stems from the Science of Reading.

Evolution of Literacy Instruction over the Years

Beliefs about the best ways to teach reading have evolved over the years. It was once believed that children are passive receivers of knowledge, and memorization and skill-and-drill approaches to reading instruction were common. Later, theorists suggested that children are active learners who construct their own meaning through scaffolded problem-solving. Literacy instruction then transitioned to focusing on reading and writing for authentic purposes. In most recent years, it focuses on phonemic awareness, phonics, fluency, vocabulary, and comprehension. This belief still acknowledges that students learn best when they are actively involved in the learning process, but there are specific methodologies to help teachers teach reading.

Current research supports the idea that students are actively involved in the learning process. They should receive a structured literacy approach to reading. Research also indicates that although children progress through typical stages of literacy development, learning is an individualized process. Differing prior knowledge and learning styles can affect the paths children take to becoming proficient readers and writers. Assessment is viewed as an important tool for helping ensure that learning is differentiated and individual student needs are met. Additionally, research indicates that language and literacy development have social components, and students benefit from opportunities to interact and collaborate with others for a variety of purposes.

Tenets of Behaviorism

The theory of **behaviorism** was shaped by several individuals, including Ivan Pavlov and B. F. Skinner. Popular in the early to mid-1900s, it centers around the belief that learners respond to external stimuli. If behaviors are reinforced, they will continue. **Reinforcement** may be positive, which occurs when stimuli are added after desired behaviors are demonstrated. Rewards and praise for completing assignments are examples of positive reinforcement. Reinforcement may also be negative, which occurs when stimuli are removed after desired behaviors are demonstrated. When teachers stop giving stern reminders to students after they begin their independent reading, **negative reinforcement** has occurred.

According to behaviorism, **punishments** are used to decrease undesirable behaviors. Taking away manipulatives from students who are misusing them is an example of using punishment to decrease undesirable behaviors.

Learning theory has evolved over time, and research now indicates that students are more actively involved in constructing meaning than suggested by behaviorism. Yet some tenets can still be applied to reading instruction. Teachers should be careful not to criticize or punish students for errors made during reading. Effort and use of reading strategies should be supported and encouraged.

Tenets of Cognitivism

Cognitivism became popular in the 1960s after the rise of behaviorism. Rather than believing that children are passive receivers of knowledge, **cognitivism** argued that there are many internal processes that affect learning. When students are confronted with new information, they attempt to make sense of it based on prior knowledge and other factors. Information that catches students' attention may proceed from sensory memory to short-term memory, where it must be processed and encoded to be transferred to long-term memory.

Cognitivism has many implications for reading instruction. Teachers should remember that learning to read is an active process. To facilitate memory transfer, students should have prior knowledge activated before reading. Attention must also be drawn to key information. This may be done using advance organizers, bolded text, or other cueing techniques. Information should also be broken into manageable chunks, and students should have opportunities to repeatedly practice new knowledge and skills. If too much information is presented at once, cognitive overload may occur. If students do not have opportunities to practice newly learned knowledge or skills, it may be forgotten. Teachers should ensure that they allow adequate opportunities for guided practice and feedback.

Piaget's Theory of Cognitive Development

Piaget's theory suggests that all children go through the same four stages of cognitive development, yet the rate at which they proceed through the stages may vary somewhat.

- From birth until about two years of age, children are in the **sensorimotor** stage. Children in this stage explore the world around them using their senses, including grabbing and chewing objects. At first, children's behaviors are caused by reflexes. Gradually, they learn that their behaviors can influence their environments, and they begin experimenting with different behaviors. They learn object permanence, meaning they understand that things still exist even when they are not visible.

- The **preoperational** stage lasts from age two until about age seven. In this stage, children begin thinking symbolically. They engage in symbolic play and begin using words to represent what they want. Children in this stage are egocentric and have trouble seeing other people's perspectives.
- The **concrete operational** stage lasts from age seven until about age twelve. In this stage, children begin to think logically but may still struggle with abstract ideas. They begin becoming less egocentric.
- In the **formal operational** stage, which begins around age 12 and continues into adulthood, people are capable of abstract and logical thoughts.

Review Video: Piaget's Cognitive Development Theory
Visit mometrix.com/academy and enter code: 100376

Applying Piaget's Theory of Cognitive Development to Reading Instruction

- Young children in the **sensorimotor stage** of cognitive development benefit from exploring types of books designed for this age group. This includes board books and cloth books containing different textures and materials to manipulate. By exploring these books using their senses, children will enjoy their first reading experiences.
- Children in the **preoperational stage** begin to think **symbolically**. The alphabetic principle can be explored in this stage. Children can also explore the purposes of punctuation marks and illustrations included in texts. They can explore using different types of texts to accomplish different purposes, such as writing letters to communicate with friends.
- Children in the **concrete operational stage** begin to think **logically**. Students in this stage can explore literary elements and text structures. They can also analyze texts deeply and comprehend relationships like cause and effect.
- By the **formal operational stage**, students should be reading and analyzing a variety of complex texts for personal and academic reasons.

Schema Theory

Schema theory suggests that when people learn new concepts, the new knowledge gets organized into units called **schemata**. These schemata include all of the information that is known about the concepts. For example, a young child's schema about cars might include knowing that they are used for transportation, they have four wheels and one steering wheel, and they are painted a variety of colors. These schemata are connected to one another when knowledge overlaps. For example, the child's schema about cars may be connected to his or her schema about motorcycles, which the child knows also have wheels and are used for transportation. When encountering new information, people look to existing schemata to make sense of the new knowledge.

Schema theory has several implications for reading instruction. It demonstrates the importance of activating prior knowledge before reading. Students can be asked what they already know about the topics of new texts. They can also complete **know**, **want**, and **learn** (KWL) charts to identify what they already know and want to learn about the topics. Additionally, students can be encouraged to make text connections. This may include text-to-self, text-to-text, and text-to-world connections.

Assimilation and Accommodation in Piaget's Theory of Cognitive Development

According to Piaget, people have existing schemata, or units of knowledge, about concepts they have learned. They look to these existing schemata to make sense of new information they encounter.

Sometimes the newly encountered information fits within an existing schema and is added to it. For example, if a student has an existing schema about baseball and learns a new rule he or she did not previously know, he or she may add this new information to the schema. This is known as **assimilation**. However, sometimes the newly encountered information challenges the existing schema. If this occurs, the existing schema must be altered. For example, a student may have an existing schema about a historical figure based on readings he or she has done from one person's perspective. Based on these prior readings, he or she may view the figure as a hero. However, the student may then read a book about the figure written from a different perspective, which highlights the negative impacts of the figure's actions on others. This new knowledge may challenge the student's existing schema and cause him or her to alter it. This is known as **accommodation**.

Teachers should model and encourage evaluating texts and consider how they affirm or challenge existing beliefs.

Tenets of Lev Vygotsky's Social Development Theory

Lev Vygotsky played a leading role in the development of the **constructivist learning theory**. According to Vygotsky, children interact in social and cultural contexts. Through their social interactions with others in these contexts, cognitive development takes place. Therefore, social interaction plays a large role in learning. Teachers can consider how to incorporate social learning experiences into reading instruction. This may include shared and interactive reading and writing experiences, collaborative projects, reader's theater, and literature circles.

Vygotsky also suggested that learning takes place when students are engaged in activities in their zones of proximal development. These are activities that students are almost able to complete independently, but they require some scaffolding or collaboration. Vygotsky explained that scaffolding should be provided by others who have higher abilities in the tasks being completed. These individuals might be teachers, parents, or other classmates. Teachers can differentiate learning activities to ensure they are within students' zones of proximal development rather than being too easy or too difficult. For example, they can select books in students' instructional reading levels for guided reading groups. Teachers can use assessments to determine how to differentiate instruction for each student.

Review Video: Zone of Proximal Development (ZPD)
Visit mometrix.com/academy and enter code: 555594

Tenets of Constructivism

The constructivist theory was influenced by several people, including John Dewey, Jean Piaget, and Lev Vygotsky. **Constructivism** suggests that learning is an active process. Rather than passively receiving knowledge from their teachers, students actively construct their own meaning through learning experiences. Meaning may differ among individual students because they each have unique prior knowledge and experiences. According to constructivism, students learn by solving real-world problems; gathering, synthesizing, and evaluating information; and testing ideas.

Constructivism plays an important role in reading instruction. When analyzing texts, teachers can encourage students to draw upon prior knowledge, consider if any existing assumptions have been challenged, and share their unique understandings with others. Teachers can also encourage students to use reading to solve realistic problems through problem-based learning activities. They can also give students some choices regarding the activities and methods used. Rather than directing all phases of assignments, teachers can instead use more collaborative approaches and provide scaffolding to students as needed.

Marie Clay's Literacy Processing Theory

While Marie Clay's **literacy processing theory** is not supported anymore due to updated research, it is important to understand what her theory suggests since it is still used throughout some schools. It suggests that all children approach learning to read with different background knowledge and experiences, which results in students taking different paths to becoming proficient readers and writers. It also suggests that reading and writing are complex and interrelated experiences, and children must read and write authentic texts to learn. Additionally, it suggests that learning to read and write are active processes, and children help create their own meanings.

Early childhood teachers should consider that all students have unique prior knowledge and experiences. Teachers can assess students' skills and build upon their existing strengths. Additionally, if students are struggling with specific literacy skills, interventions can be implemented to address students' needs. However, some tools that Marie Clay promoted are not considered to be best practice anymore. For example, she promoted the use of running records as one tool that can be used to identify strategy deficits and plan interventions, but this tool focuses on cueing systems rather than decoding words through phonics rules. Thus, teachers are now encouraged to not use running records.

John Dewey's Contributions to Theories of Reading Instruction

John Dewey greatly influenced the **constructivist theory** of education. Dewey believed that people are active learners who learn by **doing** rather than passively receiving knowledge. He believed that valuable instructional time is wasted in schools by attempts to passively transmit knowledge. Additionally, he believed that for the teaching of symbolic concepts to be effective, students need opportunities to explore the symbols in context.

Dewey's beliefs have shaped the way reading instruction occurs today. Students are expected to be active learners who complete word work activities, problem-solve to decode and encode texts, and critically analyze a variety of text types. Children are commonly engaged in guided reading groups in which they must apply strategies to decode and comprehend real stories. They are also asked to construct their own meaning from texts by activating prior knowledge and making personal connections. When teaching symbolic relationships like the alphabetic principle, students are given opportunities to explore these relationships using real words and texts.

David Perkins' Theory of Learnable Intelligence

David Perkins theorized that humans have three types of intelligence. **Neural intelligence** is determined by genetics and cannot be changed. It is sometimes measured using IQ tests. **Experiential intelligence** is developed by the types of experiences one has. For example, a child who grows up in a big city may have knowledge of how to read subway maps and bus schedules. Having diverse experiences increases experiential intelligence. **Reflective intelligence** refers to a person's ability to problem-solve and reason. It also involves self-awareness and the use of metacognitive strategies. Unlike neural intelligence, experiential and reflective intelligence can be grown and developed over time.

Teachers can consider this theory when planning reading instruction. They can create literacy-rich environments using varied activities and types of texts. These varied experiences can help students develop experiential knowledge. Print, digital texts, and media can be used to help students experience things that are distant from their own communities. Teachers can also model and encourage the use of metacognitive and problem-solving strategies.

Howard Gardner's Theory of Multiple Intelligences

Howard Gardner theorized that there are multiple types of intelligences. According to his theory, people have different strengths and prefer to represent knowledge in different ways. He outlined eight different types of intelligences.

- **Visual-spatial** intelligence includes the ability to visualize things easily, such as charts and maps.
- **Linguistic-verbal** intelligence refers to strength in using language for reading, writing, listening, and speaking.
- **Logical-mathematical** intelligence refers to the ability to reason, solve problems, and recognize patterns, often with numbers.
- **Bodily-kinesthetic** intelligence refers to skilled coordination and movement.
- **Musical** intelligence refers to the ability to recognize rhythm, sound, beat, and other musical elements.
- **Interpersonal** intelligence refers to the ability to interact effectively with others.
- **Intrapersonal** intelligence refers to strong self-awareness.
- **Naturalistic** intelligence refers to a strong understanding of nature. Gardner explained that each person may demonstrate characteristics of multiple types of intelligence.

Teachers can consider Gardner's theory when planning instruction. They can use a multisensory approach to literacy instruction and also incorporate music, art, movement, problem-solving, collaboration, and other experiences. They can allow students choices in the topics they read and write about and allow them to present their learning in different ways.

Louise Rosenblatt's Transactional Theory of the Literary Work

Rosenblatt's **Transactional Theory of the Literary Work** suggests that reading involves a **transaction** between the reader and the text. Each reader brings unique prior knowledge and experiences to the reading experience. These differences affect how the text is interpreted and the meaning that is made. Different readers may make different meaning from the same texts. Therefore, there is no one fixed meaning in any text. Instead, the meaning is determined by the reader's transaction with the text.

This theory suggests that readers must be active participants in the reading process to make meaning. For example, they should be encouraged to activate prior knowledge, self-monitor understanding, and make connections before, during, and after reading. They should be encouraged to analyze texts deeply, and the close reading process may assist with this goal. Because different students may interpret texts differently, literature circles and other opportunities to discuss meaning can be beneficial. Students can be encouraged to share what prior experiences and text clues helped guide their interpretations.

Kenneth Goodman's Socio-Psycholinguistic Theory of Reading Instruction

Kenneth Goodman explained that reading involves the interaction between thinking and language. Beginning readers do not approach new texts already knowing how to read all of the words. Instead, they combine their thinking with available language clues to guess what the words say. The **socio-psycholinguistic theory** supports the use of running records to record reading behaviors and miscues. The results of the running records can be used to provide targeted instruction in using specific cueing systems. Teachers can identify if students are using or ignoring the graphophonic, syntactic, and semantic cueing systems. Goodman also explained that teachers should observe students' reading behaviors to gain further insight into the reasons for their miscues.

In more recent studies, research has proven that the use of the cueing systems and running records are not considered to be best practice for reading instruction. Running records and cueing systems are not reliable indicators of fundamental literacy skills. Research promotes the teaching of systematic and explicit phonics instruction paired with decodable texts. This allows the teacher to encourage the students to decode words rather than guess.

Myers-Briggs Type Indicator Personality Types

There are many different theories of personality that attempt to explain differences in the ways people perceive the world and interact with those around them. One common tool to assess personality type is the Myers-Briggs Type Indicator. Based on Carl Jung's personality theory, the **Myers-Briggs Type Indicator** outlines four different scales that affect personality.

The first scale ranges from introversion to extroversion. **Introverts** gain energy from time alone and quiet reflection, whereas **extroverts** gain energy from interacting with others. The second scale ranges from sensing to intuition. People on the **sensing** side of the scale learn from interacting with their senses, whereas people on the **intuition** side rely on instincts. The third scale ranges from thinking to feeling. People on the **thinking** side apply logic and questioning to make decisions, whereas people on the **feeling** side rely more on their emotions and values. The fourth scale ranges from judging to perceiving. People on the **judging** side of the scale prefer routine and order, whereas those on the **perceiving** side prefer a more laid-back approach.

Effect of Personality Types on Literacy Instruction

Teachers should consider the role that **personality types** play in how students learn and interact with others. Information observed about students' personality types can help teachers plan differentiated instruction that meets the needs of all students.

Classes typically include students on a range of the introversion-extroversion scale. Students who are more introverted may not enjoy reading instruction if they are continually asked to read aloud or perform in groups. However, students who are more extroverted may not enjoy reading instruction if only given opportunities to read independently and complete individual assignments.

Additionally, some students think logically and may instinctively turn to text evidence for support of answers. They may have more difficulties responding personally to texts. On the other hand, students who rely more on feeling may respond to texts emotionally yet need encouragement to support answers with evidence.

Personality type can also affect how students perceive classroom routines and procedures. Some students may prefer detailed routines for reading groups and centers, whereas others may prefer more laid-back approaches. Being aware of students' personalities can help teachers plan a mixture of activity types and give students the support they need to succeed in situations outside of their comfort zones.

Learning Behaviors

There are several **learning behaviors** applicable to all subject areas that support literacy learning. Some of these behaviors include following oral and written directions, interacting appropriately with other learners, displaying curiosity and asking questions, attempting to solve complex problems, reasoning, and focusing on learning tasks. These learning behaviors support literacy development by encouraging students to seek information to answer questions and solve realistic problems. They also support the collaboration needed to participate in shared problem-based learning activities and analysis of texts in literature circles. Focus on learning tasks also helps students develop reading stamina and the ability to complete literacy-related projects. Additionally, students who attempt to reason independently may find it easier to comprehend complex texts without assistance.

Age-appropriate reading, writing, listening, and speaking behaviors also help students convey and understand meaning. These behaviors include listening purposefully, organizing thoughts before writing and speaking, and monitoring understanding.

Bloom's Taxonomy

Benjamin Bloom outlined a hierarchy of skills in each of three learning domains, including the cognitive, affective, and psychomotor domains. The domain most often applied to classroom instruction is the cognitive domain. In the **cognitive domain**, skills are ranked in the following order: knowledge, comprehension, application, analysis, synthesis, and evaluation. Knowledge is the lowest-level skill, whereas evaluation is the highest.

Reading specialists and classroom teachers should consider **Bloom's Taxonomy** while designing instruction and assessments. Learning objectives should include specific verbs in the taxonomy that accurately describe what students are expected to be able to do at the end of instruction. Objectives should include skills in all levels of Bloom's Taxonomy, not just the lower levels. When reading nonfiction texts, for example, students may answer some basic recall questions. However, they may also be asked to evaluate authors' claims and support their evaluations with evidence. Higher-level thinking skills are important for close reading activities, and they help students more deeply comprehend their reading.

Review Video: Bloom's Taxonomy
Visit mometrix.com/academy and enter code: 755020

Review Video: Learning Objectives
Visit mometrix.com/academy and enter code: 528458

Components of Balanced Literacy Programs

Balanced literacy programs teach students a variety of reading skills and strategies that can be used to decode and comprehend texts. They include a mixture of systematic and explicit skills instruction and opportunities to read and write texts for authentic purposes. However, balanced literacy programs are not supported by the science of reading since these programs encourage teachers to instruct students to use cueing systems to figure out unknown words while reading.

Balanced literacy programs include instruction in phonological awareness. This is important because phonological awareness abilities are key indicators of future reading success. Systematic and explicit phonics instruction is also an important part of balanced literacy programs. Phonics skills are used to help students both decode and encode texts. Reading fluency is also modeled and practiced in balanced literacy programs. Additionally, vocabulary is another component. Students receive explicit instruction in using context and morphological clues to figure out the meanings of unknown words. They also build connections among meanings of related words. Comprehension strategies are also taught and practiced as part of balanced literacy programs.

Phonics-Based, Whole Language, and Structured Literacy Approaches

Phonics-based reading programs use a bottom-up approach to instruction. Proponents of this approach believe that children learn best when instruction progresses from part to whole. They first teach children to identify letters and letter sounds. Next, they progress to teaching students to decode single words. Later, they decode sentences and longer texts.

Whole language reading programs use a top-down approach. Proponents of this approach believe children learn best from being immersed in authentic texts. They believe that by exploring these texts, children gradually learn the rules and patterns of language.

Structured literacy approaches are explicit, systematic, cumulative, diagnostic, and responsive. Evidence suggests that this approach is most effective for all kinds of readers. The basic elements of structured literacy instruction are: phonology, sound-symbol association, syllable instruction, morphology, syntax, and semantics. This approach can work with models like **Scarborough's Reading Rope**. This model was designed by Dr. Hollis Scarborough, and it demonstrates how different reading skills are woven together to develop proficient readers. Readers gain skills over years of instructional practice from the two main strands in Scarborough's Reading Rope, language comprehension and word recognition.

Implementing a Reading Program

Implementing Reading Programs

Implementing reading programs with **fidelity** means using them as the program developers intended. This includes following the intended pacing guides, incorporating all recommended instructional components, using the materials as intended, and more. Fidelity is necessary if reading programs are to be effectively evaluated after implementation. If not implemented with fidelity, unfavorable results may be due to causes unrelated to the quality of the programs. For example, students' comprehension scores may decline if teachers repeatedly skip the recommended comprehension components due to time constraints. Additionally, implementing the programs with fidelity helps ensure that students receive the research-based instruction promised by the programs. Presenting lessons out of sequence, omitting portions of instruction, and other changes may negatively affect the quality of instruction.

However, teachers sometimes have concerns with using reading programs exactly as intended. They may believe that some lessons are ineffective for their students, based on what they know about their students' prior knowledge and existing skills. Logistical issues, such as available time and resources, may also interfere with implementing programs with fidelity. When making instructional decisions, teachers and administrators must carefully weigh the program recommendations with their own beliefs about their students and best teaching practices.

Considerations When Selecting Reading Programs

There are numerous reading programs available, so educators should take several factors into consideration when determining which programs are best for their districts and schools. The selected programs should be based on reliable and valid research about how students learn best. Information should be provided about the research and educational philosophies the programs are based upon. Additionally, the selected programs should address all components of structured literacy instruction, including phonemic awareness, phonics, fluency, vocabulary, and comprehension. Teacher guides should be available, with plans for systematic instruction using developmentally appropriate pacing guides. Frequent opportunities for explicit instruction, guided practice, and extension activities should be included in the instructional plans.

Reading programs should also contain plans and materials to help teachers differentiate instruction. The programs should offer support for struggling, on-level, and advanced readers as well as ELLs. Leveled texts and tips for differentiating lesson plans may be included.

Selected reading programs should offer adequate professional development opportunities to help teachers use the programs successfully.

Evaluating Effectiveness of Reading Programs After Implementation

Before selecting and implementing new reading programs, districts should consider the instructional and performance gaps they hope to address. By analyzing current performance data and identifying areas in need of improvement, districts can establish specific and measurable goals for their reading instruction. These goals can be used to select appropriate programs and to evaluate their effectiveness over time. By comparing data related to the goals from both before and after the new programs are implemented, districts can determine if the gaps are shrinking.

For example, a district may determine that many of its elementary students are not meeting grade-level expectations for reading fluency on standardized state tests. They may determine that one goal for their new reading program is to increase the percentage of elementary students who meet grade-level expectations for fluency by a certain amount over the next two years. They may then select a reading program that features daily fluency instruction and leveled texts for fluency practice. The district can then analyze the data from the same tests over the next few years to determine if the percentage of students who met grade-level expectations for fluency increased by the expected amount.

Increasing Positive Results When Implementing New Reading Programs

Strategic planning and ongoing support are both necessary for new program implementation to be successful. Rushing the process initially or tapering off support too soon can lead to frustration and poor results.

It is important to have trusted reading specialists, administrators, or other educators who are well trained in the programs before they are introduced to teachers. These specialists should be available to address concerns and anxiety about the changes. These specialists should also share the research supporting the new programs and the district objectives they are designed to support.

Districts should provide opportunities within teachers' workdays to learn how to use the new programs rather than requiring them to explore the programs on their own time. The trainings should be carefully planned to maximize the use of teachers' limited time. Teachers should have opportunities to observe other teachers who are already using the programs effectively.

It is also important to provide frequent support throughout the duration of each program rather than tapering off support after the initial training period. Educators should have ongoing opportunities to share successful strategies and discuss concerns with others. Support specialists should also be easily accessible when needed.

Incorporating Literacy Centers in Literacy Programs

Literacy centers are important components of literacy programs. They allow students to practice literacy skills on a regular basis while also allowing teachers time to work with small groups for reading instruction. Teachers typically create routines that allow students to rotate through some or all of the centers each day. Sometimes they are given choices over which centers to visit. Other times, teachers may direct students to proceed through the centers in predetermined orders for management purposes.

There are several common centers in literacy-rich classrooms. **Independent reading centers** include several texts of various genres for students to read by themselves, usually in relaxing and comfortable environments. **Listening centers** contain digital texts and headphones. **Technology**

centers contain computers and/or tablets for literacy games, digital presentations, research, and more. **Word work centers** contain activities and manipulatives that allow students to explore how words and sentences are put together. **Writing centers** contain paper, dictionaries, and other materials students can use for writing. **Partner reading centers** provide places for students to read with one another. Early childhood classrooms may also contain **sensory and dramatic play centers**. Additionally, classrooms contain designated areas where teachers can meet with small reading groups.

Classroom Management Strategies for Effective Literacy Centers

It is important to establish clear routines and expectations for literacy centers at the beginning of each school year. If several literacy centers will be included, they should be gradually introduced a few at a time, especially for younger students. When introducing each center, teachers should discuss and model expected center behavior. This includes explaining whether or not group work is allowed, how the materials should be properly used, and how to correctly complete the center activities. Each center's materials should be clearly labeled and be housed in designated locations.

Clear procedures should be in place for how students should rotate through the centers, minimizing confusion and overcrowding at each location. Countdown timers can be clearly displayed on projectors while students are working, providing warnings when it is time to clean up and rotate. Both auditory and visual clues can be provided to assist with transitions.

Teachers can also occasionally rotate center activities to allow students to practice newly learned skills and prevent boredom. However, teachers should model how to complete the new activities before asking students to do them independently during center time. This is especially important for young students who may not be able to read directions independently.

Record Keeping Strategies Useful in Literacy Instruction

Record keeping can assist teachers with assessing students' progress over time and differentiating instruction. Some teachers prefer to keep separate folders for each student. These folders may contain assessment data and work samples from throughout the year. Other teachers prefer to keep separate folders for each topic. For example, a teacher may have one guided reading folder that contains a list of students' current instructional reading levels and the skills that have been highlighted in each guided reading mini-lesson.

There are many types of records that may be useful. Copies of running records can be used to indicate students' growth in the use of reading strategies over time. Anecdotal records can provide information about observed reading behaviors and areas that need further instruction. Lists of students' reading levels and flexible grouping charts can assist teachers with planning guided reading groups. Writing portfolios can be used to demonstrate progress in writing, and they may be organized by genre, chronology, or other means. Dating each writing piece can assist teachers and students with observing growth.

Teachers may also keep records of literacy center schedules to ensure that students have opportunities to rotate through each center regularly.

Qualitative vs. Quantitative Research

Qualitative research is usually used to gather subjective information about people's opinions or understandings about things. **Qualitative research** can often be used to answer the questions what and why. Information may be gathered through focus groups, interviews, and observations. Researchers gather information in a neutral manner to ensure they do not influence the opinions of the subjects. Qualitative research could be used to determine reasons why teachers have abandoned a particular reading program, for example. This information could be used to revise the program to better meet teachers' needs and address concerns.

Quantitative research is used to gather numerical data that can be used to identify patterns and relationships. It can also be used to form generalizations and draw conclusions. For example, quantitative research could be used to identify if specific literacy interventions are leading to increased standardized test scores.

Characteristics of Valid Reading Research

With the ease with which people are able to post things on the Internet, abundant and often contradictory information about best practices in education can be found. Much of this information is not reliably tested. However, there are some characteristics that identify **valid reading research**, which teachers should use when making instructional decisions.

Reading research should be **reliable**. This means that other researchers should be able to replicate the research studies and get the same results. Research that relies on qualitative responses are more subjective and may be less likely to be replicated with the same results. This reliability should be taken into consideration when evaluating research. Reading research should also be **valid**, meaning the instruments should be designed to measure what they are supposed to measure. The research should also be **credible**. This means the research uses appropriate methodology, data collection, and analysis.

Sources of Valid Reading Research

There are many sources of valid reading research available. This research is sometimes available for free. Other times, paid subscriptions or enrollment in academic institutions is required to access the information.

The US Department of Education provides information about reading research and statistics on its website. This includes information related to current reading programs, literacy progress, and more.

There are also many education-related journals that contain information about reading research. Peer-reviewed journals help ensure that the research is reliable and valid. Examples include *Language Arts*, published by the National Council of Teachers of English, and the *Harvard Educational Review*, published by the Harvard Graduate School of Education. Many of these journals are available online and are sometimes also available in print form.

There are also multiple databases containing reading research. One example is the Education Resources Information Center (ERIC). These databases are available online and are also commonly available in the libraries of educational institutions.

Chapter Quiz

Ready to see how well you retained what you just read? Scan the QR code to go directly to the chapter quiz interface for this study guide. If you're using a computer, simply visit the online resources page at **mometrix.com/resources719/aepafoundread** and click the Chapter Quizzes link.

AEPA Practice Test #1

Want to take this practice test in an online interactive format?
Check out the online resources page, which includes interactive practice questions and much more: **mometrix.com/resources719/aepafoundread**

Multiple Choice Questions

1. Assessment results often inform instructional practices. At what point should teachers begin teaching the stages of composition?

a. They should start teaching the stages of composition only after children have learned to form letters.
b. They should start teaching the stages of composition only after children have learned to spell words with reliable success.
c. They should start teaching the stages of composition only once children can generate full sentences.
d. They should start teaching the stages of composition concurrently as these writing skills develop.

2. Prior to launching a sixth-grade genre study on historical fiction, Mrs. Perez plans to create a list of vocabulary words to explicitly teach to her students. She wants to select tier-two words that will best contribute to students' overall language development and allow them to transfer their knowledge to other reading experiences. Which words fit these criteria?

a. Challenging but common vocabulary words that carry a lot of meaning
b. High-frequency, concrete nouns
c. Domain-specific words found in students' social studies textbooks
d. Student-selected words related to their interests within the genre

3. According to linguists, what do invented spellings by young children best signify?

a. Children who invent spellings lack phonemic and phonetic awareness.
b. Children's selections of phonetic spellings are due to adult influences.
c. Inventing spellings for words is evidence of phonetic comprehension.
d. Diverse children choosing the same phonetic spellings is just chance.

4. Research into instructional strategies for teaching sight words to students with moderate and severe intellectual disabilities has found which of the following?

a. Traditional approaches are effective for generalization.
b. Some orthographic approaches are better than others.
c. Classroom acquisition outpaces community acquisition.
d. Community-based instruction promotes generalization.

5. Which of the following lists of symptoms is characteristic of a language disorder?

a. Omissions, additions, substitutions, or distortions of phonemes
b. Blocks, repetitions, or prolongations of sounds, words, and phrases
c. Difficulties with the loudness, pitch, or tone quality of the voice
d. Limited vocabulary, incorrect grammar, wrong word meanings

6. Which of the following most accurately reflects the typical structure of a guided reading lesson as an alternative structure for differentiating reading instruction?

a. The text to read is selected by the students.
b. Students start reading without introduction.
c. Reading is guided, but there is no discussion.
d. Instruction for strategic activities is included.

7. Which activity would be most appropriate to teach decoding of CVCe words?

a. Covering parts of the word
b. Chunking
c. Building word families
d. Blending

8. Which of the following words contains a phonogram produced by three letters?

a. Tack
b. Hit
c. Bleak
d. Light

9. A teacher introduces a new book about water conservation to students and says, "As you read this book, locate three ways you can conserve water at home." What is her primary reason for this statement?

a. To encourage students to consider the author's purpose
b. To help students set a purpose for reading
c. To activate students' prior knowledge
d. To encourage students to make text-to-text connections

10. A teacher familiarizes students with various kinds of information sources, how researchers use them, and specific conventions they follow. The teacher compares the merits, usefulness, relevance, and appropriateness of these sources relative to a class topic. How do students benefit from this instruction?

a. Direct learning about various types of source materials is the only benefit.
b. They gain deeper understanding and critical engagement via various perspectives.
c. How to build topic-related positions using evidence is not among benefits.
d. Students gain insight into selecting materials but not into evaluating them.

11. A teacher wants to select books for her emergent readers to add to the classroom library. Which set of text features are most appropriate for emergent readers?

a. Predictable text placement, repetition, and picture support
b. Complex and varied sentence types, multiple sentences per page, little picture support
c. Sidebars and charts, several lines of text per page, descriptive words and phrases
d. Complex text structures, figurative language, technical vocabulary words

12. Which of the following is true about instructional approaches and activities for developing student phonological and phonemic awareness?

a. Direct, explicit instruction is the only effective method to teach manipulating phonemes in words.
b. Teachers cannot utilize informal interactions for these purposes because they are not systematic.
c. One instructional activity that is particularly suited for younger students is playing language games.
d. For younger students to identify spoken alliteration, they must first identify it in printed language.

13. Which of these is true about young children's preferred conversation topics and how teachers can use conversation to facilitate vocabulary acquisition and sentence completion?

a. When children speak in incomplete sentences, teachers should not extend these.
b. Young children would rather talk about other people than talk about themselves.
c. Young children prefer to talk about new things that they have not yet experienced.
d. When children misuse words, teachers can recast them showing the correct usage.

14. Which of these best describes the "during reading" phase of whole-class reading instruction with a focus on decoding phonological patterns?

a. Partners reading a text together and help one another decode new words as they encounter them.
b. Teachers monitor student progress and provide assistance when necessary while independently reading through an assigned text.
c. Students read the text as partners and take turns reading and listening to one another.
d. Teachers read sentences aloud, demonstrating decoding practices. Students then repeat together as a class.

15. A student reading a text sees the word "sow" in a sentence. Which of the following will NOT help the student figure out the word meaning and pronunciation in this case?

a. The meaning of the surrounding sentence(s)
b. The sentence's syntax and grammatical structure
c. The dictionary definitions given for the word
d. The spelling pattern of the word

16. A first-grade teacher is teaching his students about different spelling patterns that can be used to produce short vowel sounds. Which of the following words should he use to demonstrate the use of the floss rule?

a. Match
b. Glass
c. Sip
d. Trap

17. Which of the following is an example of a summative assessment?

a. Final project critiques
b. Oral question-and-answer sessions
c. Running records
d. Pop quizzes

18. During assessment, a young child is able to identify and differentiate typical English-language speech sounds. This best reflects which type of awareness?

a. Phonic
b. Phonetic
c. Phonemic
d. Alphabetic

19. Which of these statements is most applicable to instruction in phonemic awareness?

a. Instruction in phonemic awareness should be standardized across students since it is a basic skill.
b. Instruction in phonemic awareness should be uniform since children start school at similar levels.
c. Instruction in phonemic awareness should be individualized to address each child's specific needs.
d. Instruction in phonemic awareness should be less critical as it is unrelated to later reading ability.

20. In the response to intervention (RTI) framework, which recommendations from the federal What Works Clearinghouse (WWC) apply to all three RTI tiers regarding primary-grades classroom reading instruction?

a. Intensive instruction
b. Small-group instruction
c. Differentiated instruction
d. Evidence-based instruction

21. Following instruction time, Ms. Pitman provides each student with a small sign that can be hung around the waist or neck. Ten children in her class receive signs displaying a single weekly vocabulary word. Five students get signs with the following: *dis-*, *re-*, *pre-*, *un-*, and *mis-*. The remaining students have signs with the following: *-ing*, *-ed*, *-s*, *-less*, and *-ful*. What is the best choice for a follow-up class activity based on this information?

a. The students are arranged into groups to demonstrate tangibly that certain parts of the English language have fixed functions.
b. Each student must use his or her sign to brainstorm a list of possible words that include those letters.
c. Each time a bell is rung, students must find a new partner with whom he or she can combine signs to make a new word.
d. Ask each student to explain what his or her sign means and how it functions in the English language.

22. A first-grade teacher schedules 10 minutes each day for sight word practice. This daily practice will most likely improve students' reading proficiency by building which skill?

a. Decoding
b. Automaticity
c. Phonemic awareness
d. Phonological awareness

23. Meg is preparing an expository research report to share information about the costs involved in pet ownership. She shares information she printed from a website during her research that she plans to incorporate into her report. The website states, "Even though having a dog requires a significant amount of time and attention, I believe it is definitely worth it. Everyone should have a pet dog because they are the most loyal friends you will ever find." Which of the following would be the most appropriate topic for a mini-lesson based on Meg's current plans?

a. Synthesizing information from multiple sources
b. Choosing between a descriptive and compare/contrast text structure
c. Using headings and other expository text features
d. Differentiating between facts and opinions

24. Of the following, which kind of learning disability would have the most direct impact on a student's reading instruction?

a. An expressive language disorder
b. A receptive language disorder
c. An articulation disorder
d. A movement disorder

25. Among effective reading strategies, which one involves recalling relevant past experience and existing knowledge to construct meaning from the new information in text that one reads?

a. Inferring
b. Activating
c. Questioning
d. Summarizing

26. Which of the following statements regarding the acquisition of language is FALSE?

a. Young children often have the ability to comprehend written language just as early as they can comprehend or reproduce oral language when given appropriate instruction.
b. Oral language typically develops before a child understands the relationship between spoken and written words.
c. Most young children are first exposed to written language when an adult reads aloud.
d. A child's ability to speak, read, and write depends on a variety of physiological factors, as well as environmental factors.

27. Which choice is correct regarding flexible grouping for reading instruction within and across classrooms?

a. Flexible grouping within the classroom is a homogeneous format.
b. Flexible grouping across classrooms has a heterogeneous format.
c. Flexible grouping within the classroom prohibits added resources.
d. Flexible grouping across classrooms can vary teachers for reading.

28. A teacher wants his students to become familiar with a wide range of genres and text structures. Which of the following options would best help him achieve this goal?

a. Displaying posters describing different genres and text structures in the classroom
b. Rewarding students who choose to read a variety of different types of books during independent reading time
c. Selecting books from different genres and with different text structures for read-alouds and shared reading activities
d. Sending home a list of varied books and encouraging students to check them out from their local libraries

29. Kindergarten students are viewing a digital storybook on the computer. As each word is read aloud, it is highlighted on the screen. Which two concepts of print does this highlighting best assist students with developing?

a. Directionality and one-to-one correspondence
b. Letter and word concepts
c. Book awareness and book handling skills
d. Word spacing and awareness of the relationship between the text and illustrations

30. A fourth-grade teacher wants to help his students analyze word morphology in order to identify the meanings of unknown words. Which word could he use to best exemplify the strategy of analyzing word morphology?

a. Trees
b. Manuscript
c. Butterfly
d. Ceiling

31. When assessing error patterns in a student's reading, which is most detrimental to reading proficiency?

a. Substitution of "control" for "contrariness"
b. Substitution of "resistant" for "recalcitrant"
c. Substituting a noun, not a verb, for a noun
d. Substituting for errors informed by context

32. Among regular word spellings, which of these frequently recurring patterns is reflected by the spelling of *-tion* as the final syllable of many English nouns?

a. Reliable, but non-phonetic, patterns
b. Recurring phonetic spelling patterns
c. Etymological extensions to patterns
d. Spellings for Greek and Latin stems

33. To raise student awareness of the nonverbal aspects of communication, of what can teachers correctly inform students?

a. 50 percent of our communication is verbal, and 50 percent is nonverbal.
b. 10 percent of our communication is verbal, and 90 percent is nonverbal.
c. 60 percent of our communication is verbal, and 40 percent is nonverbal.
d. 25 percent of our communication is verbal, and 75 percent is nonverbal.

34. A struggling reader has difficulty comprehending vocabulary words when they are encountered in unfamiliar texts. She frequently uses a dictionary to look up the unknown words. While this helps her figure out the meanings of the words, it interrupts her fluency and affects comprehension. Her teacher, Mr. Palmer, would like to teach her other strategies she can use instead that will minimize the disruptions to her fluency and increase her comprehension. Which strategy would likely be most effective?

a. Quickly asking a classmate for the meanings of the words
b. Creating a list of the unknown words and looking them up later
c. Trying to determine the meanings of the words from context clues
d. Skipping over the words she does not know as long as the sentences make sense

35. Which of the following instructional strategies would likely help students the most in understanding the difference between denotation and connotation and help them learn to identify the connotation of a word in context?

a. Providing example sentences in multiple choice questions asking for a word's connotation
b. Filling out a Venn diagram with sets of words that have connotations, denotations, or both
c. Assigning a reading where students identify and highlight words that have connotations
d. Giving word definitions and asking students to describe the feelings elicited by each definition

36. A teacher asks students to close their eyes while she reads a descriptive, fictional text aloud. When she is done reading, students draw pictures of the story's setting and share their pictures with the class. Which reading strategy are students practicing?

a. Predicting
b. Inferring
c. Summarizing
d. Visualizing

37. Mrs. Lopez teaches second grade. After completing a science experiment, she gathers her students on the carpet to write a summary of what they learned. Mrs. Lopez asks students to help her record the responses on chart paper, sharing the marker. She provides guidance and sentence starters as needed. After everyone has recorded their responses, the class reads them aloud together. Which type of writing experience is Mrs. Lopez demonstrating?

a. Interactive writing
b. Shared writing
c. Independent writing
d. Guided writing

38. Among grouping practices, which of the following have researchers found regarding whole-group instruction?

a. It can be the least efficient use of materials and time.
b. It can make it harder for students to tune out teaching.
c. It can lead to more active student lesson participation.
d. It can enable acceleration, given effective scaffolding.

39. Which of the following sentences would best help model the concept of figurative language?

a. The sky was dark and gray, warning that a storm was approaching.
b. The snow was a wet blanket covering the earth.
c. Taking care of a puppy requires time and patience.
d. The cold, wet raindrops splashed on my glasses and made it difficult to see.

40. When should students learn how to decode?

a. Decoding is the most basic and essential strategy to becoming a successful reader. It should be introduced to kindergartners during the first two weeks of school.
b. Decoding is not a teachable skill. It is an unconscious act and is natural to all learners.
c. Decoding should be taught only after children have mastered every letter–sound relationship as well as every consonant digraph and consonant blend. They should also be able to recognize and say the 40 phonemes common to English words and be able to recognize at least a dozen of the most common sight words.
d. Decoding depends on an understanding of letter–sound relationships. As soon as a child understands enough letters and their correspondent sounds to read a few words, decoding should be introduced.

41. Which statement accurately reflects a principle regarding self-questioning techniques for increasing student reading comprehension?

a. Asking only what kinds of "expert questions" fit the text's subject matter
b. Asking only those questions that the text raises for the individual student
c. Asking how each text portion relates to chapter main ideas is unnecessary
d. Asking how the text information fits with what the student already knows

42. "Decoding" is also called:

a. Remediation
b. Deciphering
c. Alphabetic principle
d. Deconstruction

43. Students receive a new text full of technical terminology unfamiliar to them. Which reference source is likely to be most efficient in helping them understand these terms?

a. Encyclopedia
b. Dictionary
c. Thesaurus
d. Glossary

44. A kindergarten teacher is administering a reading assessment to her students. She dictates some CVC words and asks students to write them down on paper. The words she dictates are *cat* and *cot*. One student writes the following responses on her paper.

bhp
wpi

Which skill should the teacher focus on first with this student?

a. Phonological awareness
b. Alphabetic principle
c. Phonics generalizations
d. Blending

45. Which of the following statements is true regarding word walls?

a. They should mainly focus on content-related words.
b. They should contain only words that are difficult for students to spell independently.
c. They should be flexible, allowing words to be added and removed throughout the year.
d. They are only needed for students in the emergent stage of reading development.

46. A teacher wants to help her students develop metacognitive skills. Which guiding question can she prompt students to ask themselves while reading?

a. Who are the major and minor characters?
b. Were my predictions correct?
c. What happened first?
d. What is the theme of the story?

47. A teacher gives students an unfamiliar text. Without doing a picture walk or pre-teaching any vocabulary words, she asks them to read it once independently. During this first reading, students are told to identify the overall meaning of the text, as well as note their initial impressions. Students discuss these responses with their peers. The teacher then asks the students to read a specific portion of the text a second time, analyzing the author's use of figurative language. Students then discuss their thoughts again. The teacher then asks the students to reread the text a third time, comparing and contrasting the main character with the main character in another text they have read. Students once again share their responses with peers. Which type of reading activity does this example demonstrate?

a. Guided reading
b. SQ3R
c. Close reading
d. Scanning

48. What should a young child NOT be able to identify during informal assessment of print concept awareness?

a. Where the teacher should start reading aloud
b. The title of the book
c. What a period means in a book
d. All of the words in the book

49. Some experts maintain that teaching reading comprehension entails not only the application of skills but also the process of actively constructing meaning. They describe this process as interactive, strategic, and adaptable. Which of the following descriptions best applies to the interactive aspect of this process?

a. The process involves the text, the reader, and the context in which reading occurs.
b. The process involves readers using a variety of strategies in constructing meaning.
c. The process involves readers changing their strategies to read different text types.
d. The process involves changing strategies according to different reasons for reading.

50. After students have studied metaphors for several days, a teacher wants to assess their abilities to apply their knowledge of what a metaphor is. Which assignment would be most appropriate for this purpose?

a. Underlining the metaphors in a sample text
b. Explaining what a metaphor is to a classmate
c. Writing a paragraph that includes at least two metaphors
d. Critiquing the author's use of metaphors in a poem

51. Which of these is true regarding early signs of reading difficulties in young children?

a. A child's inability to form rhymes is not a concern, as long as he or she can identify rhymes.
b. A child's inability to separate words into individual phonemes can indicate a problem.
c. A child's inability to blend individual phonemes to form words is not a sign of trouble.
d. A child's inability to count word syllables or spell new words phonetically is immaterial.

52. Reciprocal teaching activities focus on four main reading strategies. What is the fourth strategy, in addition to summarizing, questioning, and predicting?

a. Evaluating
b. Connecting
c. Retelling
d. Clarifying

53. Of the following, which statement is true about instruction in the alphabetic principle?

a. Letter-sound relationships with the highest utility should be the earliest ones introduced.
b. The instruction of letter-sound correspondences should always be done in word context.
c. Letter-sound relationship practice times should only be assigned apart from other lessons.
d. Letter-sound relationship practice should focus on new relationships, not go over old ones.

54. Students in the transitional stage of reading development would benefit most from instruction in which area?

a. Sight word practice
b. Identifying the theme of abstract texts
c. Analyzing morphology to determine word meanings
d. Letter/sound correspondence

55. The Cognitive Academic Language Learning Approach (CALLA) is found to be helpful for middle school ELL students. What is true of this approach?

a. It includes content objectives but does not include language objectives.
b. It includes language objectives but does not include content objectives.
c. It has content and language objectives, but there are none for learning strategies.
d. It allows thematically based content or formats using sheltered content.

56. Of the following activities that promote building vocabulary for young children, which one is most dependent on the teacher?

a. Repeatedly singing the same familiar song over and over
b. Reciting the same familiar rhymes and chants repeatedly
c. Listening to repeated readings of the same favorite story
d. A word wall in the classroom to illustrate words/concepts

57. Which statement accurately reflects educational measurement principles relative to how teachers should design reading assessments?

a. Teachers should design tests to measure a small sample of their learning objectives.
b. Teachers should design tests to instruct as well as to diagnose or evaluate students.
c. Teachers should design tests to compare groups using criterion-referenced scoring.
d. Teachers should design tests to be either valid or reliable, as both are unnecessary.

Refer to the following for question 58:

A fourth-grade student struggles to decode several words in her science textbook, including *organism*, *conclusion*, and *prediction*.

58. Which text feature could the teacher direct the student to use to best assist with this difficulty?

a. Table of contents
b. Headings
c. Index
d. Glossary

59. What is correct about evidence-based instructional strategies to use with ELL students?

a. Asking ELL students to explain and/or retell what teachers said to classmates is useful.
b. To get ELLs to concentrate on language, teachers should avoid incorporating visual aids.
c. Teachers should not "talk down" to ELLs by presenting abstract ideas in concrete forms.
d. Teachers may have ELLs signal when they don't understand, but they should not elaborate verbally.

60. Which instructional practice would NOT be helpful for young children to understand phonics and decode words?

a. Incidental exposure to implicit phonics in instruction
b. Systematic, explicit, and direct instruction in phonics
c. Teaching main ideas or strategic integration in reading activities
d. Giving reading and writing activities to apply phonics

61. Which of the following instructional strategies helps students ask questions about text, make predictions, and then read further to confirm or deny what they predicted?

a. Gist
b. DRTA
c. Fishbowl
d. Cornell Notes

62. A teacher observes a first-grade student as she writes the word *stop* in her journal. The student says each sound out loud before writing the corresponding letter on her paper. Which process is the student exhibiting?

a. Blending
b. Decoding
c. Segmenting
d. Encoding

63. Which of the following is the earliest phonological feature to be independently recognizable in a typically developing child?

a. Syllables
b. Alliteration
c. Rhyming
d. Letter-sound relationships

64. Which of the following strategies for teaching new vocabulary best demonstrates knowledge of the Four-Part Processing Model for word recognition?

a. Reading new vocabulary words aloud and having students clap out syllables
b. Displaying sentence strips that include new vocabulary and corresponding images and reading them aloud to the class
c. Using sentence dictation exercises to develop students' receptive and expressive language skills
d. Having students create semantics features maps to learn new vocabulary and create word families

65. A fourth-grade teacher gives students a character chart to fill out while reading a fictional text. Students are instructed to record traits of the main character as they read. One student, Daniel, turns in a map that lists the following traits: short, has blond hair, has freckles, is a girl. Which strategy would be an appropriate next step for the teacher to focus on?

a. Analyzing character development from the beginning of the story to the end
b. Identifying the character as a protagonist or antagonist
c. Differentiating between internal and external character traits
d. Comparing and contrasting the character with a character from another book by the same author

66. A teacher is introducing a new phonics skill to her students. She begins with explicit instruction on the skill, followed by modeling. Which instructional component should come next?

a. Independent practice
b. Guided practice
c. Generalization
d. Feedback

67. Which of the following options represents a key tenet of cognitivism?

a. Allowing social learning opportunities to foster cognitive development
b. Reinforcing desired behaviors so they continue
c. Chunking information to avoid cognitive overload
d. Encouraging students to be actively involved in constructing their own meaning

68. One instructional strategy to help students understand nonfiction is to teach them the elements of text structure and how to identify these by "signal" words. Among common text structures, which of these signal words indicate a descriptive structure?

a. Before, initially, secondly, next, then, last, after, finally
b. For example, in particular, specifically, and in addition
c. In comparison to, similar to, likewise, however
d. Therefore, consequently, why, because, may be due to

69. Which of the following instructional strategies best demonstrates a way to prevent letter confusion in kindergarten students?

a. Introducing the letters in alphabetical order
b. Teaching visually similar letters, such as *b* and *d*, separately
c. Requiring students to master each letter before introducing the next letter
d. Focusing more on letter sounds than on letter names

70. Relative to formative and summative assessments, research reveals that the single greatest change in classroom instruction for improving student learning and achievement is effective ______, which students and teachers get best from ______ assessments.

a. comparison; summative
b. feedback; formative
c. feedback; summative
d. comparison; formative

71. In which stage of spelling development do children typically learn the alphabetic principle?

a. In Stage 1
b. In Stage 3
c. In Stage 2
d. In Stage 4

72. A student participating in a reading assessment uses information from illustrations in the text he or she is reading to support reading performance. The student is using which kind of cue?

a. A visual cue
b. A meaning cue
c. A structural cue
d. A graphophonic cue

73. When assessing pre-reading skills in typically-developing preschoolers, which of the following skills should NOT be expected?

a. They should be able to recite the full alphabet.
b. They should be able to recite all numbers from 1-10.
c. They should be able to sound out three-lettered words.
d. They should be able to tell whether or not two words rhyme.

74. In describing a literacy-rich learning environment for younger students, what is most correct?

a. Labeling everything in the classroom only distracts the attention of the youngest students.
b. Directions, calendars, signs, and schedules are organizational tools not supporting literacy.
c. Word and picture labels should be avoided for discriminating against the visually impaired.
d. Students experience lessons directly if they and teachers redo classrooms as themes or texts.

75. Regarding instruction in letter-sound associations for students having difficulty with naming or recall, which is a recommended instructional strategy?

a. They should progress to new material quickly to maintain learning momentum.
b. These students will forget associations without extensive practice.
c. Students will become bored and lose motivation with overlearning.
d. Every lesson should focus on new material instead of on reviewing.

76. Which of these applies the principle of teaching from simpler to more complex for instruction in decoding multisyllabic words?

a. Teaching open syllables first among syllable pattern types
b. Teaching closed syllables first among syllable pattern types
c. Teaching syllabication before introducing multisyllabic words
d. Teaching syllable patterns based upon spelling generalizations

Refer to the following for question 77:

For a poetry unit, a class is reading a 14-line poem in iambic pentameter. There are three stanzas of four lines each, and a two-line couplet at the end. Words at the end of each line rhyme with another word in the same stanza. After the first week of this unit, the teacher wants to determine if the instructional methods she is using are successful. If students are meeting the objectives introduced so far, she will continue with the strategies she is currently using. If students are struggling to meet the objectives, she will reteach them using a different approach. For the assessment, she plans to ask students to identify the literary devices she has introduced in sample poems.

77. Which type of assessment is the teacher planning to use?

a. Formative assessment
b. Summative assessment
c. Norm-referenced test
d. Screening assessment

78. Ms. Watson has included a variety of pointers in the classroom reading center. She instructs students to use these pointers or their fingers to point to the words when reading independently. Which of the following concepts of print is Ms. Watson addressing?

a. Spacing
b. Book orientation
c. Directionality
d. Letter concepts

79. A preschool teacher is reading aloud to his students using a big book. He wants to help his students understand that the print carries the meaning of the story. What can the teacher do to foster this understanding?

a. Show students where to start reading on each page
b. Point to the words while reading
c. Model the return sweep at the end of each line of text
d. Ask students what they see in the pictures

80. Of the three tiers of words, the most important words for direct instruction are:

a. Tier-one words
b. Common words
c. Tier-two words
d. Words with Latin roots

81. Which of the following options best demonstrates a kindergarten teacher differentiating phonics instruction for her diverse group of students?

a. Asking struggling readers to decode two CVC words and asking highly proficient readers to decode 10 CVC words
b. Asking struggling readers to decode CVC words and asking highly proficient readers to write CVC words in sentences
c. Asking struggling readers to decode CVC words and asking highly proficient readers to decode words with consonant blends
d. Having struggling and proficient readers work in pairs to decode CVC words

82. During a small-group activity, a teacher asks her students to repeat a CVC word slowly, stretching out the sounds. As students repeat the word, they slide one penny forward for each sound they hear. Which phonemic awareness skill are students practicing?

a. Blending
b. Segmenting
c. Phoneme identification
d. Phoneme isolation

83. Which of the following factors affects ELL students' English-language literacy development?

a. A Chinese student's L1 is not written alphabetically like English is.
b. A Spanish student's L1 is more phonetically regular than English is.
c. Neither one of these has any effects on L2 literacy development.
d. Both factors affect L2 literacy development but in different ways.

84. Which of the following examples best describes a predictable text that is most appropriate for emergent readers to read independently?

a. A fantasy book containing a common theme, such as friendship, that students can relate to
b. A chapter book that is part of a popular series, whose characters students are familiar with
c. A fairy tale with a clear protagonist and antagonist, which helps students to predict the ending
d. A book in which every page states, "I see a ..." followed by a picture to complete the sentence

85. Which of these correctly represents findings about research-based vocabulary instruction?

a. Children need word repetition consisting of drills for vocabulary development.
b. Children need only be exposed to new words once or twice to remember them.
c. Children learn the vocabulary in texts best indirectly through simply reading them.
d. Children require direct instruction and word exposure in various contexts.

86. Which of the following represents a main difference between the conventions of spoken and written language?

a. Syntax is more relaxed in spoken language, with more flexibility in word order.
b. Body language plays a bigger role in sharing meaning in written language than in spoken language.
c. Written language tends to be less formal and more conversational in nature than spoken language.
d. Written language includes a greater mixture of fragments and complete sentences than spoken language.

87. What is an example of the phonemic awareness instructional strategy of keyword substitution?

a. "Show, show, show your shoat, shently..."
b. "How much is that window in the doggie"
c. "'Twas brillig, and the slithy toves / Did..."
d. "Owe, owe, owe our oat, ently own the..."

88. A fifth-grade teacher introduces the skill of underlining text evidence to answer comprehension questions. He then models how to use this strategy using a sample text and related questions. Next, the class uses the strategy together to answer a new set of questions, with the teacher providing feedback on each attempt. Which activity would be the best choice to come next?

a. Give students a passage and questions to complete independently using the underlining strategy.
b. Reteach how to use the underlining strategy using different examples.
c. Ask students to use this strategy when they take tests in the future.
d. Test students on their ability to use the underlining strategy to answer comprehension questions.

89. A student is using cues in a text he or she is reading to construct meaning from it. Which of the following self-questions that the student asks indicates that the student is using graphophonic cues?

a. "Do all of these words, taken together, make sense?"
b. "Do these words, taken in this order, sound correct?"
c. "Do these new words' letter patterns match others?"
d. "Do all of these words look right to spell the sounds?"

90. Kindergarten students learn one new letter and its corresponding sound each week. They participate in songs and chants that include repetitive use of the letter name and sound. Which concept are students practicing?

a. Alphabetic principle
b. Concepts of print
c. Phonological awareness
d. Automaticity

91. Which of these accurately reflects a guideline for teaching phonemic awareness based on the research literature?

a. Explicit instruction in phonemic awareness is found to be required for all students.
b. Instruction should be driven by analysis of data from phonemic awareness testing.
c. Instruction in phonemic awareness is more effective when phonemes are implicit.
d. Effective phonemic awareness instruction is scaffolded identically for all students.

92. Which statement is a key tenet of Marie Clay's literacy processing theory?

a. Children have differing prior knowledge and previous experiences and take different paths to literacy development.
b. Literacy development is enhanced when children learn to write after developing basic reading skills.
c. Emergent readers learn best using large-group instruction, where they have models of proficient readers to emulate.
d. Children learn to read best with a whole-language approach to instruction, with little emphasis on assessment.

93. Regarding alternative lesson structures for differentiating reading instruction, for which of these should a teacher use skills-focused lessons rather than guided reading lessons?

a. For monitoring how well students apply skills to reading text
b. For helping students in mastering comprehension strategies
c. For helping students discuss the meaning of texts they read
d. For supporting students in using reading comprehension skills

94. Children first begin their vocabulary development using which skill?

a. Reading
b. Writing
c. Listening
d. Speaking

95. As a reading strategy, ELA teachers can best give students practice in making predictions to support comprehension through which activity?

a. Predicting what or whom a book is about
b. Predicting what a novel's character will do
c. Predicting a significant event in a narrative
d. Predicting (B) and/or (C), rather than (A)

96. Which of the following linguistic domains relates primarily to the meanings of words?

a. Graphophonic
b. Semantic
c. Syntactic
d. Pragmatic

97. A fourth-grade teacher is preparing her students for a reading test in which a number of words have been replaced with blanks. The test will be multiple-choice; there are three possible answers given for each blank. The teacher instructs the children to read all the possible answers and cross out any answer that obviously doesn't fit. Next, the students should "plug in" the remaining choices and eliminate any that are grammatically incorrect or illogical. Finally, the student should consider contextual clues in order to select the best answer. This in an example of:

a. Strategy instruction
b. Diagnostic instruction
c. Skills instruction
d. Multiple-choice instruction

98. What has research found about appropriately challenging, effective instruction for high achievers?

a. Low-income high achievers are less likely to attend college.
b. High achievers should be given highly directive assignments.
c. Students may collaborate across classes or even grade levels.
d. Differentiation requires more supports for the higher grades.

99. Which of the following relates primarily to how sounds are represented in a text?

a. Syntactic
b. Semantic
c. Graphophonic
d. Pragmatic

100. Strategies for establishing a verbal-linguistic learning environment include all except which one of the following?

a. Classroom discussions
b. Stories told by the teacher
c. Task cards
d. Word walls

Integration of Knowledge and Understanding

101. Kaitlyn is a second-grade student who reads a traditional version of the story *Goldilocks and the Three Bears*. After reading, the teacher asks the student to list character traits to describe Goldilocks, using evidence from the story to support her answer. Kaitlyn's response is shown below.

Well, first, Goldilocks is a girl. I know that because I saw pictures of her in the book, and she is wearing a dress and has long braids. Also, I think Goldilocks is a girl's name. She also has blond hair. I know that because her name is Goldilocks, and it says in the story that she got her name from her long golden hair. So that's my second answer. I also think she is brave. She is brave because she goes into a house that doesn't belong to her. She didn't even know who lived there, and it turned out to be bears. I would never go into a stranger's house because it could be dangerous.

Using knowledge of character analysis, write a response in which you both:

- Identify one of Kaitlyn's strengths related to character analysis.
- Identify one of Kaitlyn's weaknesses related to character analysis.

Use evidence from Kaitlyn's response to support your answer.

102. Andrew is a first-grade student who is reading a new text for the first time during his guided-reading group. His teacher is completing a running record as he reads to determine which strategies he is using and which types of errors he is making. His running record is shown below.

Sam loved animals. He had a small, spotted puppy that he loved to play with and take for walks. He even taught his puppy some tricks, like how to roll over and shake. Sometimes, he even walked his neighbors' dogs too, just for fun. That was how much he loved animals.

One weekend, Sam's neighbor came running over to his house. Her dog Max had dug a hole under the fence in the backyard and escaped. She was very worried and wanted to know if Sam would help. "Of course," Sam said. "I'll be right there."

Sam knew just what to do. He came out of his house and called for Max in an excited, playful voice. Within seconds, Sam could hear the jingle of Max's collar and knew he was nearby. "Come here, Max! I have a treat for you!" Sam called.

Suddenly, Max darted around the corner and ran right up to Sam. "Good boy," Sam said, as he handed Max a treat. Sam had saved the day.

Key

Deletion	⬭	Repetition	←
Insertion	∧	Self-Correction	©
Short Pause	|	Substitution	then / there
Long Pause	||		

Using knowledge of decoding strategies (e.g., use of semantic, syntactic, and visual cues; use of word recognition strategies; self-monitoring) write a response in which you both:

- Identify one of Andrew's strengths related to decoding words.
- Identify one of Andrew's weaknesses related to decoding words.

Use evidence from Andrew's running record to support your answer.

Answer Key and Explanations for Test #1

Multiple Choice Questions

1. D: Teachers should instruct children in the stages of composition at the same time they are developing skills for forming letters (A), spelling words (B), and generating sentences (C) rather than waiting until after they have developed them. The multifaceted approach allows for more practice in all skills and can help reduce overloading instruction into just one element of language development.

2. A: Tier-two vocabulary words are high-frequency and challenging words that hold a lot of meaning within the text. Because they appear frequently, not knowing their meanings can affect comprehension in multiple texts. High-frequency, concrete nouns are tier-one words. These are usually learned through everyday interactions and do not require explicit instruction. Domain-specific words are tier-three words. While it is beneficial for students to learn and use these words in some academic and professional contexts, they are unlikely to appear in everyday texts. Student-selected words may be used to generate interest in the topic and help students become actively involved in their learning. However, there is no guarantee that students will choose high-frequency words.

3. C: Linguists have found through research studies that not only do preschool children invent spellings for words before they have learned their actual spellings, but moreover, preschoolers from diverse backgrounds often choose the same phonetic spellings, at a rate higher than can be attributed to chance (D) or adult influences (B). Researchers have concluded that through these common invented phonetic spellings, young children demonstrate comprehension—not a lack thereof (A)—of the phonetic characteristics of words and of how conventional word spellings symbolize these characteristics.

4. D: When teaching sight words to students with moderate and severe intellectual disabilities, it has been found that community-based instruction helps promote generalization of skills. Generalization is when a student learns a skill in one context and begins to apply it to new contexts, incorporating it more generally into their thought processes. Students with intellectual disabilities may struggle more to apply skills to broader situations. For instance, they may be successful in learning sight words in the classroom, but they may leave that skill in the classroom instead of applying it out in the community. To help support the generalization process, this student's community should help reinforce that instruction out in the community to demonstrate that the skill can be used in all of life. Choices A and C are incorrect because they are not found to be as effective for students with disabilities as augmented practices, such as community-based instruction. Choice B is incorrect, as orthography refers to the actual writing of letters and less to do with reading skills, and especially sight words. Some teaching strategies may pair reading and writing skills together, but this is even less common for sight word instruction.

5. D: Restricted vocabulary, improper grammar patterns, and using word meanings incorrectly are symptoms of a language disorder, along with inability to follow directions, express ideas, or understand the meanings of seen or heard words, and difficulty getting others to understand intended communications, etc. Omitting, adding, substituting, or distorting phonemes (A) are symptoms of an articulation disorder. Repetitions, prolongations, and blocks (B) are symptoms of stuttering, a fluency or rate and rhythm disorder. Difficulties with loudness, pitch, or tone quality (C) are symptoms of a voice disorder. These three are all types of speech disorders.

6. D: In the typical structure of a guided reading lesson as an alternative structure for differentiating instruction, the teacher selects the text to read (A) by difficulty levels appropriate to the students. The teacher introduces the text to students before they begin reading (B). After students read with guidance from the teacher (e.g.; support for word decoding and identification, comprehension, meaning construction, error correction, etc.), the class discusses the text (C) meaning. In guided reading lessons, teachers also instruct students in applying specific strategies to reading activities (D).

7. C: Word families are an effective strategy for teaching CVCe words. Once students have determined the sound made by the last three letters using knowledge of the silent *e* rule, they can identify other rhyming words within the same family by changing the first letter. This increases the number of words they can easily decode. Because these words have a silent letter that affects the vowel sound, covering parts of the word, chunking, and blending are not as effective.

8. D: A phonogram is a letter or group of letters that represent a single sound. In the word *light*, the letters *igh* together produce one sound, /ī/. The longest phonogram in choice A contains two letters, *ck*. Choice B contains only one-letter phonograms. The longest phonogram in choice C contains two letters, *ea*, which together produce the /ē/ sound.

9. B: By assigning students a task that will require them to focus on key pieces of information in the text, the teacher is helping students set a purpose for reading. She is not asking the students why the author wrote the book, which would encourage them to consider the author's purpose. Choice C is incorrect because she did not ask students what they already know about the topic of water conservation. Choice D is incorrect because she did not ask students to compare or contrast this text with any other texts they have read.

10. B: Students gain deeper understanding and critical engagement by being exposed to various perspectives and learning to evaluate and compare sources relative to a topic. A is incorrect because it claims that direct learning about source types is the only benefit, which ignores the critical thinking benefits that students also gain. C is incorrect because the statement "how to build topic-related positions using evidence is not among benefits" is false; students do learn to construct evidence-based positions. D is incorrect because students gain insight into both selecting and evaluating sources, not just selection as implied by the option.

11. A: Emergent readers are learning concepts of print, and they benefit from having text in familiar places to assist with tracking and directionality. They are still developing phonics skills and may rely on one or more cueing systems, so picture support is important for determining unknown words. Emergent readers also benefit from simple sentence structure and repetition, which assists them with guessing unknown words. The features in choice B are more appropriate for early readers who are beginning to read more complex texts and are able to use phonics skills and multiple cueing systems rather than relying on picture clues. The features in choice C are more appropriate for transitional readers who are able to read a wider range of genres and text structures independently. Choice D is appropriate for fluent readers who are able to read complex, technical, and abstract texts independently.

12. C: Playing language games helps younger students to develop phonological and phonemic awareness while having fun, which better motivates them to learn. For example, teachers can ask children to see how many different rhyming words they can produce by changing the initial sound of a given word (e.g., cat, hat, mat, fat, sat, pat, bat, rat, vat, etc.). Hence manipulating phonemes in words not only can be taught in different ways, it *should* be taught using a variety of approaches and materials. Such approaches include utilizing informal interactions: these provide a meaningful context for learning, which is more important than systematically controlling their occurrence. Younger students are more apt to identify alliteration they hear before they can read. (They may be taught visual recognition of the same letter beginning multiple words in a sentence, but this does not develop phonemic awareness, which develops and/or can be taught even earlier.)

13. D: Teachers can effectively use conversation with young children to teach them grammar and vocabulary in natural contexts. When a child uses a word incorrectly in conversation, for example, the teacher can recast the word to show its correct usage (e.g. if the child says someone was driven to the hospital "in the siren," the teacher can respond, "They took her to the hospital in an ambulance with the siren sounding?"). When children speak in incomplete sentences, teachers can and should extend them by repeating what the child said in a complete sentence (A). Young children enjoy talking about themselves most (B); about what they are doing; and about familiar people, objects, and events (C) that access their knowledge. Lessons are not better than conversation for teaching grammar and vocabulary, especially for children who are too young to "sit still and listen" and learn better through natural interactions like conversations.

14. D: Teacher-directed reading is one method of instructing the whole class together. In this method, the teacher often has a passage or patterned sentences that the teacher will use to model reading practices to the class. In the "pre-reading" phase, the teacher should give the students supportive information, such as the title, topic, or new key words that the student will encounter. In the "during reading" phase, the teacher will model a sentence, then ask the class to repeat the sentence, following along with the modeled decoding and tracking techniques. In the "after reading" phase, the teacher should ask the students to apply and practice this pattern more independently on their own to gain experience decoding and tracking. In this method, the "during reading" phase takes place actively as a class, which is not represented by the other choices. Independent or partner practice usually takes place in the "after reading" phase of this type of activity.

15. D: The surrounding sentences will help the student determine word meaning; e.g., "The farmer will *sow* the vegetable seeds" vs. "She was like a *sow* nursing piglets." The sentence syntax and grammatical structure (B) will help by indicating parts of speech, which differ by meaning in this case. In the two example sentences given earlier, the first meaning is a verb, and the second is a noun. The verb has an auxiliary verb and direct object, and the noun has an article. Dictionary definitions (C) will help if the student does not already know one or both word meanings, or if the definition includes word-in-sentence examples resembling the text sentence(s).

16. B: The floss rule states that the letters *f*, *l*, and *s* are doubled when they follow a short vowel sound. In choice B, the *s* is doubled because it follows an /ă/ sound. The remaining choices contain short vowel sounds but do not have a doubled *f*, *l*, or *s*.

17. A: Critiques of final projects (e.g., art projects, research projects, music recitals) are examples of summative assessments because they measure student achievement following instruction. Oral question-and-answer sessions (b) are examples of formative assessments because they can be brief, can be administered often, and can be used to monitor ongoing student progress. Running records (c) keep track of student performance in real time (e.g., oral reading fluency) and are also formative assessments. Pop quizzes (d) are typically short, may be given at any time, and cover the most recent information during instruction; thus, they are also examples of formative assessments.

18. C: Phonic awareness, or phonics (A), is knowing how alphabet letters correspond to speech sounds and vice versa. Awareness of phonetics (B) is knowing specific individual variations in speech sounds within a language. Phonemic (C) awareness is knowing the standard, general, or typical speech sounds used in a language. Alphabetic (D) awareness is knowing the written letter symbols representing speech sounds. (The alphabetic principle is the basis of phonics.)

19. C: Instruction in phonemic awareness should be individualized to address each child's specific needs. While it is a basic skill and the main prerequisite in reading instruction, this does not mean it should be standardized across students (A), because children start school with very different levels of phonemic awareness (B). Instruction in phonemic awareness is critical because phonemic awareness strongly predicts future reading ability (D).

20. C: The WWC recommends differentiated instruction to students in all three tiers of RTI programs. However, it recommends intensive instruction (A) only for students in Tiers 2 and 3 (20-40 minutes three to five times weekly for Tier 2, daily for Tier 3). Small-group instruction (B) is common to Tiers 2 and 3 to enable more intensive intervention; Tier 1 typically encompasses independent, paired, small-group, and whole-class instruction. While the WWC panel concedes that the ideal primary-grades classroom reading instruction would be evidence-based (D), it finds insufficient research evidence on which to base it.

21. C: One-half of the class receives signs showing vocabulary words, which are probably used as root words. The remaining students are split into two general groups: those with prefixes on their signs and those with suffixes. The best approach is to get the students moving, listening, and talking in order to solidify their understanding of how roots, suffixes, and prefixes work together to make new meanings out of various root words. This approach also allows the students to participate in a game in a group context, making the activity more fun and engaging.

22. B: Automaticity refers to the ability to recognize printed words quickly and effortlessly. Because sight word practice helps increase the number of words students can recognize quickly and effortlessly, it builds automaticity. Sight words can be difficult to decode using typical phonics rules. Phonemic awareness and phonological awareness involve identifying and manipulating sounds rather than reading printed words.

23. D: Meg is creating an expository research report to share information about the costs involved in pet ownership. The information she obtained from the website contains opinions rather than facts, which is signaled using phrases like "I believe" and "most loyal." It is important for Meg to differentiate between the two so that she can support her topic with facts. While Meg will likely need to synthesize information from multiple sources, choose an appropriate text structure, and include text features, the information provided indicates that differentiating between facts and opinions is an immediate need in order for Meg to successfully complete the assignment.

24. B: Although concurrent learning disabilities and disorders are common, e.g., attentional, receptive, and expressive language difficulties often coexist, an expressive language disorder (A) would have the most direct impact on a student's speaking and writing performance and instruction. A receptive language disorder (B) would have the most direct impact on a student's listening and reading skills. An articulation disorder (C) would have the most direct impact on a student's correct or intelligible speech production or pronunciation. A movement disorder (D) could have impacts on speech production, but by itself it should not affect language or reading development.

25. B: *Activating* is the term experts use to identify the reading strategy whereby the reader activates prior knowledge and applies it to the new information in reading to construct meaning from it. *Inferring* is a strategy whereby the reader combines what the text states explicitly with what it does not state but implies, and combines these both with what s/he already knows to draw inferences. *Questioning* is the reading strategy whereby the reader engages in "learning dialogues" with the text, author, classmates, and teachers to ask and answer questions about the text. *Summarizing* is the reading strategy whereby the reader paraphrases or restates what s/he perceives as the text's meaning.

26. A: Most adults can understand the relationship between oral and written language: components of oral language have representational symbols that can be written and decoded. However, most normally-developing children acquire spoken language first and begin to develop reading and writing skills as they approach school-age. Many children are first exposed to the concept of written language when an adult introduces books or other written texts. However, a child's ability to read and write develops over time and is dependent on the development of physiological processes such as hearing, sight, and fine motor skills for writing. Written language development also typically requires direct instruction. Most children must be taught to read and write and rarely learn these skills simply by observing others.

27. D: For reading instruction, flexible small groups can be created by student skill levels within a classroom or across classrooms. Grouping within the classroom is heterogeneous (A); grouping across all classrooms at one grade level is more homogeneous (B). For within-classroom groups, schools can bring in additional materials, staff, and other resources (C) during reading block times for small-group instruction. For across-classroom groups, depending on student needs, students' original classroom teacher or another teacher may give them reading instruction (D).

28. C: By using varied books for read-alouds and shared reading activities, the teacher can ensure that students are exposed to a variety of genres and text structures. During these activities, the teacher can also help students explore the features of these texts. Choice A can be used to support this instruction, but the posters alone are not as likely to be effective as actually exploring varied types of books. Choices B and D do not ensure that all students will actually explore different types of texts.

29. A: By highlighting each word as it is read, children begin to understand that reading goes from left to right, which is known as directionality. They also begin to understand that each spoken word corresponds with one printed word, which is known as one-to-one correspondence. Letter and word concepts refer to an understanding that words are made up of individual letters. Book awareness and book handling skills include knowing how to hold a book and turn the pages correctly. Word spacing is the understanding that you include spaces between words on the page. The relationship between text and illustrations refers to an understanding that pictures provide clues about the meaning of the story.

30. B: The word *manuscript* has the Latin root *manu*, meaning *hand*, and the Latin root *script*, meaning *write*. By recognizing these roots, a reader can determine that the word *manuscript* means something written by hand. *Trees* does not contain any Greek or Latin roots that could be identified to determine the word meaning. *Butterfly* is a compound word, but the *butter* component does not assist with the meaning of the compound word. Although *ceiling* has the inflectional ending *-ing*, it is unlikely to assist students with identifying the meaning of the word when added to *ceil*.

31. A: The type or pattern of error most damaging to reading proficiency is substituting words with similar appearances or spelling but completely different meanings, because this shows a lack of reading for meaning. Substituting synonyms (B) shows some comprehension of word meaning. Substituting like parts of speech (C) shows some comprehension of grammar and syntax. Substituting correct words or closer approximations for errors based on information from the sentence context (D) shows skills in both reading for meaning and self-correction.

32. A: The common spelling *-tion* reflects the frequently recurring pattern of reliable non-phonetic spelling patterns, because letters and phonemes do not match phonically. Recurring phonetic spelling patterns (B), contrastingly, are common spelling patterns with letters matching speech sounds. Etymological extensions to patterns (C) add to phonetic spelling patterns with spellings based on word origins. Spellings for Greek and Latin stems (D) help students learn how to spell many English words sharing common roots, whose spellings may be phonetic or non-phonetic (just as the Latin suffix *-tion* is non-phonetic).

33. B: Students may be surprised to learn that only 10 percent of our communication involves words, whereas 90 percent of it involves vocal tones, facial expressions, gestures, and body language. Informing them of this statistic can help impress upon them the weight that nonverbal aspects carry in our communication, which in turn can engage their interest in developing their nonverbal communication skills.

34. C: Using context clues can help the reader determine the meanings of many unknown words quickly and also contribute to reading comprehension. Asking a classmate for the meanings of words may work in the short term, but it does not help the reader develop independent reading strategies, and there may not always be another person present while reading. Looking up the unknown words later may result in the student missing words that are critical to the meaning of the text, negatively affecting comprehension. Similarly, while skipping over the unknown words may result in sentences that appear to make sense, the missing words may play important roles in the meaning.

35. A: An effective way to teach students the difference between denotation and connotation is to provide example sentences and have students choose a given word that best expresses the connotation of a highlighted word in each sentence. For example, to show the connotation of the word *challenge*, an example sentence "This is one of the many challenges that must be faced in order to solve the problem" could be given, and students could choose whether the connotation suggested by "challenges" in this case was "threats," "obstacles," "criticisms," or "setbacks." This instructional strategy is summarized in choice A, which is the correct answer. Since words generally have denotations and may or may not have connotations depending on their use, a Venn diagram would be misleading, and choice B is incorrect. Choice C is also incorrect, as highlighting words in a passage would not require students to distinguish between denotations and connotations, nor even to identify the exact connotations of words in context. Choice D would not be logical, since not all words have an emotional connotation, and the definition alone will be of little use for determining the connotations of a specific use of a word.

36. D: When readers visualize, they use the clues and details in the stories to form mental pictures in their minds. When students draw a setting based on how they imagined it from the description in the story, they are visualizing. Predicting refers to making guesses about the text before reading. Inferring refers to using clues in the story to determine the meaning when it is not explicitly stated. Summarizing refers to retelling the main events of the story.

37. A: During interactive writing experiences, teachers and students work together to create writing pieces. Teachers and students share the writing utensils, with teachers guiding the students as they record their thoughts. In shared writing experiences, teachers record students' thoughts on paper. Students do not help with the writing. In independent writing, students utilize the strategies they have learned to complete writing pieces independently. Guided writing occurs when teachers work with small groups of strategically grouped students on targeted writing skills.

38. D: Researchers have found whole-group instruction often uses materials and time most efficiently. However, it is also most easily tuned out by students (B), frequently by those needing the most help, and allows greater student passivity (C). Solutions include intensifying classroom routines to be more useful for more students. Although whole-group assignment of the same text is harder for students reading below grade level, research finds difficult texts can accelerate their reading development, given effective teacher scaffolding (D).

39. B: Figurative language involves the use of words and phrases that differ from their literal meanings. The expression in choice B means that the wet snow covered the ground, not that it was literally a wet blanket. It is an example of a metaphor, which is one type of figurative language. The other options contain some descriptive words and phrases, but they have literal meanings.

40. D: Decoding depends on an understanding of letter–sound relationships. As soon as a child understands enough letters and their correspondent sounds to read a few words, decoding should be introduced. The act of decoding involves first recognizing the sounds individual letters and letter groups in a word make and then blending the sounds to read the word.

41. D: When students ask themselves how the information in a text they are reading fits with what they already know, they are relating the text to their own prior knowledge, which increases their reading comprehension. Students should not only ask themselves what kinds of "expert questions" fit the subject matter of the text (A)—e.g., classification, physical, and chemical properties are typical question topics in science; genre, character, plot, and theme are typical of literature questions; sequence, cause-and-effect, and comparison-contrast questions are typical of history—but also what questions the material brings up for them personally (B). It is necessary and important for students to ask themselves continually how each text portion relates to its chapter's main ideas (C) as they read to optimize their reading comprehension and retention.

42. C: The act of decoding involves first recognizing the sounds individual letters and letter groups make and then blending the sounds to read the word. A child decoding the word *spin*, for example, would first pronounce *sp/i/n* as individual sound units. She then would repeat the sounds, smoothly blending them. Because decoding involves understanding letters and their sounds, it is sometimes known as the alphabetic principle.

43. D: Found within a text, a glossary is a list of key vocabulary words or technical terms used specifically in that text, along with their definitions. This will most efficiently help students find the meanings of unfamiliar terminology. Encyclopedias (A) provide extensive information about people, places, and things rather than word definitions. Dictionaries (B) give definitions of all or most words in the language, which would be less efficient for looking up words or terms specific to one text. A thesaurus (C) provides synonyms for all or most words defined in dictionaries.

44. B: The student's responses include random strings of letters that do not correlate with the sounds in the spoken words. Additionally, she has represented the /c/ sound at the beginning of each word differently in her responses. Understanding that letters make predictable sounds is part of the alphabetic principle. Her three-letter responses indicate that she has some phonological awareness skills. She knows there are three sounds in each word, but she is not aware of which letters are used to represent each sound. Teaching phonics generalizations will be more helpful after the student has developed an awareness of the alphabetic principle and consistently matches letters to their sounds.

45. C: Word walls should be flexible, meaning words can be removed if students have mastered them, and new words can be added as they are introduced. It is also helpful if the words on word walls are removable, so students can take them to other areas of the room when they are using them for reading and writing activities. Choice A is incorrect because there are many types of words that can be included on word walls, including content-related vocabulary, academic vocabulary, and high-frequency words. Choice B is incorrect because words can be displayed on word walls for different reasons. For example, words containing the same root can be displayed to help students see relationships between words. Because word walls can contain different types of words and be used for different purposes, they can be helpful for readers in all stages of reading development.

46. B: Metacognition refers to thinking about one's own thinking. Proficient readers use metacognitive skills to self-monitor their own understanding and make corrections when necessary. Making predictions, and then later assessing and revising them if necessary, demonstrates use of metacognitive skills. The other options require students to recall and/or analyze information, but they do not ask students to reflect on their own thinking.

47. C: Close reading involves multiple readings of the same text, with students analyzing different layers of the text each time. Students read the texts independently, with no picture walks or pre-teaching beforehand. Close reading is designed to help students become actively involved in the reading process and develop deeper understandings of what they have read. Guided reading is done in small groups, with teachers focusing on targeted skills based on students' needs. Additionally, picture walks are often done in guided reading groups. SQ3R is a strategy often used to help students comprehend textbook readings. It involves students doing a quick survey of the text, followed by identification of questions about the text. Students then read the text, recite it in their own words, and review the main idea. Scanning involves reading quickly to identify specific information.

48. D: During informal assessment for print concept awareness, a young child who cannot read yet should be able to identify where the teacher would start reading the book aloud (A), the title of the book (B), the meaning of a period as the end of a sentence in the book (C), a word in or on the book as well as a letter within a word in the book and spaces between words in the book, and the front, back, and directionality of the book.

49. A: The process of actively constructing meaning from reading is interactive, in that it involves the text itself, the person reading it, and the setting in which the reading is done. These three elements influence each other, and this is the concept indicated by the term *interactive* in the question, so choice A is correct. Choice B is a better definition of the *strategic* aspect of the process. Choice C and Choice D are better definitions of the *adaptable* aspect of the process.

50. C: Writing their own examples of metaphors requires students to apply their knowledge. Identifying and underlining metaphors assesses the comprehension level of Bloom's taxonomy, and defining a metaphor assesses the knowledge level. Critiquing the author's use of metaphors assesses the evaluation level.

51. B: If a young child cannot break down a word into its component phonemes, this represents a deficit in phonological and/or phonemic awareness, which will cause reading difficulties. Likewise, the inability to do the reverse and blend individual phonemes to form words (C) is a sign the child will have trouble reading. Young children with good phonological and phonemic awareness can both identify *and* form rhymes (A). To learn to read well, they should also be able to count the syllables in a word and use phonetic spellings (by sound) for new/unfamiliar words (D).

52. D: Reciprocal teaching is an activity in which students gradually take over the role of the teacher in small groups to discuss texts. The students lead discussions focused on four main reading strategies: summarizing, questioning, predicting, and clarifying. The remaining options are also reading strategies, but they are not typically the focus of reciprocal teaching activities.

53. A: While there is no consensus among experts as to any universal sequence of instruction for teaching the alphabetic principle through phonics instruction, they do agree that, to enable children to start reading words as soon as possible, the highest-utility relationships should be introduced earliest. For example, the letters *m, a, p, t,* and *s* are all used frequently, whereas the *x* in *box*, the sound of *ey* in *they*, and the letter *a* when pronounced as it is in *want* have lower-utility letter-sound correspondences. Important considerations for the alphabetic principle are to teach letter-sound correspondences in isolation, not in word contexts; to teach them explicitly; to give students opportunities to practice letter-sound relationships within their other daily lessons, not only separately; and to include cumulative reviews of relationships taught earlier along with new ones in practice opportunities.

54. C: Although the names of the stages vary, readers generally progress through four stages of reading development: emergent reading, early reading, transitional reading, and fluent reading. The name "transitional phase" refers to the transition from having to learn to read to being able to read to learn. The greatest need for students in the transitional phase is to be able to navigate unfamiliar words in passages. To do so, they need to be able to use morphology (C), such as prefixes, suffixes, and parts of speech, to help determine the meaning of newly-encountered words. Students in the transitional stage should already have many sight words memorized (A) and have letter/sound correspondence (D) nearly mastered. Identifying themes in abstract texts (B) is probably beyond the capability of students in the transitional stage.

55. D: The CALLA is a content-based approach to language instruction that integrates academic learning strategies that students require to participate in mainstream English-speaking classrooms. It includes objectives for content, language, and learning strategies, and it allows teachers to plan lessons using content based on themes or formats using sheltered content.

56. D: A word wall uses visual illustrations of vocabulary words and the concepts they represent, and includes additional words, concepts, and pictures related to the main words and pictures to enrich vocabulary and relational thinking. The teacher would be most responsible for creating the word wall, using it in lessons/activities, and instructing/assisting young children in its use. The children themselves can and will repeatedly sing the same familiar song (A) and repeat the same rhymes and chants (B), which enhance vocabulary development for both native English-speaking and ESL students. Stories (C) may be read live by teachers, or readings may be recorded. Either way, the children play the same role of listening to repeated readings.

57. B: According to accepted educational measurement principles, teachers should design tests to measure ALL their learning objectives (including through a combination of tests), not just a few (A). While tests' primary uses are diagnosis or evaluation, another principle is that an important additional use is instructional (B), by enabling teachers to identify and re-teach important information students have missed, stimulate additional topic discussions, and integrate instruction and evaluation. Criterion-referenced tests measure achievement relative to preset criteria; norm-referenced tests enable group comparisons (C). Test validity and reliability are both equally necessary (D).

58. D: A glossary contains an alphabetized list of important vocabulary words found in a text, along with their meanings. It is similar to a dictionary. It would be the most helpful text feature for a student to use to determine the meanings of the content-related vocabulary words in the text. The table of contents helps the reader identify which pages contain which topics in the text. Headings help the reader determine the main idea of each section of the text. The index is an alphabetized list of topics in the text, along with the page numbers on which they can be found.

59. A: Research finds one helpful instructional strategy for ELL student language acquisition is to have them explain and/or retell what the teacher just said to their classmates. This not only ensures their comprehension, but it also gives them practice analyzing the English they hear, restating/paraphrasing English, and communicating to others in spoken English. Teachers should incorporate visual aids: studies show supplementing verbal input visually helps ELLs understand concepts in subject content areas as they are learning a foreign language. Research finds that students cannot grasp abstract concepts as readily in a foreign language, so teachers should give them concrete objects, pictures, and the like to illustrate and demonstrate ideas as students gradually transition from concrete to abstract in a new language. Teachers can arrange for ELLs to signal when they don't understand; they also closely observe ELLs, and if they do not indicate or demonstrate understanding, they should elaborate by summarizing, paraphrasing, and giving synonyms.

60. C: Of the options, teaching main ideas or strategic integration of ideas refer more to reading comprehension than to phonics and decoding. The best option given is choice B, systematic, explicit, and direct instruction in phonics, as phonics is not as much of an acquired language skill as it is a taught language skill. Explicit instruction in early phonics instruction is most effective. As a child becomes more fluent, increased incidental exposure (choice A) can help to improve fluency in decoding skills. Choice D represents a blended activity, using features of both explicit and implicit instruction and should prove effective in helping students understand phonics and decode words.

61. B: The Directed Reading Thinking Activity, i.e., DRTA, is a comprehension strategy that helps students ask questions about text, make predictions about it, and then read to confirm or deny predictions. Gist (A) is a comprehension strategy that helps students identify the main idea, paraphrase, and summarize text. The Fishbowl (C) is an instructional strategy that helps students participate in classroom discussions. Cornell Notes (D) is an instructional strategy that helps students take notes, read text carefully, organize, and summarize information.

62. D: Encoding is the process of translating sounds to print using knowledge of letter/sound relationships. The student is listening to each sound in the word *stop* and remembering which letter makes that sound before writing it on paper. Decoding involves using knowledge of letter/sound relationships to translate written words into speech. Blending and segmenting are both phonological awareness skills that involve manipulating spoken sounds. They do not involve identifying the letters that make the sounds.

63. C: Phonological awareness skills are developed over the course of several years, and where there may be overlap in development, recognition of rhymes (C) comes rather early, between 2 and 3 years of age. Recognition of alliteration comes shortly thereafter, whereas syllables are recognizable between 3 and 6 years old. Phonic understanding is much more complex, as it requires a coordination between auditory and visual understanding.

64. B: The Four-Part Processing Model for word recognition provides a framework for understanding how individuals acquire reading skills. According to this model, word recognition, and eventually, automaticity, occurs when four processors within the brain work together simultaneously. The phonological processor is responsible for differentiating, understanding, and attaching meaning to words and sounds in spoken language. Further, the orthographic processor works with the phonological processor to recognize and recall the meaning of written words as well as the sounds produced by written language. Through the context processor, individuals recall background knowledge and construct meaning using clues such as visual representations and surrounding words in a sentence. The meaning processor refers to one's knowledge of vocabulary, multiple meanings of words, and semantics. Helping young children become skilled readers requires that instruction incorporate all four components in the processing model. In this situation, displaying new vocabulary in a written sentence strip with corresponding images simultaneously stimulates the orthographic, context, and meaning processors. By reading the sentence aloud to the class, the teacher addresses the phonological processor, thus incorporating all components of the Four-Part Processing Model for word recognition.

65. C: Daniel has identified only external character traits, or traits related to the character's appearance. He has not identified any internal traits, or traits related to the character's thoughts, feelings, words, or actions. An appropriate next step would be to help Daniel differentiate between the two types of traits and find examples of each in the text. The remaining options would require Daniel to identify internal traits using textual evidence. For example, it would be difficult to describe how the character has changed throughout the story without using any internal traits to describe her at different points in the story. Similarly, it would be difficult to label the role she plays or compare her with other characters without using any internal traits to support the responses.

66. B: Typically, guided practice follows modeling. Independent practice and application would then follow the guided practice, and generalization would come last. Feedback should be provided throughout multiple levels of instruction, particularly during the practice phases.

67. C: Cognitivism suggests that new information should be broken up into manageable chunks with ample opportunities for practice and feedback if learning is to occur. Presenting too much information at one time can result in cognitive overload. Choice A represents social learning theory, which highlights the importance of social interactions in learning. Choice B represents behaviorism, which focuses on the role that reinforcement plays in the continuance of certain behaviors. Choice D represents constructivism, which highlights the role of students being actively involved in the learning process.

68. B: The signal words in (A) indicate a sequential, chronological text structure. The signal words in (B) indicate a descriptive text structure. The signal words in (C) indicate a comparison-contrast text structure. The signal words in (D) indicate a cause-and-effect text structure.

69. B: Children tend to confuse letters that are visually similar, such as *b* and *d*. Introducing them separately helps to prevent confusion between them. While there are differing theories on which order to use when introducing letters, generally alphabetical order is not the most effective. Letters are sometimes grouped for instruction by the difficulty of their sounds, their formation, or relevance to the students (such as introducing letters in their names first). Letters may be introduced in small groups to allow students to practice them in context, and both letter sounds and letter names are important for students to learn.

70. B: Research finds that the single greatest change in classroom instruction for improving student learning and achievement is feedback, which students and teachers get best from formative assessments. Summative assessments are best for comparison (A) of students to normative student samples, classes to statewide/nationwide classes at the same grade level, and schools to other schools, but they do not give such immediate feedback during ongoing instruction (C). Although they yield more individual student data, formative assessments are typically informal and not standardized and hence are not used to make comparisons (D) the way that standardized summative assessments are.

71. C: In the five established spelling development stages, in Stage 1 (A) children learn the difference between drawing and writing, letter formation, writing directionality, and some letter-sound correspondences, but not the alphabetic principle. In Stage 3 (B), they learn long and r-controlled vowel spelling patterns, more advanced consonant patterns, diphthongs, and other less familiar vowel patterns. In Stage 2 (C), they learn the alphabetic principle, i.e., that letters represent corresponding speech sounds, and they also learn consonant and short vowel sounds, consonant blends, and digraphs. In Stage 4 (D), they learn grammatical suffixes and rules, syllabication, and homophones.

72. B: Although the illustrations themselves are visual images, using the information available from them to inform reading is not using a visual cue (A). Word appearance and length, familiar-looking phrases, and word-initial letters or phonemes—i.e., visual aspects of the verbal text itself—are examples of visual cues. Because the student uses information from illustrations, he or she uses a meaning cue (B). A structural cue (C) would involve using knowledge of syntax (sentence structure) to inform correct reading. A graphophonic cue (D) would involve using knowledge of sound-to-letter correspondences.

73. C: When assessing pre-reading skills in typically developing preschoolers, they should be able to demonstrate some benchmarks. Though they are somewhat flexible, most pre-schoolers are able to demonstrate knowledge of the full-alphabet, often in song-form. They are usually able to count from 1 to 10. They are often able to recognize some sight words, though these are not usually tied to phonetic skills at this age. Preschoolers may recognize some words as whole units, but it is unlikely that they will be able to sound out words from their letter components. Preschoolers do usually have a good grasp of similar sounds and can usually distinguish between rhyming word pairs and non-rhyming word pairs.

74. D: To establish literacy-rich environments, experts advise teachers to label everything in the classroom with words and pictures. This helps students connect all things and places with written language representing them, rather than distracts (A). Directions, calendars, signs, and schedules are not only everyday organizational tools; teachers can also have students use them to understand everyday language use (B). Word and picture labels should not be avoided, but should include textured materials, Braille, large fonts, etc., enabling access for visually impaired students (C). If teachers and students redesign classrooms to reflect themes or books they have studied, students "live in" lessons, experiencing them directly (D).

75. B: Experts advise teachers not to advance to new letter-sound association material too quickly (A) with students who have recall or naming difficulty, because they need extensive practice or they will forget the associations they were taught before (B). Overlearning is recommended for these students (C). They should perform not only perfectly, but automatically to enable good decoding and encoding. Teachers should not focus only on new material, but combine reviewing earlier instruction with new instruction in every lesson (D).

76. B: Closed syllables, i.e., those ending in a consonant and typically preceded by a short vowel sound (e.g., *fabric, rabbit*), are the syllable pattern type used most often, so they should be taught first, before open (A) or other syllable types. To teach from simpler to more complex, instruction in decoding multisyllabic words should also teach strategies for syllabication divisions after introducing multisyllabic words, not before (C). Also, teachers should teach spelling generalizations based on syllable pattern types, not vice versa (D).

77. A: Formative assessments are given during a unit of study to identify students' existing knowledge and gaps. They are used to guide instruction by helping a teacher determine if current instructional strategies are successful or if changes need to be made. Summative assessments are given at the end of a unit or after another extended period of time. Norm-referenced tests are standardized tests that compare students' performances to sample groups of similar students. Screening assessments are used to identify students who may be at risk for future academic difficulties and may benefit from interventions.

78. C: Following the text with a pointer and pointing to each word with a finger both help with the concept of directionality. Directionality includes the understanding that you read from left to right, from top to bottom, and from the left page to the right page. Spacing refers to the understanding that you include spaces between words and between sentences. Book orientation refers to knowing how to hold and open a book correctly. Letter concepts include recognizing letters and knowing the difference between a letter and a word.

79. B: Pointing to each word as it is read aloud will help students understand the relationship between the printed and spoken word. They will begin to understand that the meaning of the story is contained in the text. Showing students where to begin reading on each page and how to complete a return sweep will help them track the text appropriately. Asking students what they see in the pictures encourages the use of the semantic cueing system.

80. C: Tier-two words are words that are used with high frequency across a variety of disciplines or words with multiple meanings. They are characteristic of mature language users. Knowing these words is crucial to attaining an acceptable level of reading comprehension and communication skills.

81. C: Differentiation involves instructing students according to their individual strengths and needs as indicated by assessment data. Instruction should challenge students in their zones of proximal development to ensure that they learn new skills without becoming bored or frustrated. Choice C provides both groups of students with words at their appropriate levels of difficulty. Choice A involves simply giving extra words to highly proficient readers. If they have already mastered decoding CVC words, decoding many of them is likely to be boring and unchallenging. Similarly, if highly proficient readers have already mastered CVC words, writing them in sentences is likely to be less challenging or beneficial than learning to decode more complex words. While paired experiences can be beneficial in many situations, choice D does not provide more challenging words for the highly proficient readers, nor does it ensure that they will scaffold the struggling readers rather than decoding the words for them.

82. B: By taking a whole word and breaking it into its individual sounds, the students are practicing segmenting. Blending is the opposite process, where students take individual sounds and combine them to form a whole word. Phoneme isolation refers to identifying the beginning, middle, or ending sound in a word. Phoneme identification refers to identifying a common sound in a group of words with either the same beginning, middle, or ending sound.

83. D: The concept in question is known as language transfer, also known as L1 interference, in which language features from the first language affects the acquisition of a second language. This is particularly noteworthy in language features that exist in one language, but not in the other. For instance, in English, plural nouns are usually marked by adding *-s* to the end of the word, whereas Chinese does not make use of a plural indicator. This grammatical feature, therefore, is commonly difficult to accurately acquire. Regarding the options in the question, the Chinese written language is ideographic rather than alphabetic (A)—that is, its written symbols represent concepts visually rather than being letters representing speech sounds. Also, the fact that Spanish is much more phonetically regular than English (B) (i.e., many more words are pronounced the same way as they are spelled than in English) contributes different effects to ELL students' English-language literacy development. Therefore, choice C is incorrect.

84. D: Emergent readers are beginning to understand concepts of print and read very simple texts independently. Using short, repetitive sentences with picture support allows students to read these texts independently and practice concepts of print, such as one-to-one correspondence and understanding that the print carries the meaning. The other options contain predictable structures or characters that could assist emergent readers with comprehension if the texts are read aloud, but they would be too complex for students to decode independently.

85. D: Research-based vocabulary instruction findings show that children need ample word repetition, but not through drilling. Multiple exposures to the same words in different contexts are more effective. Multiple and repeated exposures are important because children do not learn vocabulary through only one or two exposures to a new word. Research finds that they do not simply learn vocabulary in texts indirectly from reading; instead, teachers must give them direct instruction in the new vocabulary words they find in their texts.

86. A: Spoken language is generally less formal and more conversational in tone than written language. As a result, syntax is more relaxed, and there is greater flexibility in word order. Spoken language also tends to contain a mixture of sentences and fragments. For example, a typical conversation among friends may contain several shifts between speakers, along with brief comments and replies rather than fully developed sentences. Body language plays a greater role in spoken language, as it can either affirm or contradict the meaning of the spoken words. For example, if a person says they are looking forward to something, yet they are frowning and avoiding eye contact, the recipient of the message may not believe the speaker is sincere.

87. A: Keyword substitution involves replacing a phoneme in key words of song lyrics or other common phrases and sayings. This gives children practice in wordplay and is entertaining. After singing the revised lyrics, teachers can discuss with children how changing one phoneme changed the meanings of words in the song. Changing /r/ to /ʃ/ in "Row, row, row your boat" (A) is an example. Choice B transposes the two nouns in the lyric. Keyword substitution refers to substituting different phonemes in key words, not substituting different whole words or transposing existing words. Choice C quotes the first line of Lewis Carroll's poem "Jabberwocky," famous for using many nonsense words. Choice D uses the same song as choice A but deletes initial phonemes rather than substituting.

88. A: Generally, the sequence of instruction is as follows: explicit instruction, modeling, guided practice, independent practice and application, and generalization. The teacher has already completed the explicit instruction, modeling, and guided practice portion of the sequence. Therefore, independent practice and application would come next. Choice A best demonstrates this stage of instruction. Reteaching is only necessary if informal or formal assessments indicate that students did not learn the skill after the first attempt at instruction, which is not indicated in this example. Choice C represents the generalization stage, which typically comes after students have had independent practice with the skill. A formal assessment, such as a test, should also come after independent practice opportunities.

89. D: Choice A indicates that the student is using semantic cues to construct meaning. Choice B indicates the student is using syntactic cues to construct meaning. Choice C indicates the student is using phonics cues to construct meaning. Choice D indicates the student is using (visual) graphophonic cues, i.e., whether word spellings match their phonetic sounds.

90. A: Alphabetic principle is the understanding that each letter of the alphabet makes a predictable sound. Students are practicing this by repeating the letter name and sound each week. Concepts of print are conventions used to convey meaning in text. Examples include knowing how to hold a book and track text correctly. Phonological awareness is the ability to identify and manipulate sounds in words. It does not involve letter/sound relationships. Automaticity refers to the ability to recognize whole words quickly and effortlessly.

91. B: Based on the research literature, guidelines for phonemic awareness instruction include using analysis of data from phonemic awareness assessments to drive instruction, because only a minority of students requires explicit instruction in phonemic awareness (A). However, effective instruction in phonemic awareness does explicitly label phonemes (C), as well as demonstrates phoneme blending and segmenting processes. Effective phonemic awareness instruction is also differentiated to account for individual differences, including various levels of scaffolding for different students (D).

92. A: A key tenet of Marie Clay's theory is the understanding that children take different paths to becoming readers based on differences in prior knowledge and experiences. As a result, teachers must meet the needs of individual learners rather than using a one-size-fits-all approach to instruction. Choice B is incorrect because Clay's theory also explains the interrelationship between reading and writing. Choice C is incorrect because Clay's theory emphasizes the importance of individualized instruction based on students' unique needs and experiences. Choice D is incorrect because frequent observation and data collection are important components of individualized instruction, as they allow teachers to determine students' strengths and needs.

93. B: A teacher should use guided reading lessons, not skills-focused lessons, to monitor how well students are applying the skills they have learned to reading text (A). Guided reading lessons are not the best format for helping students master comprehension strategies (B), phonics knowledge, phonemic decoding strategies, key vocabulary, or other fundamental reading skills if students have basic knowledge gaps in these. Skills-focused lessons are more effective to develop these skills before students can apply them to read for and discuss text meanings (C) with teacher support (D).

94. C: Long before babies are able to speak, read, or write, they learn language skills by listening. Through listening, children learn rules of grammar, syntax, and pragmatics. They also develop their vocabularies.

95. D: Predicting what (like a quest or a war) or whom (such as a prince or three animals) a book is about is a common practice of students who fall back on the easiest answer to a teacher's request to make predictions. It is more useful for teachers to challenge students to try to predict what a character in a novel will do or a significant event that may occur in a story. Teachers can explain to students that they can make predictions by looking for clues in book titles, front-cover illustrations, and illustrations inside a book before even reading it. They can also have students read just one passage from a book, and then have them predict what will occur next.

96. B: Semantics is the branch of linguistics that deals with meaning. The semantic system in language includes all aspects of language use that carries meaning. Semantics include words, phrases, sentences, and further contexts that help to convey meaning. Semantics are involved in both receptive and expressive language processes. Choice A is incorrect because the graphophonic system is largely related to the sounds of a language and their written representations. Graphophonics study the relationship between phonics and orthography (writing system). Choice C is incorrect because the syntactic system refers primarily to sentence structure, word order, and other elements of grammar. Syntax does impact meaning, but in a more indirect way than semantics. Choice D is incorrect because pragmatics refers to practical application of language in a variety of contexts. For example, pragmatics is interested in language shifts between social and academic contexts. In reading, this involves being aware of how writers use language to convey moods and draw out more subtle implications.

97. A: Strategic instruction involves teaching a methodic approach to solving a reading problem. It consists of strategies done in steps which aid the reader in eliminating incorrect responses.

98. C: Research has found the potential of many gifted and high-achieving students wasted when schools do not engage and challenge them sufficiently and appropriately. Studies show that 90 percent of high achievers from all income levels attend college (A); however, low-income high achievers have less likelihood of graduation. Experts advise giving high achievers less directive, more open-ended questions and assignments (B) for greater challenges, and, since abilities vary widely, they also advise letting them collaborate across classrooms and grade levels (C) to find ideal matches. Differentiating instruction is as important for high achievers as struggling students, requiring more support personnel in lower grades (D) where children cannot work independently.

99. C: Graphophonic cues are based on the speech sounds in words and their alphabetic representations in print, so choice C is correct. Syntactic cues (A) are based on how words are arranged and ordered to create meaningful phrases, clauses and sentences. Semantic cues (B) are based on the meanings of morphemes and words and how they combine to create additional meanings. Pragmatic cues (D) are based on the readers' purposes for reading and their understanding of how textual structures function in the texts that they read.

100. C: Task cards are a strategy best used as a manipulative for tactile-kinesthetic learners. While a task card may have writing on it, the value to tactile learners is that a card is something that the students can touch, which makes the writing more real to them. Students who are dominantly verbal-linguistic learners will learn best when listening, speaking, reading, and writing. Consequently, activities such as classroom discussions, listening to a story read by the teacher, or reading the words listed on the classroom word wall are good strategies for reaching the verbal-linguistic learners in the class.

While learning styles do vary some from person to person, all people do need to learn from visual information, auditory information, and by hands-on learning. Different materials lend themselves to a different format, but where possible, the best practice when presenting information to others is to use a mixture of formats, including hands-on materials, visual, and auditory information to keep the materials engaging to all learners.

Integration of Knowledge and Understanding

101. Sample Response:

Kaitlyn's response shows some strengths and weaknesses regarding character analysis. She uses text evidence and personal connections to support her choices, yet her selection of traits represents a mostly superficial analysis.

One of Kaitlyn's strengths is that she uses text evidence and personal connections to support her choice of character traits. She describes knowing that Goldilocks has long blond hair because the story described how she was named after a description of her hair. She supports her description of Goldilocks being a girl with clues she obtained from the picture support in the story, noting that she saw Goldilocks' dress and long braids. Additionally, she supports her decision to describe the character as brave by saying Goldilocks did not know who lived in the house when she entered it, and she herself would never enter a stranger's house because it could be dangerous. This indicates a personal connection and Kaitlyn's ability to use prior knowledge to influence her choices.

However, describing Goldilocks as a girl with long blond hair indicates a mostly superficial analysis. These are external character traits, or things you can tell just by looking at the character. Internal traits, or traits based on the character's thoughts, beliefs, or actions, are needed for a deeper analysis. Describing Goldilocks as brave was the only internal character trait mentioned. Therefore, Kaitlyn would need to select two more internal character traits for Goldilocks and support them by citing specific thoughts, beliefs, or actions described in the story to demonstrate a deeper level of understanding and analysis.

102. Sample Response:

Andrew is showing a combination of strengths and weaknesses regarding his use of decoding strategies. His main strength is his use of graphophonic, or visual cues, to assist with decoding unknown words. However, a major weakness is that he is not consistently cross-checking his word choices with semantic or syntactic cues to ensure that his guesses make sense and sound right in the sentences.

When he comes to an unknown word, Andrew often looks at the first few letters and guesses a word that begins with those letters. For example, he said *field* for *fence*, *home* for *house*, *wondered* for *worried*, and *danced* for *darted*. This shows his use of visual, or graphophonic cues, though he concentrates on the beginning letters only. His use of visual cues would be enhanced if he looked at the middle and ending letters in the words in addition to the beginning letters.

Andrew's main weakness is that he does not stop to ask himself if these visual guesses make sense or sound right in the sentences. For example, he read "she was very *wondered*" instead of "she was very *worried*." While *wondered* and *worried* begin with the same two letters, *wondered* does not make sense or sound right in the sentence. However, Andrew continued reading without noticing his error. In another example, he read "*danced* around" instead of "*darted* around." While this sounds right, it does not make sense because Max is a dog. Andrew is therefore not consistently cross-checking his visual cues with semantic cues and syntactic cues, causing his errors to go unnoticed and uncorrected.

AEPA Practice Test #2

To take this additional practice test, visit our online resources page:
mometrix.com/resources719/aepafoundread

How to Overcome Test Anxiety

Just the thought of taking a test is enough to make most people a little nervous. A test is an important event that can have a long-term impact on your future, so it's important to take it seriously and it's natural to feel anxious about performing well. But just because anxiety is normal, that doesn't mean that it's helpful in test taking, or that you should simply accept it as part of your life. Anxiety can have a variety of effects. These effects can be mild, like making you feel slightly nervous, or severe, like blocking your ability to focus or remember even a simple detail.

If you experience test anxiety—whether severe or mild—it's important to know how to beat it. To discover this, first you need to understand what causes test anxiety.

Causes of Test Anxiety

While we often think of anxiety as an uncontrollable emotional state, it can actually be caused by simple, practical things. One of the most common causes of test anxiety is that a person does not feel adequately prepared for their test. This feeling can be the result of many different issues such as poor study habits or lack of organization, but the most common culprit is time management. Starting to study too late, failing to organize your study time to cover all of the material, or being distracted while you study will mean that you're not well prepared for the test. This may lead to cramming the night before, which will cause you to be physically and mentally exhausted for the test. Poor time management also contributes to feelings of stress, fear, and hopelessness as you realize you are not well prepared but don't know what to do about it.

Other times, test anxiety is not related to your preparation for the test but comes from unresolved fear. This may be a past failure on a test, or poor performance on tests in general. It may come from comparing yourself to others who seem to be performing better or from the stress of living up to expectations. Anxiety may be driven by fears of the future—how failure on this test would affect your educational and career goals. These fears are often completely irrational, but they can still negatively impact your test performance.

Elements of Test Anxiety

As mentioned earlier, test anxiety is considered to be an emotional state, but it has physical and mental components as well. Sometimes you may not even realize that you are suffering from test anxiety until you notice the physical symptoms. These can include trembling hands, rapid heartbeat, sweating, nausea, and tense muscles. Extreme anxiety may lead to fainting or vomiting. Obviously, any of these symptoms can have a negative impact on testing. It is important to recognize them as soon as they begin to occur so that you can address the problem before it damages your performance.

The mental components of test anxiety include trouble focusing and inability to remember learned information. During a test, your mind is on high alert, which can help you recall information and stay focused for an extended period of time. However, anxiety interferes with your mind's natural processes, causing you to blank out, even on the questions you know well. The strain of testing during anxiety makes it difficult to stay focused, especially on a test that may take several hours. Extreme anxiety can take a huge mental toll, making it difficult not only to recall test information but even to understand the test questions or pull your thoughts together.

Effects of Test Anxiety

Test anxiety is like a disease—if left untreated, it will get progressively worse. Anxiety leads to poor performance, and this reinforces the feelings of fear and failure, which in turn lead to poor performances on subsequent tests. It can grow from a mild nervousness to a crippling condition. If allowed to progress, test anxiety can have a big impact on your schooling, and consequently on your future.

Test anxiety can spread to other parts of your life. Anxiety on tests can become anxiety in any stressful situation, and blanking on a test can turn into panicking in a job situation. But fortunately, you don't have to let anxiety rule your testing and determine your grades. There are a number of relatively simple steps you can take to move past anxiety and function normally on a test and in the rest of life.

Physical Steps for Beating Test Anxiety

While test anxiety is a serious problem, the good news is that it can be overcome. It doesn't have to control your ability to think and remember information. While it may take time, you can begin taking steps today to beat anxiety.

Just as your first hint that you may be struggling with anxiety comes from the physical symptoms, the first step to treating it is also physical. Rest is crucial for having a clear, strong mind. If you are tired, it is much easier to give in to anxiety. But if you establish good sleep habits, your body and mind will be ready to perform optimally, without the strain of exhaustion. Additionally, sleeping well helps you to retain information better, so you're more likely to recall the answers when you see the test questions.

Getting good sleep means more than going to bed on time. It's important to allow your brain time to relax. Take study breaks from time to time so it doesn't get overworked, and don't study right before bed. Take time to rest your mind before trying to rest your body, or you may find it difficult to fall asleep.

Along with sleep, other aspects of physical health are important in preparing for a test. Good nutrition is vital for good brain function. Sugary foods and drinks may give a burst of energy but this burst is followed by a crash, both physically and emotionally. Instead, fuel your body with protein and vitamin-rich foods.

Also, drink plenty of water. Dehydration can lead to headaches and exhaustion, especially if your brain is already under stress from the rigors of the test. Particularly if your test is a long one, drink water during the breaks. And if possible, take an energy-boosting snack to eat between sections.

Along with sleep and diet, a third important part of physical health is exercise. Maintaining a steady workout schedule is helpful, but even taking 5-minute study breaks to walk can help get your blood pumping faster and clear your head. Exercise also releases endorphins, which contribute to a positive feeling and can help combat test anxiety.

When you nurture your physical health, you are also contributing to your mental health. If your body is healthy, your mind is much more likely to be healthy as well. So take time to rest, nourish your body with healthy food and water, and get moving as much as possible. Taking these physical steps will make you stronger and more able to take the mental steps necessary to overcome test anxiety.

Mental Steps for Beating Test Anxiety

Working on the mental side of test anxiety can be more challenging, but as with the physical side, there are clear steps you can take to overcome it. As mentioned earlier, test anxiety often stems from lack of preparation, so the obvious solution is to prepare for the test. Effective studying may be the most important weapon you have for beating test anxiety, but you can and should employ several other mental tools to combat fear.

First, boost your confidence by reminding yourself of past success—tests or projects that you aced. If you're putting as much effort into preparing for this test as you did for those, there's no reason you should expect to fail here. Work hard to prepare; then trust your preparation.

Second, surround yourself with encouraging people. It can be helpful to find a study group, but be sure that the people you're around will encourage a positive attitude. If you spend time with others who are anxious or cynical, this will only contribute to your own anxiety. Look for others who are motivated to study hard from a desire to succeed, not from a fear of failure.

Third, reward yourself. A test is physically and mentally tiring, even without anxiety, and it can be helpful to have something to look forward to. Plan an activity following the test, regardless of the outcome, such as going to a movie or getting ice cream.

When you are taking the test, if you find yourself beginning to feel anxious, remind yourself that you know the material. Visualize successfully completing the test. Then take a few deep, relaxing breaths and return to it. Work through the questions carefully but with confidence, knowing that you are capable of succeeding.

Developing a healthy mental approach to test taking will also aid in other areas of life. Test anxiety affects more than just the actual test—it can be damaging to your mental health and even contribute to depression. It's important to beat test anxiety before it becomes a problem for more than testing.

Study Strategy

Being prepared for the test is necessary to combat anxiety, but what does being prepared look like? You may study for hours on end and still not feel prepared. What you need is a strategy for test prep. The next few pages outline our recommended steps to help you plan out and conquer the challenge of preparation.

Step 1: Scope Out the Test

Learn everything you can about the format (multiple choice, essay, etc.) and what will be on the test. Gather any study materials, course outlines, or sample exams that may be available. Not only will this help you to prepare, but knowing what to expect can help to alleviate test anxiety.

Step 2: Map Out the Material

Look through the textbook or study guide and make note of how many chapters or sections it has. Then divide these over the time you have. For example, if a book has 15 chapters and you have five days to study, you need to cover three chapters each day. Even better, if you have the time, leave an extra day at the end for overall review after you have gone through the material in depth.

If time is limited, you may need to prioritize the material. Look through it and make note of which sections you think you already have a good grasp on, and which need review. While you are studying, skim quickly through the familiar sections and take more time on the challenging parts.

Write out your plan so you don't get lost as you go. Having a written plan also helps you feel more in control of the study, so anxiety is less likely to arise from feeling overwhelmed at the amount to cover.

Step 3: Gather Your Tools

Decide what study method works best for you. Do you prefer to highlight in the book as you study and then go back over the highlighted portions? Or do you type out notes of the important information? Or is it helpful to make flashcards that you can carry with you? Assemble the pens, index cards, highlighters, post-it notes, and any other materials you may need so you won't be distracted by getting up to find things while you study.

If you're having a hard time retaining the information or organizing your notes, experiment with different methods. For example, try color-coding by subject with colored pens, highlighters, or post-it notes. If you learn better by hearing, try recording yourself reading your notes so you can listen while in the car, working out, or simply sitting at your desk. Ask a friend to quiz you from your flashcards, or try teaching someone the material to solidify it in your mind.

Step 4: Create Your Environment

It's important to avoid distractions while you study. This includes both the obvious distractions like visitors and the subtle distractions like an uncomfortable chair (or a too-comfortable couch that makes you want to fall asleep). Set up the best study environment possible: good lighting and a comfortable work area. If background music helps you focus, you may want to turn it on, but otherwise keep the room quiet. If you are using a computer to take notes, be sure you don't have any other windows open, especially applications like social media, games, or anything else that could distract you. Silence your phone and turn off notifications. Be sure to keep water close by so you stay hydrated while you study (but avoid unhealthy drinks and snacks).

Also, take into account the best time of day to study. Are you freshest first thing in the morning? Try to set aside some time then to work through the material. Is your mind clearer in the afternoon or evening? Schedule your study session then. Another method is to study at the same time of day that you will take the test, so that your brain gets used to working on the material at that time and will be ready to focus at test time.

Step 5: Study!

Once you have done all the study preparation, it's time to settle into the actual studying. Sit down, take a few moments to settle your mind so you can focus, and begin to follow your study plan. Don't give in to distractions or let yourself procrastinate. This is your time to prepare so you'll be ready to fearlessly approach the test. Make the most of the time and stay focused.

Of course, you don't want to burn out. If you study too long you may find that you're not retaining the information very well. Take regular study breaks. For example, taking five minutes out of every hour to walk briskly, breathing deeply and swinging your arms, can help your mind stay fresh.

As you get to the end of each chapter or section, it's a good idea to do a quick review. Remind yourself of what you learned and work on any difficult parts. When you feel that you've mastered the material, move on to the next part. At the end of your study session, briefly skim through your notes again.

But while review is helpful, cramming last minute is NOT. If at all possible, work ahead so that you won't need to fit all your study into the last day. Cramming overloads your brain with more information than it can process and retain, and your tired mind may struggle to recall even previously learned information when it is overwhelmed with last-minute study. Also, the urgent nature of cramming and the stress placed on your brain contribute to anxiety. You'll be more likely to go to the test feeling unprepared and having trouble thinking clearly.

So don't cram, and don't stay up late before the test, even just to review your notes at a leisurely pace. Your brain needs rest more than it needs to go over the information again. In fact, plan to finish your studies by noon or early afternoon the day before the test. Give your brain the rest of the day to relax or focus on other things, and get a good night's sleep. Then you will be fresh for the test and better able to recall what you've studied.

Step 6: Take a Practice Test

Many courses offer sample tests, either online or in the study materials. This is an excellent resource to check whether you have mastered the material, as well as to prepare for the test format and environment.

Check the test format ahead of time: the number of questions, the type (multiple choice, free response, etc.), and the time limit. Then create a plan for working through them. For example, if you have 30 minutes to take a 60-question test, your limit is 30 seconds per question. Spend less time on the questions you know well so that you can take more time on the difficult ones.

If you have time to take several practice tests, take the first one open book, with no time limit. Work through the questions at your own pace and make sure you fully understand them. Gradually work up to taking a test under test conditions: sit at a desk with all study materials put away and set a timer. Pace yourself to make sure you finish the test with time to spare and go back to check your answers if you have time.

After each test, check your answers. On the questions you missed, be sure you understand why you missed them. Did you misread the question (tests can use tricky wording)? Did you forget the information? Or was it something you hadn't learned? Go back and study any shaky areas that the practice tests reveal.

Taking these tests not only helps with your grade, but also aids in combating test anxiety. If you're already used to the test conditions, you're less likely to worry about it, and working through tests until you're scoring well gives you a confidence boost. Go through the practice tests until you feel comfortable, and then you can go into the test knowing that you're ready for it.

Test Tips

On test day, you should be confident, knowing that you've prepared well and are ready to answer the questions. But aside from preparation, there are several test day strategies you can employ to maximize your performance.

First, as stated before, get a good night's sleep the night before the test (and for several nights before that, if possible). Go into the test with a fresh, alert mind rather than staying up late to study.

Try not to change too much about your normal routine on the day of the test. It's important to eat a nutritious breakfast, but if you normally don't eat breakfast at all, consider eating just a protein bar. If you're a coffee drinker, go ahead and have your normal coffee. Just make sure you time it so that the caffeine doesn't wear off right in the middle of your test. Avoid sugary beverages, and drink enough water to stay hydrated but not so much that you need a restroom break 10 minutes into the test. If your test isn't first thing in the morning, consider going for a walk or doing a light workout before the test to get your blood flowing.

Allow yourself enough time to get ready, and leave for the test with plenty of time to spare so you won't have the anxiety of scrambling to arrive in time. Another reason to be early is to select a good seat. It's helpful to sit away from doors and windows, which can be distracting. Find a good seat, get out your supplies, and settle your mind before the test begins.

When the test begins, start by going over the instructions carefully, even if you already know what to expect. Make sure you avoid any careless mistakes by following the directions.

Then begin working through the questions, pacing yourself as you've practiced. If you're not sure on an answer, don't spend too much time on it, and don't let it shake your confidence. Either skip it and come back later, or eliminate as many wrong answers as possible and guess among the remaining ones. Don't dwell on these questions as you continue—put them out of your mind and focus on what lies ahead.

Be sure to read all of the answer choices, even if you're sure the first one is the right answer. Sometimes you'll find a better one if you keep reading. But don't second-guess yourself if you do immediately know the answer. Your gut instinct is usually right. Don't let test anxiety rob you of the information you know.

If you have time at the end of the test (and if the test format allows), go back and review your answers. Be cautious about changing any, since your first instinct tends to be correct, but make sure you didn't misread any of the questions or accidentally mark the wrong answer choice. Look over any you skipped and make an educated guess.

At the end, leave the test feeling confident. You've done your best, so don't waste time worrying about your performance or wishing you could change anything. Instead, celebrate the successful completion of this test. And finally, use this test to learn how to deal with anxiety even better next time.

Review Video: Test Anxiety
Visit mometrix.com/academy and enter code: 100340

Important Qualification

Not all anxiety is created equal. If your test anxiety is causing major issues in your life beyond the classroom or testing center, or if you are experiencing troubling physical symptoms related to your anxiety, it may be a sign of a serious physiological or psychological condition. If this sounds like your situation, we strongly encourage you to seek professional help.

Online Resources

Due to our efforts to try to keep this book to a manageable length, we've created a link that will give you access to all of your online resources:

mometrix.com/resources719/aepafoundread

It's Your Moment, Let's Celebrate It!

Share your story @mometrixtestpreparation